A RENTED WORLD

A Novel

by

Merle Temple

Southern Literature Publishing
www.southernliteraturepublishing.com

A Rented World

Copyright ©2014 Southern Literature Publishing

ISBN: 978-0-9911475-3-3

Printed in the United States of America

Unless otherwise noted, all scripture references are taken from the Holy Bible, New International Version. Copyright 1973, 1978, 1984 International Bible Society. Used by permission. All rights reserved.

Where noted, scripture references taken from the Holy Bible, King James Version, kingjamesbibleonline.org. Used by permission. All rights reserved.

Also where noted, scripture references taken from the Holy Bible, English Standard Version. Copyright 2001. All rights reserved.

Southern Literature Publishing
www.southernliteraturepublishing.com

www.merletemple.com

Reviews for *A Rented World*

"Merle Temple weaves another totally captivating tale of intrigue and treachery! The demons he faces are completely unexpected… truly A RENTED WORLD!"—Jim Clemente, Writer, *Criminal Minds*

"Leave the gun, take the cannoli, and buy this book!"—John Martino (Paulie), *The Godfather*

"Writing is spellbinding, haunting…broke my heart."—Lisa Love, Writer, *Southern Reader Magazine*

"The next 'superstar author'…a remarkable talent…a must read!"—Susan Reichert, Editor, *Southern Writers Magazine*

"Writing hums with the pulsating rhythm of the New South, where gangsters and ghosts no longer lurk in the shadows but reach out and grab you by the throat in broad daylight. A gripping read from an emerging author with a true gift for words."—Robert Lee Long, Editor, *De Soto Times*

"…betrayal, heartache…the wrong side of powerful men who thrive in the dark shadows of power. Merle Temple dives deeper into the depths of the underworld he survived…"—Mark H. Stowers, *Clarion-Ledger*

"Whether a man is Goliath, or a White Knight covered by armor, there is one point of vulnerability…right between the eyes…even better than *A Ghostly Shade of Pale*."—Jan Ballard, Yarnspinners Book Club

"…a master at delivering spiritual messages within secular bindings…deep within the company of the finest Mystery-Suspense writers in the Southern Tradition."—K.B. Schaller, Author, *100+ Native American Women*

"…provocative, powerful…the dark underbelly of humanity…begs for Temple's third book to complete the trilogy."—Bob Chrismas, Canadian police officer, Author, *Canadian Policing in the 21st Century*

"I ask my students, 'Can you picture that?' Merle Temple's descriptive writing makes it so much easier for them as he creates spectacular mental images."—Jonelle Gillette, Speech Pathologist

"I tell my clients who think life is over, 'I have two words for you—Merle Temple.'"—John Garcia, Attorney (former prosecutor)

To all who helped me find the treasures hidden
in darkness, the threads of God's purpose
woven into blankets of crushing pain.

—Merle Temple

PREFACE

The dawning of the twenty-first century was greeted with high hopes and fresh resolutions by those who labored beneath the polluted firmaments of the Gotham of the New South. Atlanta's empire builders crushed all who threatened their way of life and their religion—the mysticism of materialism. A pilgrim in this foreign land, former Mississippi Bureau of Narcotics Captain Michael Parker, finds an unholy trinity of politics, crime, and business humming the same secular hymn—"Everyone and everything is for sale."

Political barkers promised the fruits of the tree of good and evil. Souls were ransomed for tokens of pleasure. Prophets of utopianism, peering like Narcissus into the muddy waters of the Chattahoochee River, saw only their own image—not that of their Creator—and whistled their anthem: "I Did It My Way."

All that was necessary to lose your soul in the city of darkness was to turn around once with your conscience muted. All that was necessary to find redemption and your way home was to enter the sanctuary of brokenness, where the noise of the world was silenced that man might hear the inescapable voice of lost love—agape love—whispering, *"Who do you say that I am?"*

The cops counted corpses, the courtiers buried truth beneath flattery, and political grifters brokered Faustian deals in a rented world as they asked their own question—"How long can we go on with lies on our lips, perjury and larceny in our hearts, and shotguns in our laps?"

A restless Michael Parker, looking for meaning in all the wrong places, decides he's willing to march into this maelstrom for what he's sure must be a heavenly cause.

"Every human is in the process of becoming a noble being, noble beyond imagination; or a vile being beyond redemption...an immortal horror or an everlasting splendor."–C.S. Lewis

"Show me a hero, and I'll write you a tragedy."—F. Scott Fitzgerald

CHAPTER ONE

*"Satan, your kingdom must come down. I
heard the voice of Jesus say, 'Satan, your
kingdom must come down.'"—Robert Plant*

*"After reading history…investigate the
mystery of allegories, restrain their
subtlety…so not to lose judgment in what
they discern…"—Hugh of St. Victor*

The club on the north end of Peachtree Boulevard was far from the gleaming lights of the Braves' stadium, the gold of the Capitol dome, and the venerable Fox Theater where locals swore they saw the ghost of Margaret Mitchell.

Patrons of Atlanta's Cougar Club could barely see the clock that registered 4:09 a.m. The incandescence of the stage footlights couldn't cut through the pungent odor and strange amalgamation of smoke, sweat, drug cookers, poor hygiene, casual intimacy, and broken hearts—a toxic stew in Hotlanta's most notorious strip club.

The antique air conditioner barely moved the dense air, creating an eerie churn of the combustible fumes that seemed to form the outlines of spirits which swirled into existence and then were gone. Some said they were ectoplasmic echoes of strippers and hookers lost to the hot shots of heroin, the hepatitis of bad needles, or the violence of jilted lovers.

The club with the emerald-green door and the peephole for admittance sat squarely in the middle of an area of cultural convergence that locals called the Twilight Zone. The TZ was bordered on one side by the Atlanta Museum and the Atlanta Symphony, on another by the large park that had become the central recreational site for the gay community, and on the other by several strip clubs and bars. The nightspots were the hives of peddlers of the forbidden that attracted the curious tourists of suburbia, professional politicians, and the Dixie Mafia.

At the apex of this triangle rose the peach tower and olive roof of the Peachtree Condominiums, standing like a modern Tower of Babel. It was home to all the worker bees of this cosmopolitan area. Elevators in the tower house seemed to go so high that passengers might kiss the balcony of heaven—that is, if they could see the Celestial City through the yellow-green haze of Atlanta pollution. A ticket to ride might mean sharing a car with concert pianists, strippers and enterprising hookers, military officers, wrestlers, professionals in demure business attire, or even older men with their concubines. From tuxedos to fishnet stockings and military surplus to wrestling tights, it was a cosmopolis where travelers did not speak the same language but moved past each other like ships in the night.

Billy Joe Estes was a portly man with a receding hairline, penguin body, and rosy-red cheeks that hinted of long hours, bad diet, and a penchant for hard liquor. He sat motionless and expressionless at a table filled with dirty glasses in the Cougar nightclub. Darlene Darling, an exotic dancer at the club, delivered a grotesque imitation of intimacy in an opera of the absurd where mechanical and contrived gyrations were passable for intoxicated patrons. Her moves were more or less choreographed to the beats of Carl Perkins on the jukebox: "It's almost dawn, and the cops are gone. Let's all get Dixie fried."

Billy Joe had seen it all before as the gofer for "Big Jim" Martin, the undisputed boss of Georgia politics as Georgia's Speaker of the House—a man who bore an uncanny resemblance to Colonel Sanders.

Everyone called Billy Joe "Hoss," not for his size or resemblance to Dan Blocker or his reputation as a "take no prisoners" political enforcer, but for a horse farm he invested in near Bonanza, Georgia. It was a front group buying old horses and selling them to glue factories, and it took all the speaker's clout to rescue him when the Feds found out.

Each time he was asked (for the umpteenth time) to explain his nickname, people hee-hawed, brayed, and then inquired, "Where's the rest of them Cartwright boys? Why'd they shoot Trigger and Buttermilk?" The double entendres and guffaws were endless. Billy Joe just hated it.

Tonight, Billy Joe was working—sort of. His job this night, as many evenings, was to ride herd on three drunken legislators who were unshackled from the restrictions and conventions of their home districts.

Far from the front pews of the churches where these Pharisees parked on Sundays, they were free to indulge their proclivities for whiskey and wild women, to rub shoulders with the rich and famous who proved that money can't buy happiness.

They also collected "get out of jail free cards" from a local federal judge who frequented the club with a young female defendant he had shown leniency to in his court. To show her gratitude, she furnished him with her favors and all the cocaine he could ingest. At the Cougar Club, legislators and judges could take that anonymous walk on the wild side that they had only dreamed of before their call to serve the people.

Billy Joe, who wheezed now and then when he walked, was there on orders from Big Jim, who told him, "Just make sure these boys don't break anything, hurt any gals, or run afoul of the law. But if they do, it's your job to remind the local boys in blue that all our legislators are in session and, therefore, immune to the laws that we make for the common folks."

Big Jim told him that the ancients of tender, state-government beginnings passed session immunity because adversaries were always having their rivals arrested by friendly *gendarmes* on the day of critical votes. In modern times, enterprising legislators pumped up with grandiosity and arrogance used their immunity as a weapon and a shield—the absolute power that Lord Acton warned could corrupt absolutely.

Some of these juveniles fancied themselves as supermen or demigods entitled to breach the rules of civilized society. It was difficult to cover up some of their addictions and excesses. Lots of money was paid to squelch rumors and to salve injured parties. If the people knew it, they would never stand for such abuses. The old arguments for immunity shields weren't that strong.

Billy Joe was shepherding three legislators from East Georgia, as well as Bill Cook, a newspaper editor from Augusta, who enjoyed the spoils of the boys he protected in his daily columns. Ricky Garcia, a rotund legislator from Augusta who looked like the Pillsbury Doughboy's long-lost twin brother, brought Cook to the party. Representative Joey Tomlin, a diminutive, baby-faced alcoholic with a penchant for crashing his car into Georgia Power Company poles, was along for the ride.

Steve Palmer, a silver-haired pharmacist and committee chairman, was there as well. He frequently warned women he encountered in Atlanta clubs that just because there was "snow on the roof" didn't mean there wasn't "fire in the chimney." Palmer couldn't handle the pills he brought to Atlanta from his store back home—the same store he allowed enterprising drug dealers to burgle as cover for his inventory shortages that turned up when auditors came to call.

In the midst of the night's performance, Doughboy lurched suddenly toward the dance stage and Darlene, whom he nicknamed Honeysuckle. He thrust a wad of money into the young dancer's immodest outfit just above a slight roll of baby fat. The glassy-eyed, flaxen-haired child—that was what she was when the makeup was scraped away—was new to the game and startled by the move. Her fatuous smile showed more gum than teeth and contorted into a scowl, betraying the semi-permanent pout of her stage persona.

"Ow, Billy Joe! He pinched me!" the nubile dancer cried.

Billy Joe waved off Rex, the burly bouncer and former tight end for the Falcons. Coming out of the University of Georgia, he had great promise until he blew out his knee. Rex puffed his chest out in his too-tight muscle shirt, but deferred to Billy Joe and the reflected power of his patrons.

"Ricky, make nice with the dancer. No touching!" Billy Joe scolded.

"Aw, Hoss…I just wanted to show her some appreciation," a contrite Ricky whined.

"Shut up, Ricky, and sit down. Big Jim needs you sober and ready to vote on the highway bill at ten this morning. You can't do that in jail, now can you?" Billy Joe admonished the baby-faced legislator as a distant grumble of thunder punctuated the moment.

Ricky swayed to and fro, almost fell, then bowed before young Honeysuckle and said, "I am so sorrrrrrrreeee, missee."

Just as things seemed poised to return to normal, a red-faced, middle-aged man who apparently had a thing for the young dancer came from the rear of the club and charged the legislator. The man bellowed like an enraged moose and brandished a flash of cold steel from the knife suddenly produced from his back pocket. Veins swollen with blood protruded from his temples and forehead. He was infused with a rush of adrenalin and the righteous anger of a guy whose woman-girl had been wronged.

"That's my girl, you cheap suit," he yelled as he reached for Ricky. Tables went flying, and shattering glass from the whiskey tumblers and beer mugs fractured the normal night-spot murmuring and chattering. The bouncer was too far away to stop him.

Patrons who didn't know Billy Joe were surprised by what followed. Seen by some as an unlikely intervener, he jumped into the path of the offended Romeo and hobbled the raging bull by stepping hard on the man's instep as he passed. He brought the thunder of the storm raging outside the club indoors with lightning-quick claps to both ears and an elbow across the side of the man's head. The anguished knight crumpled to the concrete floor of the Cougar Club with a thud, as a trickle of crimson blood oozed from his right ear.

Billy Joe bent to retrieve the knife, exposing the blue steel of his snub-nosed Smith & Wesson .38 beneath his belt. An antique watch of pitted gold had fallen from the man's pocket; it popped open on the scarred concrete floor and chimed a haunting ode to his "Beautiful Dreamer." The Speaker's "babysitter of wayward legislators" snapped it shut and shot the crowd a challenging look. Hushed patrons, suddenly sober, looked on with wide eyes and raised eyebrows—exhibiting a new respect for Billy Joe.

The bouncer rushed in to make a show, muscles rippling, but the drama and theater was over. The local blue-and-white Atlanta police cruiser arrived as if on cue, and the officers, who were regulars on the strip club beat, asked the perfunctory questions with rote efficiency, strutting around as if they had never laid eyes on the usual suspects.

Carmen Rodriguez, the club owner of record and front for the real owners and investors, nodded at the bouncer, who slipped the senior officer a wad of Federal Reserve notes. Carmen was given the Cougar Club to manage, along with controlling interest in two others. He was rewarded for taking the fall for tax charges and Mann Act violations for both city politicians and Dixie Mafia members out of Biloxi. The Dixie

Mafia laundered money through the clubs and used them as hideaways after armed robberies ranging from New Orleans to Miami. Carmen served eighteen months at the Atlanta federal prison camp for his silent partners, and they rewarded him as promised.

Billy Joe whispered sweet nothings in the second officer's ear. "The Speaker is eternally grateful for your help. Here's something for your trouble and some passes for you boys and your families to attend House sessions. You can even eat free in the section of the state cafeteria reserved for legislators."

The man they nicknamed "Romeo" was cuffed amidst his protestations about the legislator from Augusta. The police dragged him to a cursory stop at Grady Memorial's emergency room, the depository for Atlanta's trauma cases, and then to a night in the drunk tank for disorderly conduct, where he was encouraged to forget it all.

Everyone settled down, tables were righted, and the music cranked up, just as the bartender announced last call and "a round on the house." The rhythm of the dirty dance of the used and the users began again: actors taking their places and reciting their lines as the planet spun on uninterrupted.

Billy Joe finally loaded his legislative cargo into his van for a ride to the apartment the politicians shared while in Atlanta. As he drove, he thought of how he came to be in this sorry business.

He grew up in the Delta of Mississippi in rural Bolivar County near the village of Alligator. His folks were dirt-poor sharecroppers who lived in a small, white frame house weathered to gray. The shack sported a slightly bent, shiny silver television antenna. Because the Delta was so flat between Alligator and Memphis, Billy Joe could point it north and pick up WHBQ and WMC on a good day. When asked "Just how flat was it in the Delta?" he answered, "It was so flat you could sit on top of your house and watch your dog run away from home for two or three days."

Billy Joe's golden-haired sister, who was a few years older, ran away from home after laying out their father with a shovel blade to the head. They found him unconscious and bleeding in the cotton field where she left him as she took money from her mother and made it to the bus station. They never told Billy Joe why she left, but years later she wrote and told him that she still had nightmares every night about their father and often awakened screaming.

Billy Joe picked cotton until his hands bled from the sharp and unforgiving blades of the cotton bolls. The furrowed rows seemed never-ending and miles long in the hot Mississippi glare, which had left his neck a permanent red-bronze. He felt the red neck stigmatized him as one of the great unwashed "crackers" of the South and would often wash and scrub his neck until it was raw.

Billy Joe got tired of poverty and equated his bad luck with indifference on the part of Jesus, who he felt didn't live up to the sermons and promises of the prosperity preachers. "I don't like boundaries," he told people. "I seek other diversions that have all the advantages of Christianity but none of its restrictions and defects."

So he left home as his mama cried and his daddy slept off a drunk from home brew on the front porch. After many misadventures and a short stint in the U.S. Navy, he came to work for the gangster Ace Connelly in his nightclubs around Memphis and North Mississippi.

Ace had pulled up one day in front of the National Guard Armory where Billy Joe worked after the Navy. There to hold a fundraiser to improve his image and buy protection from the local authorities, Ace spied Billy Joe and asked him if he wanted a job. Billy Joe was tired of the "weekend warriors" and his sergeant, whose motto was, "If it don't move, paint it!" So he left that day to become a gofer for Ace.

Ace asked him if he was crazy like people said. Billy Joe answered, "I know they say that I ain't *right* in the head, but they ain't proved me *wrong* yet."

When Ace inquired as to his qualifications, Billy Joe said, "I left home like the Prodigal Son, but won't be back—the pig pen's fine with me." That sealed the deal.

Everything was fine until Ace started dealing with the governor of Mississippi and that devil-worshipping freak Fredrick Hammel. He brought that narc, Michael Parker, down on them when he killed that girl in Memphis. Ace went to prison and left Billy Joe high and dry. Death followed Fredrick, and he almost killed Parker in Tupelo. The Grim

Reaper claimed Fredrick instead. Fredrick was always talking about moving to a warmer climate, and Billy Joe figured he got his wish.

That's when he decided to head to Atlanta—too much heat; not the kind Fredrick spoke of but too many aggressive law dogs. Now and then he swore that he could still hear Fredrick in his head recruiting him.

The dimmycrats, as Billy Joe called them, had ruled over Georgia with an iron fist for a hundred years, and his move to Georgia had worked out well, but things began to change in 1994. Strange people were moving to Georgia, and Republicans, who once could have held their conventions in one of those old phone booths, were causing trouble. Worst of all, one had just been elected state superintendent of schools—a woman to boot.

"What's the world coming to?" Billy Joe asked Carmen one day over a beer. "Women don't know their place anymore," he reckoned. "Maybe it was that Adam and Eve thing, but something has to be done about her. She's been firing people who've been on the payroll of the Education Department for twenty years as payment for loyal service to the dimmycrat machine. She even had the audacity to require that they show up for work! Unbelievable! Those boys and gals didn't sign on for no job—just a check. Now this woman is violating contracts of good standing. Something has to be done, for sure.

"I know just how to do it, too...frame folks, plant stuff, and have our friendly cops arrest people. Pour a little liquor on 'em after a quick slap-jack to the head. Yes, suh, resisting arrest, faces in the tabloids, would be the end of them for good. Even if she's exonerated later, it'd be buried on the back page of the sports section in fine print in an article so small they'd have to use a magnifying glass to find it. Folks only remember the front page and the first story, never the second. It works so often, I can't imagine how the public keeps buying it," he mused.

He had favor to curry, not only from "Big Jim" but from Governor Henry "Hank" Holcomb, who was building a kingdom in Georgia. "King Hank" they called him, and he didn't like anyone getting in his way, particularly this uppity woman.

Play ball or go back to Podunk Hollow. This is Atlanta—Sherman couldn't keep us down, and a skirt sure enough ain't going to, Billy Joe ruminated as he looked up at the high-rise condominium where that very woman lived.

"This ain't no job for sissies," he muttered as he cranked the dusty old white van to leave the club with his arrested juveniles pretending to be adults. A flock of pigeons caused him to look up and see a peregrine falcon making a dive at them.

"The hunter is out to prey on the weak. Just like us. Natural, isn't it?" he asked, but the boys' blood alcohol levels precluded any coherent answer. No matter. He owed his soul to his political masters; no more time to waste on sentimental musings and abstract discussions of right and wrong. Billy Joe reckoned that he was never more right than when he was wrong.

As he pulled onto 14th Street, the first dim rays in an overcast sky struggled to relieve the night lights of their duty. Sooty-gray chimney swifts were ending their nocturnal sweeps to find cover in the uncapped chimneys of some of Atlanta's older buildings. The savvy political enforcer paused to look up at the message on a large blinking sign in front of the ancient Georgia Mission Church that anchored the far end of the same block as the club. "Our Savior won't be arriving by Air Force One. Under new management—Can't be impeached and won't resign."

The brewing storm blew in from Buckhead. The gale-like wind whipped Billy Joe's van, and the semiconscious boys with him muttered complaints—"Whazza matter?" The towering condominiums—monuments to the corrupt officials who taxed elderly couples from their lifelong nests so contractors could raze their homes to build these money-making condos—swayed before the storm. This was the city where the languages were all confounded, but where the conflicting cultures all integrated in a strangely functional dysfunctional madness.

Billy Joe, the refugee from Mississippi, popped a disk in his player and moved off into the night as his mama's favorite, Tennessee Ernie, rattled the worn speakers in the old van: "Saint Peter, don't you call me 'cause I can't go. I owe my soul to the company store."

* * *

Ironically, just at that moment, insomniac and early riser State Schools Chief Mary Ruth Robinson stared down at the first stirrings of the city that dozes but never closes and the approaching storm from the balcony of her 35th-floor condo.

This wasn't the city of Rhett and Scarlett which the incurable romantic from Millen, Georgia, had dreamed of as a young girl. She hated Atlanta but ran for office at the urging of Senator Thaddeus Alexander, who was trying desperately to field a full Republican ticket in Democrat Georgia. She was the longest of long shots to upset the genteel incumbent patrician; but as every devotee of the track knows, even the nag comes in first once in a bookie's worst nightmare.

Mary Ruth did it for adventure, because she loved to please strong men, and to put distance between herself and her husband's alcoholism and abuse. She was not only trying to escape him but to flee the voices that tormented her at home—the voices that had followed her to "Asphalt Atlanta" and were beginning to become more invasive. Years of worshipping at the altar of the libertines, that night of drunken silliness, and the incantation to the prince of darkness had exacted a terrible price. The excesses of the '70s wouldn't release her and were as fresh as the odors of Sheol outside the gates of old Jerusalem.

Extraordinary efforts were required now to keep the guttural whispers at bay. Each night, the ritual began as she carefully placed scented candles around her bed in an attempt to erect a barrier to the approach of a legion of her demons. Other recreational rituals were employed with only limited and decreasing effectiveness. The casual and meaningless encounters had failed to mute the pain, and like an addict who needed more and more, the balm of the quick fixes of the flesh were fleeting, and had at last gone cold.

Could the God of my childhood still love me? No, she thought. *That dream, like old Atlanta, is—gone with the wind.* The accidental politician with tousled blonde hair leaned over her balcony in her chartreuse bathrobe, astonished to see a lone white van below moving slowly up the frontage road toward I-285. She wondered what fool would be out so early and driving into the eye of the coming storm. Playing behind her on the drive-hour oldie show was Simon and Garfunkel: "Coo, coo, ca-choo, Mrs. Robinson, Jesus loves you more than you will know."

And then the storm front and a howling wind engulfed the van and Peachtree Towers. Mary Ruth was driven inside, where familiar voices also howled in her own private hell. The rain fell and whipped the streets in angry, sweeping surges, trying in vain to wash clean the streets of Sodom and Gomorrah.

CHAPTER TWO

"It's the soul afraid of dying that
never learns to live..."
—Amanda McBroom, *"The Rose"*

"The cross is real wood, the nails are real
iron, the vinegar truly tastes bitter, and the
cry of desolation is live—not recorded."
—Malcolm Muggeridge

Fifteen years earlier, as the revelry and fireworks of New Year's Eve yielded to 1980, the black smoke from Billy Joe's oil guzzler shrouded his exit from Mississippi as he hastily crossed the state line. He was headed toward Georgia. He told everyone, "It's a dog-eat-dog world, and I've been wearing Milk Bone britches." He hoped Georgia might be different.

When Billy Joe first saw the skyline of Atlanta, WPLO and Tom T. Hall provided the perfect soundtrack for a hopeful immigrant to this new land of plenty. "Faster horses, younger women, older whiskey, and more money" pretty much summed up his philosophy of life.

* * *

Mississippi Bureau of Narcotics Captain Michael Parker had been discharged from the North Mississippi Medical Center in Tupelo just weeks earlier. He had a jaundiced color, uncertain and darting eyes, and a deep scarring of the soul, but all agreed—a miracle nonetheless.

While in the hospital, he had to learn to walk again, and to speak without raw terror and emotion betraying him. There were times when he could still smell the fear he felt the night the pale slasher, Fredrick, attacked him—a fear that violated his self-image, his view of who he was. He could still feel the knife as it cut and short-circuited his wiring, severing nerves from muscle and muscle from bone. It was there within him—the skitter and scrape of the blade along his bones, a sound and sensation that can reduce tough men to whimpering children.

In moments of false bravado or healing, he weakly joked that it would be years before he could ever watch another infomercial for Ginsu knives. In his nightmares, he was bound to a rudderless ship sailing in circles on the Sea of Doldrums as sea creatures with stilettos slashed and killed all that he held dear.

Lodged in his ears was the sound of his skull as it banged the floor that night, a jarring thud accented by the shrieks of the women who looked to him as their sorry excuse for a defender. He saw something at the back of Fredrick's eyes that was evil and without conscience, a thing that recognized no entreaty to love or peace, an entity that knew only death with no negotiation for life. Like the shepherd boy David in the valley of Elah, Michael was called to be a champion—"in between" in ancient language—a soldier in-between the armies of good and evil.

Though he prevailed, his self-image was diminished, and he withdrew in humbling, emasculating, terror as he confronted his most primal doubts, all the things that go bump in the night. He faced the goblins, the monsters of B-horror movie nights at the Lee Drive-In theater in Tupelo, and the faceless Grim Reaper carrying a ticket to forever—a ticket with his name on it. Each time the nightmares came, he tasted fear.

He had to swallow hard at the reflux of pure terror that burned in his mouth and ate away at the lining of his throat. Titania, the Queen of the Fairies in *A Midsummer Night's Dream*, appeared to him in his nocturnal vignettes and demanded, "What have you done?" He could only answer her question with a question: "Where can you go to hide from yourself?"

It was at those moments of awakening from dreams when he took his pulse to make sure it was still there and found it racing. He felt his head and found it throbbing with pain memory etched forever in the neural pathways of his mind. He knew that something in him had died that night—that he might never be the same. It was at those intersections of incongruence where he tasted the guilt steak that condemns and shouts "Quit!"

He wailed mournfully, "Why did I live and not Dixie Lee? Why should I go on? Why, why, why?" There was no answer except a faint whisper from beyond—"One day it'll be payday."

All manner of visitors came to see him in the hospital. Some were welcome faces: co-workers, local citizen activists, and his best friend Clay, the MBN intelligence chief; others were uninvited intruders breaching hospital security. The dramatic death of Fredrick birthed a media circus where reporters vied to get an interview before Michael "kicked the bucket." Only tight security kept the jackals at bay, but late one night, Michael awoke from his drug-induced haze to hear a rustling at his side, a shuffling of papers. Harry Stein, a pimply-faced reporter from the *Jackson Clarion-Ledger*, slithered up to his bed and told him (rather than asking) that he was there for an interview.

After the perfunctory "How are you?" and an uplifting "You don't look so good," Stein got right to it. He was the kind of neo-journalist, Columbia University graduate who sees a thin man and assumes that some fat man must have taken something from him. He whipped out a tablet and a number 2 lead pencil that he licked repeatedly, signaling he was ready to write.

"Did you know Mr. Hammel before that night? Had you been stalking him? Sources tell us you had persecuted him for his demon-strations of conscience in the anti-war movement, and he snapped from your vendetta against all who were not part of the imperialist war machine." Stein rambled as Michael peered at him through bandages and life-sustaining drips.

Querulous and pettish, more shadow-in-the-night than substance, he continued, "Did you know that he was mentally and physically challenged? Misunderstood really, his professors told me. Was it his appearance that you disliked? Does it bother you that you murdered a man crippled by albinism and schizophrenia?"

Michael wanted to run away, but he couldn't walk. He wanted to hit him, but he couldn't make a fist.

I just put a big Band-aid on all of this, Michael thought. *Here's this little pompous puff ball...trying to rip it off.* Fighting the urge to yield to the profanity that he abhorred, he said, "Excuse me...I'm not the bad guy here."

The reporter cleared his throat twice and adjusted his rimless spectacles. "This isn't about good and evil, Mr. Parker. All such terms are relative and subjective. This is about the privileged and the powerful representatives of the oppressive establishment disenfranchising people like Mr. Hammel, whom our society has failed."

A faint cackle of laughter came from a nearby bed somewhere in the ward. Michael recoiled at Stein's emotional poverty and his subjectivizing of reality. Death was only an abstraction to him, not the final stillness—the knowing that you had caused the clotting of black blood and the foul smell that can never be forgotten. Michael stared at him incredulously, finally hit the nurse call button and said, "You come uninvited. You seem to think there are no absolutes while stating absolutes. You've contradicted your own logic. Time's up."

Then the inevitable moment came when the crew-cut arrived—a jar-headed agent with parched, blonde arm hair over rolling muscles. He identified himself as Tommy from some Federal alphabet agency. One night near midnight, he more materialized than entered the gloom of the hospital room, flashed impressive credentials, and showed Michael pictures with a penlight, asking if he recognized anyone. Michael shook his head slowly. Then the man cautiously asked if Fredrick said anything about a trip to El Salvador.

Clay had shown Michael papers recovered from Fredrick's car after the fight. Although they were fairly innocuous notes, there was an itinerary for a flight to El Salvador, along with two ticket stubs from a sleazy nightclub, which Fredrick noted that he and Agent Tommy had visited in San Salvador. The strip club had featured "The Snake Lady," who danced with a python in her act.

Michael, grown weary of such mendacity, rasped, "That trip in the old plane…in the club after the show…with the snake lady when you got drunk."

"Yes, yes…" the agent said as he leaned closer.

"Fredrick said she was fine, but…" Michael began to cough and choke.

"Yes, yes, but what…" the anxious agent asked.

"Come closer," Michael whispered.

As the agent leaned close to hear Michael, he whispered a dry confidence: "Fredrick said that she was fine—but the snake died!"

The agent flushed red even in the dimness of the room and drew back abruptly with a balled fist. Michael could hear him grinding his teeth so hard that he expected bone to crack. "We have your name. Yes! Yes, we have your name, and we know where to find you!" he stammered. Then he disappeared into the night, and Michael drifted back to the sleep of morphine, praying for forgiveness for that moment of self-indulgence. Thundering laughter came loudly this time with uproarious abandon from behind the curtain—a grizzled, bedridden octogenarian, a World War I vet, cursed the government in a way that Michael never could.

* * *

All such intrusions ended when a temporal angel with a winsome smile was assigned to his ward and policed all access to him. Glossy, reddish-brown hair and warm, brown, deep pools for eyes—such were the features of a young, freckle-faced beauty named Susan, who came and went in his room, attending to his needs. She was too young to be a Gray Lady but past the age of the teenage candy-stripers. He learned not to argue with her orders to drink this, take that, and seek the Lord.

"If the Lord be for you," she told him in a shy but certain whisper of a voice, "who can be against you?" She was always pushing spinach on him as she sat by his bed with a bowl of the goop and spoon at the ready.

"Why must I eat this stuff?" Michael whined.

"Because, Agent Parker," she said firmly, "it's good for you." There was something about her—the curve of her lips, the shape of her throat, but more than that—the light that emanated from her soul. He decided that she was Van Morrison's "angel of the first degree, as sweet as Tupelo honey."

He eventually gave up resisting her orders and told her that arguing with a woman was like trying to blow out the light in a bulb. He dubbed her Olive Oyl and swallowed another spoonful of the wretched mush as he told her, "After all, Olive, I yam what I yam!"

His Florence Nightingale brought warm blankets when he was cold and cool drinks when his throat was parched. She radiated goodness and warmth in stark contrast to the coldness and sterility of the tomb of the hospital. He woke one morning to find her quietly administering a syringe full of insulin to herself as she steeled her response to the prick and stab of the needle, a ritual since she was a child of eleven, he learned. *She is a diabetic*, he thought, but quickly withdrew that to say—*No, she's a brave young woman with diabetes.*

She became the sun of tomorrow when the angels rolled away the stone from his medical sepulcher. When he succumbed to pain and drugs, she was the last face he saw, and when he returned from the outskirts of forever, she was there praying. She was the reason he lost his belly full of butterflies and why the rats that gnawed incessantly at his guts finally went away.

Each time Susan left, she smiled and said, "See you later, alligator."

He knew she was drawing him out, but he would dutifully answer, "After while, crocodile."

The deal was sealed when she walked into his room just before he was released from the intensive care unit and found him getting out of bed in one of the flimsy, backless hospital gowns that concealed little.

"Hey," he said, clutching the white cotton sheet around him. "I am exposed here!"

He was captivated when she smiled a mischievous smile and replied, "Why do you think they call it—ICU?!"

* * *

On D-Day, as they dubbed departure day from the hospital, Susan processed his discharge papers and wheeled the reluctant and reticent hermit to the door. Clay's car waited under a firefly-yellow sun hanging in a sky as blue as robin eggs. A chorus of chattering house sparrows nestling in the hospital eaves sounded a sympathetic symphony.

Reentry into the land of the living was almost too much for Michael. Everything was too loud and objects moved too fast. The world rushed at him like a universe in fast-forward. It was jolting and jarring to his senses and flushed up the sense that danger was all around—lurking, watching, and waiting to attack him again.

His daily therapy was not all contingent on the visits with physical therapists in Tupelo. There were many days of fishing on the banks of the pond in Parker Grove and the slow savoring of BBQ plate dinners made by his uncle at TKE soda fountain. Then came the movies with Susan at the Lyric Theater, where they saw *Love Story*, and she told him, "Remember, love means never having to say you're sorry." When she said it, he almost believed it. So one night, he gave her one of his grandmother Pearl's King Leo peppermint sticks and told her, "This is for when you just can't bring yourself to say 'I'm sorry.'"

The day finally arrived when he gave up his fear of loving again and his inability to fix, correct, and arrest the random variables of a transitory life. He made an uneasy peace with his inclination to hold back and guard against loss and grief.

Michael journeyed alone to the worn paths of the old cemetery in Memphis and stood beneath oak trees with too many circles of life to count. He lingered there under branches that seemed to strain toward heaven, to knock on the door of home and origin. Leaving the filter of the tree leaves that scattered the sparkling beams of sunlight, he once again climbed the lonely hillside smoldering with memories where Dixie waited in sunshine and shadow in the thin veil between the here and the hereafter: a place of allure despite the pain. It was all that was left of her.

The last drops of an ocean of tears fell as he knelt at her gravesite. With a trembling voice of hello and goodbye, he began to recite to her a song of closure and an ode to hope. It was the last poem he had begun before her young life of promise had been snatched from her.

> *The Heart*
> *The heart tis a complex creature;*
> *Men are born and die ignorant of its feature.*
> *What seems evident is often contradiction;*
> *Where lies truth, where begins fiction?*
> *Navigate its channels, try its tides;*
> *Ebb and flow, its currents seldom confide.*
> *Mystery shrouds like fog, tis the heart's master;*
> *Peer through the mist in vain, pursue faster.*
> *Circle the world, bridge the seas, cry in twilight;*
> *Lovers repeat the eternal prayer tonight:*
> *Protect the seekers and searchers, who the heart would tame…*
> *Tis fraught with riches, replete with danger, but worth the game.*

Chalky white clouds formed and re-formed above him, and black crows lazily flapped along, casting passing silhouettes over his silent vigil. He laid a wreath on Dixie's grave and tucked the poem within its delicate white flowers. Without looking back, he turned and walked in forced briskness down the soft, willow-green slope of the hillside with an aching and tentative finality. Shadows of pitted monuments and majestic oaks caressed him. Ancient angels and cherubs, standing guard over masters long gone, seemed to mark his passage from the dead to the living with a silence that was deafening.

A sudden, clamorous wind, birthed from nowhere on a windless day, plucked his poem from the cradle of flowers, bore it upward like a wild, errant kite, and swept it down the rolling knoll to a private memorial service on the far side of the cemetery. There, a young couple had just buried their son, and with him their broken marriage: an unjust interment of fragile, husband-and-wife love and affection.

"We can't go on. This must end," the young woman with the dishwater-blonde hair and puffy face said to her husband. Her bloodshot eyes wrongly accused him. She knew it was unfair, but someone had to pay for all the pain and answer all the "Whys" of life gone terribly wrong.

Her husband looked older than his years. His mouth had a slackness, his skin appeared dry, and his suit hung loosely around his shoulders. Weary and defeated, he weakly protested, "This isn't my fault."

"I know, but I can't look at you anymore without seeing him. I can't live with that pain, that constant reminder," she replied in tones laced with a corrosive bitterness.

In those chilly moments as the fading mulberry sun painted the sky in pinks and mauves, the now avian-like poem fluttered and danced over their heads. They looked up at the object that momentarily blocked the sun. Shielding her face, the woman swatted at the paper as she would an angry wasp buzzing her head, but the air-borne paper that bore Michael's affirmation of life and love combed her hair, brushed her cheeks, and then stuck to her blouse like stubborn flypaper.

She pulled it from her and began to crumple the poem when she saw the title…"The Heart." Despite herself, she began to read the words. When she did, the snuffling began. The tears came, and they wouldn't stop. She looked at her husband and suddenly knew she didn't want to give up on love. It was her first glimmer of knowing that he was the one person she couldn't survive loss without, her only chance to rediscover innocence—her first understanding that redemption was possible.

She handed it to him, and as he read it, he began to tremble. They embraced, tenderly at first, and then they clung to each other and wept as one for the first time in many years. They hugged like they had before tragedy fractured their world. They were pilgrims, like Michael, who had been to the City of Destruction, where it seemed always the depths of a bitter winter with no island of joy called Christmas. But now, they were one step closer to the Celestial City.

CHAPTER THREE

"I'm gonna tell you racketeers, something
you can understand. Don't let your tongues
say nothing that your head can't stand."
—Richard "Rabbit" Brown,
"The Downfall of the Lion"

"The unholy trinity—politics, crime and business…"
—Thomas Jones, Big Daddy in the Big Easy

"I need you…like roses need the rain."

Sad song lyrics played repeatedly in a loop in Michael's head as he drove to the northern headquarters of the MBN. Susan called it the jukebox of his mind. Like Michelangelo carving to free the angel from the marble, Michael was seeking himself within the alabaster of his tenuous existence—the overlapping of past, present, and the "twelfth of never" that promised to set him free from the poisons fermenting within his soul.

"For he's a jolly good fellow, for he's a jolly good fellow. That no one can deny." Out-of-tune caterwauling of agents and staff greeted Michael upon his return to duty in Oxford. They scuffed into his office, drinking too much—all wound up like old Timex watches that had taken their lickings but kept on ticking.

The "Welcome Back!" banner was tacked above Michael's door. A box of iced catfish from Sheriff "Monty" Monteith sat on his desk, suggesting that it had been too long since they had eaten the greasy delights of the Blue and White Café in Tunica.

Monty's note said, "C'mon over, Michael, and we'll party. Our bumpers may be dragging but our batteries are still charging!"

John Edward Collins sent a dog-eared copy of Charles Portis's *True Grit*, and there was an anonymous letter from Missouri containing a newspaper article and a photo of a girl handing out Bible tracts at a tent revival.

The girl in the picture looked like Ruth, the waitress at Ace Connelly's club in De Soto County, the same young woman-turned-informant who called to warn of the planned hit on Michael at Horn Lake. Her long, rust-colored hair had been close-cropped, and her dress was now demure, modest and sackcloth in appearance.

He was certain that it was her, and he was glad. On the back of the clipping was a note that said, "Praying for you, Agent Parker."

He received a call from Clay the first day he was behind his desk, something familiar to assure him that he was back in the saddle again.

"Hey, buddy. How're you doing?" Clay asked with the warm tones of a best friend.

"Good. Well, okay, I think," Michael answered honestly.

"It's good to have you back. There's much to do. Pat said to tell you that we are looking forward to the big day—long overdue!"

"Hey, I'm just happy to be out of the hospital. Did I tell you that they put a bell on me when I was in ICU? They didn't want me getting up without them," Michael said.

"Hey, that's disgusting!" Clay replied.

"I thought so. I pulled it off one night and just roamed the hospital," Michael said.

"Yeah? What happened?" Clay asked.

Michael laughed. "They caught me and said they were going to nominate me for the No Bell Prize! Get it, Clay—the No Bell Prize!"

"Oh, man. You had me going," Clay said through his goofy chuckles.

"Thankful to be alive, Clay. A preacher at Parker Grove Baptist told me, 'It's not right to pull in single harness all your life. You'd better get the horse out of the barn. You're getting too old to be horsing around!'" Michael's smile was one to inspire Polaroid or Hallmark moments.

"You sound as if you're just lost in happy today, Michael," Clay said.

"Yeah, I am, Clay. Susan's the one," Michael said.

After a long talk with Clay and a day full of too many memos, memories, and sanguine faces full of forced cheer, Michael was drained, pasty white, but anxious to talk.

He picked up Susan in Tupelo, and they parked on the knoll above the tiny house where Elvis was born. As a silvery moon played peek-a-boo through the trees and a lone mockingbird whistled a tune of insomnia, Michael spoke of the days of yesteryear and of the people who had become his extended family in a world that seemed without mercy or boundaries.

He saw a path to healing in revisiting the familiar ground of his covert projects with Clay. They were echoes of his vivid hospital dreamscapes—not normal dreams, but time machine trips to the isle of memory, where a house of mirrors bled with the rainbow-colored emotions of another time. They were magic carpet rides where yesterday was only a good dream away. Old friends and old enemies waited to replay the game again and again in epilogues that falsely and cruelly promised a next time, when history might be rewritten.

Michael had read the script and seen the movie before, and he knew the beginning and the end. None of his dream pleadings of "No, don't do it" could change one thing about it all, but walking through the vignettes in slow motion did reveal subtleties missed in the living years.

As a gentle, gray drizzle began to mist the windshield of his car, he turned to Susan. "Did I ever tell you about the time…?" he began and then laughed. "Sounds like a tall fish tale or war story coming on, huh?" They both laughed.

"Yes, probably, but I never tire of your stories," she said with her enchanting smile. "They get better each time you tell them."

As "True Love Travels on a Gravel Road" played on his new eight-track player, he began to tell her of a dusk-to-dawn mission with Clay in Jackson.

"Clay's nervous informants fed him sketchy details of a likely midnight visit to Governor Hal Davidson by a mysterious visitor from New Orleans. So Clay asked me to run a two-man surveillance with him," Michael told her.

* * *

Clay explained, "Michael, these sources have given me some good information. Two weeks ago, they told me to watch the home of Lieutenant Governor Bill Melton, the political patron of our old friend, State Patrol Investigator Red Winter. Red still procures women and whiskey for the legislators in Jackson.

"As a result of this heads-up, I watched a Mafia underboss and two of his soldiers from the Big Easy arrive at the home of our smiling and jovial lieutenant governor. They whisked the lieutenant governor away to a long and cozy late dinner at the Jackson Country Club. So I think our time might be well-spent following up on this new information," he said with that child-like air of excitement he would get when the hunt was on.

Clay was tight-lipped about who the visitor from the Crescent City might be, reluctant to jinx it. He would only say that he was "big, very big." Whether this bit of information proved reliable was of no concern to Michael. It was enough to spend time with someone about whom the word "friend" was not a conditional term.

Surveillance with Clay included the usual industrial-strength black brew of toxicity he called coffee. His car was cluttered with intelligence-gathering devices and reams of paper. His car smelled musty and foul, like an old wet dog, but it was always time well spent.

As they waited, nestled in a recessed spot at a rest stop off the interstate, a soupy gloom of fog reminiscent of 1940s film noir seemed to mysteriously materialize just before midnight. As veterans of many long, late-night vigils watching various dusk-to-dawn deviants, Michael and Clay sat in the bird-dog car illuminated by the green wash of spook devices on, in, and under the dash. They traveled the happy trails of yesterday.

They knew the days grew short for their time on the stage, and the retelling of it all might somehow freeze the stories that would one day end. Like thieves in the night, illness and corruption were the twin armies approaching the castles of their world.

The wispy, gray mist covered the secret agents of Mississippi like a gentle curtain. Michael and Clay remembered the brume of another similar night over in Tylertown, and they spoke of the Grand Weaver who had intervened so many times.

"Michael, we've been lucky—blessed really," Clay noted. "I don't know any other way to explain how we fell into so many briar patches and came out without a scratch."

They sat silently reflecting on it all as male cicadas, freed from their seventeen-year exile below the surface, chirped like click toys in the trees above the Bureau car. The radio softly played Johnny Rivers' ode to those secret agent men who "lead a life of danger."

Clay suddenly killed the radio at precisely 11:45 p.m. and leaned his ear toward the window. Off in the distance, the humming sound of an approaching heavy vehicle grew louder and louder, and the ground cloud was suddenly parted by ghost-like headlights reflected against the smothering murk. A Rolls Royce Silver Shadow II with Louisiana plates thundered by the rest area where Michael and Clay waited, bursting the shroud of fog like football players roaring through paper banners on Friday night fields all over the Magnolia State.

"That's our target," Clay said in a raspy voice weakened by illness and radiation treatments. He slid the Bureau car into the ocean of vapor. Like some silent submarine easing into the vast emptiness of a silver sea, he dropped in behind the Rolls. Clay used his cutting-edge display—so essential to one-car surveillance—to change the appearance of their headlights to mimic many different vehicles.

It was soon evident that the car was headed for downtown Jackson, followed closely by the one-eyed dragon that stalked the visitors. True to the tip received, the Rolls headed for the historic building now cast by fog and street lamp in eerie outlines—the Governor's Mansion. The car arrived with a sudden squealing of brakes as clocks struck midnight.

A beefy man with no neck and thick shoulders, a crooked nose, and only three fingers on his right hand stepped from the driver's seat. In the tint of the night-scopes, Michael thought he looked like a professional Italian wrestler he had once seen wrestle BoBo Brazil, but the "Green Lantern" lights cast everyone as your Martian cousin.

The driver looked left and then right and opened the back door. A stocky man about 5′4″ in height (two inches of that the stacked heels he was wearing) stepped regally from the car. Clay tapped Michael's shoulder and pointed at the photos in his folder of Carlos "Little Man"

Marcello, the squat, self-professed tomato salesman who was also widely recognized as the Godfather of the New Orleans Mafia family.

Michael whispered quietly, "Oh, man!"

Marcello had close-cropped hair and was clad in a shiny, undertaker-black suit that reflected the incandescent blue-white from the lone streetlight. He walked toward the gate with the confident stride of a man who knew that he was expected and would be welcomed.

The redheaded highway patrol officer on duty opened the gate without pause for the undisputed crime boss of New Orleans, the "Midget of the Mafia." With all the flurry and pomp that might be afforded a visiting head of state, the gates opened to one of the "men of respect" New Orleans Mayor Joseph A. Shakespeare once singled out as "the most idle, vicious, and worthless among us…"

Marcello had been the face of crime in New Orleans and the South since the day he and friends robbed a bank in 1929, as much a part of a Louisiana subculture of prostitution, gambling, violence, and drug trafficking as gumbo, étouffée, crawfish, and po'boy sandwiches on Bourbon Street. Here he was in the lime colors of MBN night scopes, poised to enter the mansion of the governor of the great state of Mississippi.

Michael said, "Clay, it's Red on the gates."

He noted for the record that the officer on duty for this historic visitation was Red Winter, a cagey, freckle-faced wiretap specialist for the governor, as well as the procurer of women and whiskey for the arrested adolescents in the legislature while they were far from the home fires. Winter had been a part of the team that raided Ace Connelly's joint and, unbeknownst to Michael, had helped himself to dozens of guns and custom-made pool sticks in the aftermath of the raid that night.

"Not surprised," Clay nodded. He pointed his new boom mike at Marcello to capture and record any snippets of conversation as he shook Winter's hand. Clay's mike followed Marcello as he turned to walk to the door of the mansion in the grainy light.

Winter and some compliant members of the patrol had been used to ferry syringes full of morphine to the Governor's Mansion in their patrol cars. Prescriptions were written in the name of the governor and others in his inner circle by his own doctor and filled at multiple drugstores by unquestioning pharmacists. The narcotic was needed after the governor's announced acute appendicitis, in reality a gunshot to his posterior by his wife. Now the drugs were just for recreational use.

The MBN had no recourse under the state statutes. A doctor wrote the orders, pharmacists filled them, and the user was under a doctor's care—technically legal under state laws designed to go after street drugs while protecting favored dispensers.

The State Medical Board, populated by doctors, refused to hear the evidence against the physician supplying the governor with morphine. The Board of Pharmacy, comprised of pharmacists, wouldn't look at the record of abuses by their peers in Jackson and Meridian. The U.S. Attorney, an appointee of the governor's political party, had effectively removed the blindfold from the eyes of Lady Justice when he declined to get involved.

Michael dubbed this political triumvirate "Hear No Evil, See No Evil, and—Evil."

And as he and Clay watched, the door to the mansion opened and there was Davidson, embracing the Godfather who was first convicted of drug trafficking in 1938. He had been deported by Attorney General Bobby Kennedy and suspected by some for involvement in the assassination of Bobby and his brother, President Kennedy. Marcello, blessed by Frank Costello, Meyer Lansky, and La Cosa Nostra, had cultivated friendships with powerful political figures since the days he lavished money and favors on police chiefs for a free hand to run his many criminal operations in Jefferson Parish.

In the graininess of the night scope, he now kissed Mississippi Governor Hal Davidson on the cheek.

The fish-eyed governor said haltingly, "Don Carlos, I didn't know if you were going to make it in this weather. It is late or early, depending on your view. You don't have any yapping dogs, uh, those unfriendly agents following you, I hope?"

With his bodyguard at his side, translating to impress the governor, Marcello answered in Sicilian. Marcello shrugged at the governor's question, and with a flip of the wrist, said, *"A un povir'omo, ogni cani cci abbaja."*

The driver said, "The Don says that every dog barks at a poor man."

Davidson nodded, laughed, and said, "Well, it was getting so late, I thought you might be staying for church with us tomorrow."

Marcello smiled and said, *"Lu Signiuruzzu li cosi, li ficci dritti, vinni lu diavulu e li sturclu. Jiri n celu ognunu vo; l'armu cc'e, li forzi no."*

"The Don says that God made things straight, the devil came and twisted them. Everyone wants to go to heaven. The desire is there but the fortitude is not," his driver answered, punctuating his translation with dramatic gestures to capture the Don's meaning. They all laughed, Davidson bid Marcello to enter, and the doors of the Governor's Mansion opened again like the mouth of a hungry beast, feeding on morsels of misery.

Two hours later the door opened again, and Marcello bid Davidson farewell. As the Godfather turned to walk to the waiting limo, a sudden, heavy rain and gusts of high winds, fed by a tropical storm off the coast of New Orleans, blew into Jackson and rocked the Bureau car. The squall seemed to sweep into Jackson to reclaim one of its own who had escaped the tempest.

Then Clay did something totally out of character for the former Army officer. With his jaw set, he violated all protocol. He stepped from the car without warning and approached the gate to the mansion, just as the driver and the highway patrolman produced umbrellas to protect Marcello from the gale.

With water pouring from his gaunt face, Clay appeared out of the night like some lightning-bleached apparition and shouted above the wind, "We know who you are and what you're doing here. Get out! Get out and don't come back!" Clay's voice prickled the flesh on the back of Michael's neck and stood his hairs on end.

It was a surreal moment, and everyone froze. All the actors in this touring production of "Rednecks and Gangsters" seemed to be moving in slow motion, strobe-like images illuminated by intermittent, ghostly flashes of thunderbolts. Stunned men, who lived lives expecting assailants to emerge from the shadows at any moment, contemplated drawing weapons. All the players looked at each other for seconds that seemed like an eternity.

Marcello's driver moved his hand toward the .45 that hung beneath his left armpit, but he paused at the sobering and unmistakable *rack-rack* sound of Michael loading a round of buckshot into his Bureau-issued 12-gauge, Remington pump shotgun.

"Freeze, fat boy, or go home in a body bag!" Michael yelled.

The Mafia soldier made like a statue. Marcello was drenched in the downpour, but he remained the same expressionless man that agents of Bobby Kennedy had left in the jungles of Guatemala to live or die.

Red Winter, gray uniform soaked and silver badge reflecting the white bursts of lightning, looked Michael in the eyes and raised questioning "what now" red-orange eyebrows. Michael nodded as the curtains near the front door of the mansion opened, in one flash revealing—just for a frozen moment—the face of a wild-eyed Governor Davidson.

Clay turned suddenly and left the soaked gangsters and officer under the rumble of thunderheads and heavenly fireworks, captives of a whipping wind and a driving downpour. He marched slowly back to the car, soaked to the bone, and breathing in gasping, gulping inhalations. Michael lowered his shotgun, backing away from the mobsters as he followed his mentor. As they drove away, he looked at Clay in silence and handed him a towel. Michael knew there would be no reprisals. No one would want the questions that Davidson would have to answer about a bewitching-hour visit from the nation's most powerful mobster and the culture of corruption that flourished behind the scenes in Mississippi. In any event, the old Don would soon be convicted on racketeering charges in Louisiana and bribing a judge in Los Angeles.

"I'm a little tired, Michael…tired of all of it," Clay sighed. "These politicians make a mockery of all we do and think there's not a thing we can do about it. Tomorrow, Davidson will probably talk about Mississippi being free of organized crime. The U.S. Attorney, who no self-respecting folks would ever associate with in polite society, will vouch for him. People will believe their line because they read it in their know-nothing newspapers."

* * *

As the strains of memory and a tsunami of introspection faded away, Michael turned to Susan and smiled. "Some story, huh? Who would believe that these things happen in the good ole U.S. of A.? How many would deny their lying eyes if they had seen it?"

Susan squeezed his hand and Michael sighed. "You know, I didn't know what to say to him that night. My fingers gripped my shotgun so tightly that my fingers ached. My voice sputtered and trembled, and my palms were sweaty at what I'd seen. There are moments when the right words at the wrong time can become the wrong words. So I just told him, 'I know, I know.'"

At that moment, a falling star streaked across the sky, and the talk shifted from yesterday's sorrows to tomorrow's clean slates when two would become one.

CHAPTER FOUR

*"I want to hide a while behind your smile and
everywhere I'd look, your eyes I'd find."—Donovan*

*"Mom always said that I was born to sit in
the electric chair, but I'm proving her
wrong. I'm going to die on my knees,
begging for my life."—Bauvard*

The day finally arrived.

Like the process of entrainment where body parts placed close together begin to beat in unison, like clocks in a room that synchronize to the same time and rhythm, like two people who know what the other is thinking without the necessity of spoken words—so it came to be between Michael and Susan.

With Clay as best man and Timothy Charles, Bureau Director and ordained minister, officiating, they wed in a simple ceremony. Clouds flowed like water in a stream above the gnarled and ancient catalpa tree that had seen generations of Ole Miss students come and go. Their wedding tree was there when the University Greys marched off to death at Gettysburg, seeds from the campus to slumber forever young between past and present.

Their ceremony was filled with the mystery, wonder, and paradox of the script now playing out in their lives. A smattering of freckles on her cheeks accentuated Susan's eyes and smile. Michael caught himself in a moment of connect-the-dots on a radiant face framed by the white netting of her tulle veil and the satin dress her mother, Stella, had created. It was a traditional gathering, but they read from personal lines when each said, "I love who you are and the why of our love."

After the nuptials had ended, well-wishers, including Glenda and Linda, the nurses forever bonded with Michael from the night of Fredrick's horror, finally wandered off to The Grove to a reception for the newlyweds. As dusk fell across Ole Miss, Michael sat alone with Susan under the same old bean tree that had shaded Faulkner, Manning, and Confederates of old.

Michael looked at her. She was gentleness encased in a fragile binding. Susan asked him, "A Confederate penny for your thoughts?"

"Just wandering here and there," he said. "Did you know this was the same type of tree Washington and Jefferson planted at Mount Vernon and Monticello—the same trees we had in Parker Grove? I used to pass this old tree every day on the way to class here at Ole Miss. Some preferred the giant magnolias with the beautiful white blooms—not me."

He picked up one of the fallen, heart-shaped leaves with ruffled, white flowers. "These twisted old trees held the catalpa worms Pearl and I harvested for the bait that catfish so dearly loved in Parker Grove. We'd grab our buckets and cane poles and head to that muddy, old snake-infested pond. I learned to swim there, dog-paddling amidst the turtles slip-sliding into the waters and the daddy bullfrogs croaking from their pulpits of mud."

He smiled and she smiled back at him with a sweetness accentuated by the line of her temple and the set of her warm eyes. There was so much he wanted to say—tales of Tylertown, the ambush the day of the ice storm, near-death by the hands of would-be assassins at Horn Lake, the real evil that stalks the earth—stories of those who were gone but not forgotten, and the journey that brought him to the hospital and her.

He worried for her because he had seen how the stress of work at the hospital and a part-time job wreaked havoc with her blood sugar and sent her into some serious tailspins. He smiled back at her and shrugged his shoulders. Susan squeezed his hand and hung on his every word. Her eyes, full of quiet strength, spoke volumes when she said nothing at all.

After the reception, they left for Ft. Walton Beach and Okaloosa Island for their honeymoon. They passed through many towns in Alabama where the directions always began, "When you get to the Waffle House…" In what would become their sanctuary in storms of life to come, he looked at her that first night as if he had never seen her before—this woman-girl who had come to rescue him. An aching tenderness overcame him as they sat on their lanai under a million stars. They held hands and listened to the *shoosh-shoosh* of the tide rushing in to eat away the white sands of the beach. The wind blew against the glass doors behind them, flopping the fronds of the palms near their condo, and a whistling sound vibrated and tweeted the metal tracks.

After a long silence, she said, "Michael, you know I'm not as fragile as you might think. You don't have to be so tenuous with me, physically or emotionally. I won't break."

"I know," he said at the subject he wanted to avoid. "I just want to understand how we manage this disease."

"I've been managing it or being managed by it since I was eleven," she said. "I did have some moments of denial. Once I passed out at Mississippi State when I decided to see what would happen if I didn't take my insulin."

She paused and said with a little-girl smile, "I woke up in the infirmary.

"I'll go with you wherever life calls us," she said, "but you would do well to keep good health insurance. Otherwise, one day I'll break us. The prognosis isn't good for any of us who have juvenile diabetes."

He looked at her and thought her face would still be beautiful at sixty, if she lived that long. The fragility of happiness haunted him.

"I'll make a deal with you," Michael said. "Let's try to live on one salary. You stay home and see how that works. Deal?" he asked, as he took her hand and felt the warmth of her pulse.

"Do we have to talk about it now?" she asked.

He became the hero in their favorite movies that night, and she the heroine in a world where second chances were still possible. They held on tight to one another until the dawn broke over the white sand beaches, when a squall-fed rain swept in from the sea and raged against the windows of their sanctuary. He slipped out of bed and parted the curtains to see the white churn of the surf as it pounded the sand crabs trying to find their homes.

He turned to watch her, the rhythmic rise and fall of her chest. She opened her eyes, this angel of his mornings and nights, and blinked away the waking fuzziness. She smiled at him, raised the covers, and held out her arms…and the rhapsody began again.

* * *

After the honeymoon, Clay and his wife joined Michael and Susan for a picnic and softball game hosted by Tim Charles and his family at Sardis Lake, west of Oxford.

Charles approached Michael away from the others and pulled at the brown-blonde beard on his chin. "Michael, I thought I'd tell you before anyone else does. We've taken Tommy Tindall into our home at Tchula. We helped him get released from Parchman on early parole. It's something I believe God wants me to do. He's redeemable, Michael."

"Tindall? Isn't that the former KKK bomber?" a confused Michael asked.

"Yep, they called Tommy the 'Mad Bomber' of the Ku Kluxers," Charles said.

"And yes…he was in that infamous shootout with police when he was caught trying to bomb a synagogue in Meridian. He could've died that day but didn't. He had a tough life of abuse and manipulation growing up. So much hate preached at him that it twisted him. He found God in prison, and though it angers many of our old buddies in law enforcement, I believe it's sincere, and I want to see if he can be brought to the service of God."

Michael listened and nodded, amazed at Charles, who had been threatened by the Klan when he was a young investigator and ballistic expert on the Medgar Evers murder. Now, here he was, risking his reputation to help a member of the organization that left threatening notes on his windshield and rattlesnakes in his mailbox while he and his family were in church.

"Yeah, a 'jailhouse conversion,' some judged it," Tim said with a quiet, matter-of-fact observance as the wind blew his thinning hair. He brushed it back with his hand while a bright-red cardinal reassured him from a nearby pine tree, "Pretty, pretty, pretty."

"That includes your old boss in Washington—J. Edgar Hoover," Tim added with a grin. "I took Tommy to a prison ministry gathering with Chuck Colson. You know who was there? Eldridge Cleaver, the former Black Panther who also once hated people for their skin color—whites in his case. You know what he told Tommy? 'We both got a lot to live down, don't we?'"

Tim paused and said, "Michael, you know Reverend Will Campbell spent a lot of time with Tommy behind the barbed wires of Parchman. Will told me, 'We're forever arguing people must be restrained, so we pass a law and set about enforcing it. But if the law is for the purpose of preventing crime, of securing a just and civilized society, then every wail of the siren calls out its failure.' Will would look at me, and say, 'For God's sake, let's try something else, Tim.'

"Naïve, our friends might say, or radical, and they might be partially right on both counts, but Will has seen the executions, as I have, where the prisoners are dragged, bound and gagged, to be strapped in the electric chair. I've heard some of our friends say that it's beautiful, artful justice in its purest form…It isn't.

"There's that uneasiness about us holding the power of life and death, wondering if the state got it right. They often don't, you know. That twenty-five-hundred volts of electricity hits the man and scorches his skin. Smoke fills the room. His hands turn black, and then they hit that second surge when the first fire bolt fails to kill him. That smell is something you can never wash from your nostrils, and it's all so ghastly that you want to vomit. Then you hear the chanting of those gathered like the spectators in the old Roman coliseums to celebrate death. They call for the BBQ sauce—exalting death, reveling in it, so sure the state has judged the right man."

Tim sighed and pawed the ground with his ostrich boots. "Are they innocent? I don't know, Michael. Some proclaim innocence to the end, and some not, but to me it just sounds too much like 'Crucify Him! Crucify Him!'

"Boil it all down at those moments, or now with Tommy; it doesn't matter if it's Klanfolk or kinfolk. What really resonates isn't the temporal right and wrong of it all, but knowing that, as Campbell put it, 'Mr. Jesus died for the bigots as well.'"

Charles looked at Michael with a deep peace that burned in his soul and said of his own critics, "You know, Michael, it's just mind over matter. I don't mind, and they don't matter."

Sensing he was getting too serious, he got a sly smile on his face and said, "To my way of thinking, the real miracle might not be that

Tommy and Eldridge became religious, but that Cleaver has become a Republican!" He laughed the hearty belly-shaking cackle he was known for.

Timothy Charles had something that Michael was desperately seeking—something the world hadn't been able to shake since that first whimpering cry in a stable in Bethlehem.

CHAPTER FIVE

"A time of innocence…Preserve your
memories; they're all that's left."
—Simon and Garfunkel

"You don't know about sadness 'til it's
chiseled in stone."—Vern Gosdin

A trip to Memphis with Clay and his wife followed the picnic. James Walker, the proprietor of the Bottom of the Blues Club on Beale Street, sent free passes and dinner coupons for all as a belated wedding gift. The mallard ducks were marching at the Peabody, where everyone called you sir or ma'am if there was any chance you might be even thirty minutes older than they were, and foamy, root-beer-colored water lapped at the shores of Mud Island.

The day began with a slow trip over the muddy waters of Old Man River on the stately old Memphis Queen. With its red paddle wheels churning the tawny froth, they paralleled Riverside Drive and the bluffs that seemed to guard Memphis from the ravages of nature.

When they made land, a visit to Graceland followed. Fans of all ages were milling around the gates. Many were walking up the hill as far as the sawhorse barricades allowed. The Memphis police arranged for Uncle Vester Presley to meet the refugees from the MBN and escort them up the hill for a private visit to pay respects to the man who saluted Dixie on the cemetery hillside so long ago.

A sudden shower came and went, leaving a humid mist rising from the hot markers for the Presley family. There seemed to be something lingering in the air, suggesting too many premature interruptions of life. Michael looked at Susan and saw that she had been crying. The emerging sunlight touched the tears on her face, turning them a mercury color. He looked at Clay, who had been somber all day. He stared at the inscription on Elvis's tombstone—"God saw that he needed some rest and called him home to be with Him."

He turned to Michael and asked, "Buddy, when we get back to Oxford, do you think you might dip into your collection and see if you have his song 'Lonesome Cowboy'?"

"Sure thing," Michael answered as they walked back down the hill, savoring the peace at the end of the day. The sun warmed his face. A sudden rustling of the leaves above him whispered a murmuring message, and images of Dixie's funeral at the church down the street flooded over him. Suddenly everything about living and dying seemed as wrong as Christmas in a hot, Mississippi summer.

At home in Oxford, they played what was to be the requiem for the lonesome cowboy. Clay was a mile deep down inside himself. He looked up with a wrinkled forehead under coppery-colored, thinning hair and asked, "Remember when the outlaws hired people to kill you, and I took the money man for a ride and explained life to him?"

"How could I forget it? I fussed at you in the hospital, as I remember," Michael answered.

"I wonder what happened to him…what happened to all the players in our dramas?" Clay asked with an air of wistful fatalism.

The day they had all dreaded suddenly seemed near. It had hung over them ever since Michael left Dixie in Memphis to rush to Clay's side in the Jackson hospital several years earlier.

* * *

Six weeks later, Michael went to visit Clay for what he hoped was one more victory over the invading cancer. As night shaded State Street in Jackson, he sat alone with Clay in a musty room in Baptist Hospital, a place Clay had taken to calling Hotel California. "You can check out anytime you like, Michael," he said, "but you can never leave."

Trim and tidy nurses in starched, ivory-white dresses and matching flat-heeled shoes came and went. Then the grim-faced doctors appeared in their official smocks with news as evident as the epitaphs etched in their tightly drawn physician faces.

With the hushed tones of undertakers, they asked Michael to leave, but Clay said, "No, Michael and I have no secrets."

The doctors with evasive eyes spoke of tests, of treatments attempted over the years—a tortuous stalling of the final report on the cancer that Clay had been exposed to in Vietnam ten years prior.

They finally got to it. "The cancer's back. There's nothing more we can do. We're sorry."

A deafening silence followed their news and departure. A clock ticked loudly in the void, and somewhere below, the wail of an ambulance siren announced its arrival at the emergency room. Michael couldn't actually hear the air system, but the antiseptic smell of recycled air was overwhelming, and the drapes moved ever so slightly. An eerie orange seeped in from the outside as the daystar hid its face from the awful news: Clay was dying.

A robin in a holly bush melodiously signaled the end of another day, but death, so long back there somewhere in the rearview mirror, was now staring at them just over their shoulders, binding the neck muscles and staining the very fabric of that time and place.

"Clay, I…" Michael began and faltered.

He struggled to find the words that would comfort, but choking, suffocating grief subdued him. It rendered him speechless and useless, but the best friend he'd ever had rescued him one last time. "Michael, we know how we feel about each other. Words aren't necessary. We've been expecting this for a long time, buddy, but it's been a good ride."

Clay's eyes looked dead, and he began to speak of a life that had lost its charm, petty worries that now seemed comical. In a long, rambling monologue, he said all he could while he could.

"We lost our innocence and our way in the fifties and rebelled against our parents," he said in a rattling whisper. "In the sixties, we rejected all authority and dropped out. In the seventies, we forgot love, no difference between love and sex. Life became all about us, the "Me" generation, and hyphenated words like self-esteem replaced honor, duty, and country. Like cows satisfied chewing their cud and dogs happy with just an old bone, people became carnal and instinctual.

"Everyone pretends to be happy in their false gaiety. They watch each other and ask, 'Am I doing it right? Are we having fun yet?' They seek meaning and assurance from the know-nothing crowd, while they polish their mirrors of self-worship, and believe this is all there is or ever will be. They are coreless captives of a prison of their own making who ask, 'How can I escape my prison when there is nothing and I am nothing?' They wake from their dreams crying, 'Oh no, oh no…This isn't the way it was supposed to be.'

"It's just no place anymore for an old cowboy like me," he said with a deep sigh of resignation and finality.

Michael was stunned. He'd never heard him talk like this.

Clay continued as a strand of graying hair fell across his forehead, "They think truth is expendable, that there is no truth. They travel on their dustless roads, polish their rustless cars, and attend the chapels of their Godless religiosity. These birds of a feather flock together for mutual assurance. 'I'm okay, you're okay.' Boredom's their curse, and they populate the mental wards and suicide watches; when relativism fails, they finally reach out to God in their prayers of contradiction: 'Dear God, if you're real, save my soul, if I have one.'

"When the times get hard, these feckless, soulless people will turn on you like pullets in a henhouse attacking a new chicken that's sick or intruding. They won't give the cock time to crow three times—or even once. They'll peck that little rooster until he is a bloody pulp because it—you—are a threat to the established order.

"Be careful, buddy. It's not easy to be a hero, and that's what you want to be. I won't be here to watch your back. Remember, in life there are only two pursuits—love and power. No man can have both."

He sighed and looked a hundred years old. "Don't worry about me, Michael. What can they do to me? Threaten me with eternity? Heck, that's no threat at all. Go home, buddy. We'll talk some more tomorrow."

* * *

There were more tomorrows to talk, but time began to bleed away the twilight of Clay's life. He was in and out of the hospital until one inky night, when it seemed the angel of death was near and the blood of the Lamb marked the doors of the redeemed.

Michael and Susan visited Clay in the hospital that night, and Pat told them to go home, get some rest, and return the next day. As they prepared for bed, grief subdued words, and they fell into a fitful sleep.

Michael hyperventilated in the midst of pain and panic. Over-breathing and unable to catch his breath, he moved across the edges of sleep and waking.

He had taken one of the pills his doctor had prescribed for panic attacks, but he couldn't sleep. He could hear Susan's soft snuffling, choking half-sobs in the night. The silence in the room seemed to highlight the creaks in the house as it stabbed at their bleeding hearts.

He finally rose and fumbled in the dark to select an FM radio station on their RCA stereo for some low-volume white noise. He fell back into bed in a dream-drenched, fitful sleep where he saw his own face—the face of a stranger.

In the storms of his nightmares, the albino was chasing him again, men ate razor blades and swallowed fire in Tylertown, and sniper fire rained down on Michael and his agents. A cold sweat poured from his body, drenching the night clothes plastered to him like Saran Wrap. His heart pounded like a timpani against the walls of his chest, startling him awake at two in the morning.

When he sat up in his bed with fear all around, Elvis was singing a tune of goodbye on the radio. It was a poignant recitation of parting that received little airplay, only performed in concert near the end of his life— a story of a man who's dying in a hospital room as his wife is sleeping near him. The man takes his pen to write her a note and says, "Softly, I will leave you…though my heart would break if you should wake and see me go, and beg me stay, for one more hour, for one more day…"

Michael tried to arrest his gasping breaths until he could separate the dreamscape from the fuzziness of the waking world. He drifted back into a tortured sleep for a few hours until he rose at six to call Clay's wife at the hospital.

"Pat, I'm on my way. How is he this morning?" he asked with apprehension.

"Michael, he left us for Zion…at two a.m.," she replied softly.

There was only the *swoosh, swoosh, swoosh* of the ceiling fan, the deafening *drip, drip, drip* of a leaky faucet in the master bath, and the warmth of Katie the cat against Michael's ankle.

The song was no dream…the lonesome cowboy—dead at 2 a.m.

* * *

The final roundup for the best lawman Michael knew and the truest friend he ever had was scheduled for two days later. A glittering sea of sapphire blue as far as the eye could see punctuated the slow, crawling funeral procession that stretched and snaked for miles along Interstate 55 in Jackson. It finally arrived at the verdant cemetery nestled in the rolling hills and deep hollows surrounding Clay's remote ranch.

Clay left instructions to bury him in his western shirt and jeans with his pointy-toed cowboy boots straight from Texas. Clay's daughter, Jenna, had his eyes and fine, blonde hair that she raked nervously with her fingers. She captured how her family's loss diminished all whom her father had touched. In trembling timbres, she read Procter's poem of those who seek to stave off or explain loss, that last transcendent and calming chord sent from heaven, to be found again there:

"I have sought and I seek it vainly—That one lost chord divine— Which came from the soul of the organ, And entered into mine. It may be that death's bright angel will speak in that chord again, It may be that only in heav'n, I shall hear that grand Amen!"

She sighed and added, *"Rock of Ages, let me hide myself in thee..."*

After everyone had gone, Michael and Susan lingered and held hands at the grave site. They looked at each other and at the fresh grave and whispered, "See you later, alligator."

* * *

Another part of Michael died that day when he lost his partner. He drove to Oxford after the funeral, sat in the quiet of his office, and looked at a picture of all of the original Bureau personnel from that first year. The founder/director, who was like a father figure to him, had been banished from the Bureau, and Chris, who had once dated Cybil Shepherd, was lost to a scandal. Lonnie was killed in Corinth. Larry Burnside had fallen to politics. Many of the agents had become jaded, disillusioned, or sought solace in the depths of the bottle. Remnants of the Davidson regime were still trying to find the means to wreak revenge on Michael. While he stared at yesterday's still, it was as if his own image in the photo began to fade and disappear.

* * *

A month after Clay's funeral, the Bell System offered him a job as a manager in telephone security. Some asked him to stay, but he knew it was his appointed time to leave the crusade that was much more than a job.

In a tearful farewell, a leaden and pale Captain Parker laid down his gold shield in a wake of sorts. Loud, nervous agents laughed too hard, tried too hard, and drank too much in a pseudo-masculine ritual to cover the pain of passage, separation, and yet another loss that diminished the whole.

After most had left the office, abandoning garbage cans filled to overflowing with party favors, Merlene Johnson, the first black female agent in the state, wandered into his office. She plopped down into a chair and seemed to bear the discomfort of someone about to say something personal. Her massive, mahogany pupils were afloat on salty pools of emotion propping up the angst etched into her face.

"It's not going to seem right without you here," she said, scuffing her shoes on his floor and looking down like a kid trying to say something hard.

"I'm going to miss you guys," he answered.

"I wouldn't have made it in the Bureau under another supervisor," she said, in what he could sense was the beginning of a prepared speech.

"That's not true. With your talent, you would've made it under anyone," he protested.

She would have none of it. "No, I remember how some said they would never have a black agent working for them. No one wanted me when I left the academy...no one, but you. All the other black agents are gone. I'll never forget what you did for all of us. You showed us the right way. That's why everyone wanted to transfer up here with us."

"You were our secret weapon," he said. "None of the old gangsters thought you existed—no such thing as a black female agent in Mississippi. You sneaked up on 'em, and they never knew what hit them." He smiled a big smile, desperate to steer the conversation away from the disconcerting moments of real emotion that always induced a fidgety, twitchy anxiety.

They shook hands, and after a quick and awkward side-to-side embrace, she was gone. Though such tenderness made him uncomfortable, he would return to that moment of innocence again and again through the years, especially when the world turned against him.

He finally left the valedictory farewells at MBN's Northern Headquarters, mementos in hand, and wandered onto the campus he loved. As the evening light began to fade, he sat near The Grove watching students come and go. A bright-blue snap of lightning suddenly delineated the heavens from the terrestrial, and a distant rumble of thunder sounded like the cannons at Gettysburg as it echoed across Ole Miss.

A lone ROTC bugler played Taps over the end of the day and what had been his life. Michael nursed old memories and grieved ones that would never be—one last mourning for what might have been. Like Jonah, he was about to be swallowed by a whale called the Bell System for an unexpected journey into the unknown.

Time to pause from questioning his questions, reshuffle the deck that seemed stacked against him, and indulge what Susan called his "gypsy restlessness."

Up ahead—Nineveh.

CHAPTER SIX

*"He's a well-respected man about town, doing the
best things so conservatively."—The Kinks*

*"It is better to have your head in the clouds and
know where you are…than to breathe the clearer
atmosphere below them, and think that you are
in paradise."—Henry David Thoreau*

Gusts of early morning wind whipped dust and papers down Capitol Street in Jackson, Mississippi. A newspaper boy sped along on his old JC Higgins three-speed bike, throwing papers left and right with unerring accuracy. Automatic sprinkler heads popped up to mist the ornamental shrubs and hardy lantana that anchored the windowless Bell switching center.

Michael Parker, the newest Bell System security manager, squinted into a rising, pale-orange sun that had subdued the night, casting a golden hue along the street and down the walls of the slate-gray buildings of downtown.

In his mind, he returned to the scene of the crime, so to speak, and could almost hear the chants of the marchers years ago when he joined their parade down Capitol Street—an undercover agent in an anti-war protest peppered with drug dealers and revolutionaries. It was here that he first encountered Fredrick, the day when Fredrick's lifelong obsession and hatred for him began, culminating in the death of Dixie Lee, the woman Michael loved.

He had only been gone from the Mississippi Bureau of Narcotics for six months, but already, his replacement as captain had suffered a heart attack—Michael's heart attack if he'd stayed. He and Susan made their nest in a grove of pecan trees on New Post Road, a modest three-bedroom ranch design. As agreed, they lived on his income so she could stay at home and control her diabetes, free from the stress of the nine-to-five grind.

In his new position, Michael needed information that only he police could unearth. Brad, who replaced Clay in the MBN Intelligence unit, was helping as he could with such requests. The loss of the trappings of a cop, once seldom considered, now seemed strangely unsettling. The loss of the image of who he had been evoked a sense of impotency—even danger—at the thought of the state. Government was no longer "we" for him; it was now "they."

Today Michael was not wearing an old Army jacket and peace symbols. He carried a brown leather briefcase as part of the garb of his new culture. His short haircut, tastefully understated navy-blue suit, and white button-down Oxford shirt (paired with the requisite red tie) captured his new corporate look—red, white, and blue. It was, he decided, the clothing of the indigenous people.

Harvey Smoot, the rotund Bell personnel manager who lived to ring cowbells at weekend Mississippi State football games, yelled at him across the street. "Hey, Mr. Parker, whose future are you carrying around in that briefcase today?"

"Wouldn't you like to know?" Michael answered.

"What'd you say?" Smoot called back. The infernal cowbells had ruined his hearing.

Bell Security managers, he found, had the air of the internal sleuths of the system—just enough sleuthing for the corporation to claim the mantle of completeness and a veneer of integrity. They were a cross between agents of the law, as he once had been, and a kind of secret corporate police with their own mystique. It was a self-contained universe with its own mores and folkways, an entrenched culture that could churn out dazzling telecommunications innovation, but one that also resisted organizational change with all its might. He felt like an alien in a foreign world when he arrived.

Suspicious of intruders and all new entrants, the organism viewed him with a skeptical eye. They suggested that he acted like a "lone wolf" and were unsettled by his apparent lack of need for the normal bonding rituals—the drinking and parties bureaucrats seemed to hold sacred. The corporate culture operated on the dictates of Bell System practices: reams and reams of instructions and regulators of free thinking written by the ancients of Bell to be passed down from generation to generation with virtually no updates.

There was a binder of directives to instruct new managers how to think, act, dress, converse, and breathe on a cloudy day, a sunny day, a warm day, a cold day…all conceivable situations were covered in the Bell "bible," eliminating the need to ever "think." Enforced by the corporate culture and the dictates of social and political pressure, it bred a comfortable stagnation and the unique type of manager Michael came to label as the "Bell-shaped head."

Such devotion was given to the mandates of long-dead gurus of telecom that the new inhabitants had forgotten how to be nimble and innovative in both the small and large decisions of the day. They were numbed by a contagion of sameness and isolated culturally in a world where there was little change: a cocoon where a kind of cradle-to-grave immortality was granted. "You got a job for life now, son," they assured him.

This mentality of no drive, no incentive, and worshipful homage to deceased corporate gods was reminiscent of the inhabitants of Jonathan Swift's Struldbrugs on the island of Luggnagg, who couldn't die and envied those who could.

All that concerned many in Bell was that subtle calculation—would life or money run out first? So each day they followed the ritual of checking their Bell stock and multiplying the gains versus the losses to reassure themselves that they were in control of their destiny. With breathless revelation, they would announce to all they saw, "Have you heard? Bell's up three cents today!"

Michael observed that the inhabitants possessed a kind of industrial-strength smugness, but he wondered if it wasn't a carefully constructed mask worn by those who proclaimed, "Look at us. We have it all!" There was always the whispered and uncertain echo from the question mark—"Don't we?" He'd been taught to use things and to love people, but in this land, many loved their toys and used people in an alternate universe of excess and self-indulgence, where lots of meetings and seminars imitated life…lots of talking, but only to people like themselves—no contamination and no growth.

Lips moved and people jawboned, but nothing was ever said that had not been said before. The Muzak in their elevators seemed befitting in their world where gluttony, the cousin of avarice, was ingrained. The restaurants they recommended had a variety of names, but all the menus were from Café Limbo.

Even worse, systemic corruption was a way of life. Department heads and managers had become accustomed to swimming pools and houses (courtesy of contractors they supervised), and the local tire stores just slipped a new set on the manager's personal car in return for the company business. Paramours were given apartments and promotions; construction companies bought Bell supervisors, buried cable at half the required depth, and then billed hapless farmers who snagged the phone lines with their plows. The money flowed, and the damage from illegal placement only insured more business for contractors and new kickbacks to managers. It was an incestuous monopoly where the purifying doctor of free enterprise had yet to arrive.

They'll probably one day pass a law as an answer to their own systemic failings, he thought. *They'll probably call it something like "Call before you dig!"*

But the first rumblings of the ugliest word known to monopolists was already looming on the horizon—competition. Graft and girls were an unstated package of perks that Bell would soon not be able to afford. From the beginning, the dinosaurs were always trying to force Michael into a mold he didn't fit and never would. They looked upon him as a threat, though they weren't quite sure why. Somehow the pack could always smell a lone wolf. His department head told him with a sneer, "You were a big fish in a little pond. Now, you're just a little fish in a big pond."

I should probably be grateful, he thought. In a sense, the game provided a slot for him in a farcical contest, where the simple chopping of the snake's head could have averted the need for so many investigators. But the offenders at the top would have lost their goodies. So people like Michael were employed to nibble at the snake's tail and be a token testimony to corporate ethics.

And the gods of corporatism surveyed all they had created and said, "It is good."

* * *

Joseph Spencer, Ole Miss Law School graduate and head of Bell legal, called Michael and asked him to look into a lawsuit pending by some farmer in Davis County.

"Our contractors were plowing in some cable and left the pit open. This guy says he fell in it and has been unable to work for a year, and that he can't run his construction company and farm. See if you can find anything to mitigate the damage. They look at us and see deep pockets. So they're asking for a ton of money. You can earn your money for the corporation if you can do anything with it. Be careful down there! We've had lots of cable and copper theft."

So Michael headed to rural Davis County on his first case for the legal department.

On the *bump-de-bump* of a worn, blacktop highway, he entered the city limits of Jefferson, the sleepy county seat. A wooden sign welcomed him to the "Hamlet where time stood still." A flock of white cattle egrets passed overhead as they dipped and wheeled toward a nearby pasture. The narrow road seemed to be the lone exhausted, asphalt path in and out of the city that time forgot. Massive oaks surrounded the town like a wall of some olden fortress.

It looked more like the '50s than the '80s as he drove past old dairy bars, old men playing checkers in front of a hardware store, a barber shop replete with the old turning striped barber pole, an outdoor movie theater where drive-in Lotharios plied their trade, and everywhere—people who absentmindedly waved at everyone they passed. No fast food chains and no golden arches had contaminated the area.

His first stop was the local building supply shop. The proprietor, Del Smith, was a tanned man with white hair, a broad smile, and a perpetually furrowed brow accented by a wide, Stetson hat. He was forthcoming and seemed to have no affection for Harold Davis.

"Harold Davis hasn't had credit to buy supplies from me in over two years. He had no business to lose, son. His company, like his farm, was more a figment of his imagination than reality."

"Can you tell me how to find this R.J. James, who Davis supposedly hired to manage his farm?" Michael asked.

"They call him Bull. Yeah, I'll tell you, but you need to be careful, son. Bull is not to be toyed with," Smith warned.

So Michael took the directions and headed down the two-lane highway that went through miles and miles of undeveloped forest land. He followed the paved road until it ended. He picked up a dirt road until it also ended. Finally, he bumped along a rutted path of sorts through heavy thickets that shrouded whatever lay beyond. From what he'd been told, he knew he must be close to the home of Bull James. He could feel it—a sixth sense he had developed over many years of searching for fields of dope, remote airfields, drop sites, and distribution mills.

After bouncing along, he finally saw it—off to the left, situated high on a wooded hill. Under low-hanging mimosa trees, heavy with pink flowers, was a ramshackle wood-frame house with a tin roof. Three wooden pillars held up the roof over the front porch, and purple clematis vines that seemed oddly out of place adorned each one. Off to the side, an old rusted car—windows smeared and broken—rested on blocks in front of an ancient smokehouse, now falling down. Off to the other side, underneath a large fig bush, was a Bell cable reel full of copper.

Michael exited his car after trying his mobile phone. He was out of range with the new company device that he felt was almost decadent. In an amazing bit of tunnel vision and paradigm blindness, a Bell official had once said only 50,000 licenses would be needed for all of America. To think there would ever be any market or demand for mobile telephone devices beyond that, he said, was…"unthinkable."

He walked up the slope carrying his briefcase. A pack of dirty black-and-tan hounds rose at his approach. Sooners, he thought. Sooner eat than sleep, but not much eating by their emaciated look. Immediate sniffs of the air and barking and growling ensued, with menacing snarls revealing dirty teeth and red gums.

A barefooted and flat-nosed Bull James came out on the porch wearing no shirt and jeans riding just above the hip line and just below the roll of fat that must have required quite an intake of belly in order to button the pants. A shock of receding, greasy black hair on a sloping skull accented small, crazy black eyes. His skin was a deep, red-brown tone with some deceptive fat over musculature, cords of muscles that protruded in ridges and knots along his shoulders, arms, and back. The dogs cowered before him, whining as they bowed their heads and tucked their tails in total submission...learned behavior the hard way, Michael imagined.

"Now who you be and what can I do for you, mister?" he growled as he picked up an old .22-caliber, single-shot rifle lying in the rotting front porch swing.

"I'm Michael Parker, a security manager with South Central Bell. I'm here to talk to you about work Harold Davis said you did for his farm when he was laid up in April and May of last year."

"Well now, fancy that," he sneered, sizing up his guest and glancing at the visible Bell reel of copper.

"I do lots of things for Harold. Besides, what's a city boy like you doing way out here in our little county?" he challenged. The bicep in his right forearm began to twitch, causing the girl in the tattoo there to appear to dance.

Before he could answer, Bull moved closer. "I stayed in one of dem Jackson hotels once that had bellboys, but you some kind of different Bell boy, ain't you? A college boy, I bet. That's what's wrong with your company."

Okay, I'll bite, Michael thought. "How do you figure that, Mr. James?"

"Watergate!" he bellowed incredulously, as if it were self-evident. He leaned the rifle against a tree and moved closer.

"What does Watergate have to do with the company's problems?"

"It was them college boys that caused all of that mess!" Bull snorted and guffawed, now only three feet away.

Michael could imagine that Bull had been the bully on the school yard: a big kid who terrorized scrawny ones and took their lunch money. Beatings probably followed any complaints to teachers. *Here I am*, he thought...*no badge, no gun, no deterrent to bullies*. He longed for the weight of the .357 on his hip. He had felt naked and vulnerable since he left all that behind—never more so than now.

"That may well be, Mr. James, but it doesn't take a college education to figure out that you couldn't have done any work for Harold during that period, because you were in the county jail in Pascagoula for drunk and disorderly and assault on a police officer," he shot back.

Just then, Bull lowered his head, bellowed like a water buffalo, and charged like his namesake in the old rings of Spain—like the legendary old high school linebacker he was. Back in the day, Bull would wrap those arms around the quarterback in a rib-cracking vise, and like a pile driver, just slam him into the ground. He would take the quarterback out of the game, no matter if Bull was offside or got a penalty. If, by some miracle the quarterback returned, he would hurry every pass and overthrow his receivers when he saw Bull coming again.

Michael felt every bit the matador facing an enraged bull. He sidestepped the charge and, as Bull passed him, he hooked the big man's ankle with his own, much like he did with charging linemen in high school when blocking seemed insufficient. Bull went tumbling end over end, and landed with a *whoosh* of air—atop a huge fire ant mound. The South American invaders swarmed him immediately, and Bull came up dancing wildly—swatting, brushing, and screaming in a frantic, high-pitched, almost girly voice. Then his eyes rolled back into his head, and he fell to the ground—eerily silent.

A young woman in a too-short, sheer housecoat came out of the house—bleached-blonde dry hair with black roots showing...the outline of a child's bosom and a mouth so thin that she painted it with a heavy red smear of lipstick to enhance it. She had a pockmarked, puffy face, a slight double chin, and dull, vacant eyes—the slack-jawed look of a woman who was unloved and emotionally abandoned.

"Never seen anyone do that to Bull before, mister," she said, as she moved quickly to Bull's side. She pulled a syringe from her housecoat pocket and jabbed Bull in the shoulder with the anti-venom.

"Anaphylactic shock, they call it. He's allergic to them ants," she said in a matter-of-fact, emotionless tone.

She looked at Michael as she massaged the serum into Bull's arm from the injection site. "He bout killed several city folk come out to serve papers, sell stuff, and such. One salesman liked me way back when. Bull bout beat him to death. They say he still throws up if someone just mentions Bull's name. He was going to take me away from here. He thought I was pretty. Bull won't like this when he comes to. His cousin is the sheriff, you know?"

She paused. "Do you think I'm still pretty, mister?"

Michael said, "There's a big world away from here and men who would love to have a good woman like you." She smiled through teeth that needed the attention of a dentist, blushing red against her pink housecoat.

He took the lot numbers on the copper reels, tagged each reel with his name, gathered samples of the copper, and photographed Ma Bell's property for evidence. He left the woman-child kneeling by her man. He worked his way back down the dirt road in his blue Chrysler until he heard the wail of the siren.

He pulled into a logging truck road and parked behind a thick stand of pine trees and low-lying bushes as the cruiser whizzed by, flashers going. Michael hit the blacktop and took the back way to a neighboring jurisdiction, the shortest route to the county line. No time to get caught in a place like this and suffer any time in a jail that could be deadly.

Yes, sir, no badge, no gun...no respect, he thought. This is what he had come to. Today was what passed for a rip-roaring tale in the lore of Bell Security.

His exit from Davis County was only noted by a small metal sign alongside an overgrown ditch in the middle of nowhere. This stretch of highway was an area of sparse meals for the circling buzzards that prayed for the infrequent motorist to have a chance encounter with a stray rabbit crossing the road: dinner courtesy of road kill.

Finally in range of the mobile tower, he dialed Virgil Layton, the only state highway patrol investigator he'd ever trusted, to tell him that he would like to meet him to file charges on the reels of Bell copper he saw at Bull's place. Michael suggested warrants be obtained immediately from the district court outside of Davis County.

He phoned Joseph Spencer, Bell's legal eagle, who said he'd already had calls from the irate attorneys on the lawsuit to say that if Michael ever returned to their little slice of hell, they knew how to handle such city boys. The young lawyer was aghast that another member of the court could say such vile things. Michael told him it was a good thing and said, "We have them now."

"Yes, I think so," Joseph said. "After they finished cursing you, they lowered their figures by half…we are negotiating down from there. Good job! Your department head will receive a generous commendation for you, and it will be copied to the state president."

Michael smiled. Then he called Susan…

"Hello," she answered, a crackle of excitement in her voice, mixed with anticipation—the memory of the gentle night before fresh in her mind. She knew that he was the only one who had their new number for their first real home.

"Hi, honey, it's me, your lone wolf."

"Hey, how's your day been today? Anything exciting? Been howling at the moon?" she asked with the little-girl giggle that so soothed his heart.

"Nah, nothing much. Just a routine day, pretty boring," he said. "I'll be home soon."

After he hung up, he thought again about Bull. He was a thief and a brute for sure, but was he only a reflection of the brutality deeply seated in the human collective? If he'd been born in a different time, Bull might've been one of the lucky thieves who hung next to Jesus of Nazareth.

He knew something was missing in the equation of his new life. There was still the faint melody that he couldn't quite hear; just out of his view was a lighthouse or fogbow—that arc of light he could see at a distance but couldn't bring into focus. It was a riddle he could almost solve, but then it slipped away. He had the feeling that in all the tragedy of his life, he was at once the pursuer and the pursued, both running from and to the same inescapable force. Like a logger dancing on trees floating on a roaring river, he hopped from one to the next, spinning precariously as he sought safe harbor and answers.

Impulsively, he pulled over to the side of the road and stood beneath a brilliant pink sun. Three turkey vultures circled over the remains of a dead possum whose bones they would pick clean and leave to whiten in the searing heat. The chirping of lowland bugs serenaded him with a cacophony of hungry songs.

He looked intently at his scarred hands, pierced by Fredrick that night so long ago, and he suddenly asked, "Are You there?" No answer came, only the honking of a flock of Canada geese, flying in a perfect V-formation above. He heaved a deep sigh, and as he stepped back into his vehicle, a new butterfly, still trailing some of the evidence of its past life, winged its way toward the heavens—born again, having shed its former husk.

As he drove away, the question still nagged at his soul: *Is it, is He—gone forever?* And the Rolling Stones' anthem for a rented world played on his radio…"I tried and I tried, but I can't get no satisfaction."

CHAPTER SEVEN

"My nightmare. My sorrow. My past. My mistake.
My regret. My love."—Shannon L. Adler

"…so sleep, silent angel, go to sleep…"—The Hollies

After Michael's trip to Davis County, all heck broke loose over the following weeks. Mississippi Highway Patrol Investigator Virgil Layton, a folksy man who claimed to be the only MHP investigator to earn his job through merit, was fond of saying, "Police work ain't no Tupperware party, you know." He got his search warrants from the circuit judge and served them at Bull's place with state Alcohol and Beverage Control agents.

They found the cable reels, tons of copper, and C-wire used to run phone service to protectors. The ABC agents found moonshine stills in the thickets behind Bull's house. It seems that a local Bell supervisor had been selling material on the side and letting Bull have keys to the work center. The supervisor was indicted, arrested, and fired by Bell.

Bull James squealed on his friends. The sheriff was served with a notice from the IRS for tax evasion, calculated from Bull's testimony about protection payments. In the midst of it all, Michael heard that the brute's abused wife decided this was her chance, so she left for parts unknown with the salesman that Bull had thrashed. Local sages and watchers marveled at it all and asked highway patrol investigator Virgil Layton, "You mean all this was stirred up by some telephone boy nosing around down here?"

Michael pondered all this as he approached 341 Millbury Lane in Jackson. Bright daylight had faded to pink and surrendered to the curtain of the purple-black night. The sounds of last-minute lawn mowers purred in the distance. Venus bobbed like a cork floating on an astral sea. A faint siren moaned on the thoroughfare above the subdivision as an ambulance carried a patient to Hinds General Hospital, another possible interruption of the cycle of life. Nighthawks soared and dived for bugs to feed hungry babies waiting in the nest on the roof of the flat-topped grocery store down the street.

The smell of the dusts and sprays of earnest gardeners lingered in the air, suggesting roses were once again safe from black spot, immaculate lawns would be the most vibrant green, and hopeful residents might receive the coveted "Lawn of the Month" sign reserved for the perfect yards of suburbia. Somewhere beneath a bank of shrubs, the liquid whistle of a towhee searching for insects salted the stillness. A deliberately slow-strolling Himalayan cat with flame points crossed the street and stared at him with a regal air and haughtiness. He thought of Katie at home with Susan. It seemed a "too-perfect" setting for a case of obscene and threatening phone calls.

Jenny Stuckey tentatively opened the door of her tidy, squarish brick home to his knock. She wore the look of crushing grief and immeasurable loss—a twenty-six-year-old widow, too young and too unprepared for sudden aloneness. She was a slender, blue-eyed blonde with pursed lips, deep vertical lines between once-pampered brows—now unattended—and gray circles under guarded blue eyes that had been leaking for a long time. Her hair was as lifeless as she was, and it held the odor of smoke. She knew he was coming but stared at him through foggy blue lenses as if she had forgotten their appointment.

Jenny's husband, Jackson Police Captain Mark Stuckey, had been an up-and-comer in the department—strong, Marine-jawed, and Quantico-cut. He knew the ropes, knew the streets, and knew what to do and not do. Then one night he forgot it all for a split second.

In a routine domestic disturbance, he backed up officers removing an abusive alcoholic from a rickety, wood-frame dwelling on the wrong side of nowhere. As the officers cuffed and led the man away, Mark offered kind words to Cecelia, the battered wife with bright, black-and-blue marks on her face and arms.

When he turned his back to leave, Cecelia pulled a Saturday night special from under her pillow and shot Captain Mark with a pistol that retailed for the price of a good meal. It was a gun that had exchanged hands countless times on the streets of inner-city Jackson—an impersonal tool of death. Witnesses said Mark looked stunned, grabbed his shirt, saw the blood, turned to her with a questioning look of "Why?" and smiled an ironic smile at the thought that he had violated the very caution he had drilled into countless rookies. He seemed almost amused that he could now be felled by such a small and inferior weapon. Then he tumbled into the finality of death—the endless sleep.

The newspaper and television coverage showed the funeral procession that backed up traffic from Capitol Street to the interstate. The service was filled with the military rituals of death—folded flag for the widow, bagpipes playing "Amazing Grace," and a wave of centurions in blue searching for meaning in the unique bonding of a profession set apart from society—defiantly saying, "We have our brothers, we don't need you." Then after the crowds of mourners had abandoned the young widow to the deafening silence of a home without her husband and best friend, the calls to Jenny began.

Whispering, hissing utterances of depravity stabbed the vulnerable young widow at the lowest ebb of the tides of life, causing her to question if she was being punished somehow—killing what little was left of her in the deepest recesses of her psyche. The world had moved on and left her with the reality of emptiness, alone with small children who wanted to know when "Daddy" was coming home—and now this knife to what was left of her heart as she struggled to "tidy up her life."

As he watched her watch him from some remote place where broken hearts live, he said, "Mrs. Stuckey, I am Michael Parker with Bell Security. I'm so sorry for your loss."

"Come in, please," she said. "Mark would have known just how to handle this, Mr. Parker. I have no clue how or why this is happening." Two carbon copies of her—a blonde girl about four and a sandy-haired boy about two—hung on to her and peeked from behind her skirts.

"We see it all the time. Predators seem to know when to attack, but they are almost always harmless. Most are people who could never look a person in the face and say anything like this. The anonymity is what they use…the shock value from people who are often insecure and wrestling with their own demons."

They talked for a while, and he explained to her how the call traces would work. If she had a suspect, she didn't volunteer that information, but she talked of her job at a local college—a job that was vital to providing for her children now that her husband was gone. She had his life insurance, but the job provided a financial lifeline. Her overwhelming vulnerability was palpable. He felt the urge to reach out as she teetered near the edge of the abyss, but he retreated to the safety and comfort of the routine, acquiring her permission to "tap" her line.

The oldest of Bell System switching centers served her home. Tracing calls was arduous and had to be done piecemeal between offices or "step-by-step" as the switching office was called. The recipient of a call had to lay the phone down without hanging up to "trap" the call and keep it open for technicians to work back to the source. The first time she tried it, they found it came from outside her area. It originated in another switching center, a crossbar office in South Hinds County. A bridge was put up to that office to prepare for the next call.

She repeated the procedure that weekend, but the caller came to her home at midnight and cut down the drop wire from the pole to her house to break the connection. Michael knew then he wasn't dealing with the ordinary obscene caller. When the next call came in, it was trapped and the trace made to a college town. The phone was on the campus of Hinds Community College at the home provided to the dean of the school where Mrs. Stuckey worked—her boss.

Michael told Mrs. Stuckey that they had the trace, and the phone used by the caller was locked open and unusable. He asked her if she would prosecute but told her he couldn't, by law, tell her who the call came from. Someone in Kentucky had once taken the information from Bell and then took a baseball bat to the caller. It was an effective deterrent but also tremendous liability for Bell, which changed the company's practices.

"No, Mr. Parker, I want this to end. You have my permission to handle it. No police. No FBI." She was listless and passive, a woman playing solitaire now. Her dreams were shattered. He wanted to tell her…make new ones.

As he turned to leave, she touched his arm and whispered in a faraway voice, "You don't have to tell me, but I know who it is. At work after the funeral, he said he wanted me to trust him for everything, but in his disguised obscenity on the phone, he said he wanted to—truss me." She laughed a sardonic laugh. "Trust to truss…when all I wanted was truth, Mr. Parker, the why of it all…But I don't know what truth is anymore." He thought she was diminishing right in front of him, collapsing inwardly, fading from view but wanting to talk.

So before he left this third visit with her, he listened as she began to tell him about Mark. She had been a gangly girl, all arms and elbows, bookish and shy. She had no boyfriends but began to blossom into the beauty she became at seventeen.

Mark, the star quarterback, asked her out. As they became inseparable, she awakened from a sort of slumber. They married young. He went to Vietnam with the Marines, and after the fall of Saigon, they came home to Jackson. He was accepted into the Jackson Police Academy, where he graduated with honors—a natural for police work. Mark gave her identity—wife, mother, lover, and friend. She knew who she was, but now he was gone.

As she talked, Michael looked at her and knew the suitors and manipulators would come soon. The beautiful young widow had a house free and clear due to Mark's life insurance, a pension from the city for her husband slain in the line of duty, and a stable income. Some would see her as a pliable woman to be exploited in her grief. If she got lucky, maybe one would come who would be good and true, but after talking with her, he knew that none would ever be—Mark.

When Michael walked up to the door of the house on the Hinds College campus, he could hear the bird-like chirping of children inside as he rang the doorbell. A man answered who filled the picture of a dean. He was professionally attired and resembled the picture hanging in the foyer—though with a little more belly and a little less hair, which demanded creative combing. Over his shoulder Michael could see children at the supper table and a matronly woman who looked like wife and mother with bowls and dishes setting the table.

"Are you Mr. Stevens?" Michael asked.

"Why, yes, I am. Can I help you?"

"I'm Security Manager Parker with Bell Telephone. Is your phone out?"

He looked hesitant but said, "Uh, yes, I believe it is."

Michael walked to the phone, picked up the receiver, and spoke to a Bell manager on the other end at Mrs. Stuckey's house, confirming the two phones were connected by the trap they had placed on the line.

He turned to the dean and said, "Would you like to talk about this outside?"

The pink suffused his face. "Yes, yes, I would," he said as he glanced at his wife and children. He closed the door behind him, separating his perfect life from the corners of his secret world.

"Mr. Stevens, I'm here to tell you that calls violating the law have been made to Mrs. Stuckey from your house. She has opted not to prosecute as of now. Do you want me to assure her that this will stop, or do we have to file charges?"

"No, Mr. Parker, they'll stop!" he said anxiously as he peered again through the prominent whites of his eyes at his wife and children, visible through the glass of the storm door.

"Will she, will she…know it was me?" he asked.

"No, we're not allowed to tell the customer. She has authorized us to handle it."

He turned to watch the man as he went into his home. The dean wiped his sweaty palms on his trousers, looking this way and that to see if anyone had seen it all to catch a glimpse of who he really was. He looked diminished but not really contrite. No evidence of remorse was to be found in him. Michael didn't feel good about how easy the man got off.

Michael called Mrs. Stuckey to tell her she would receive no more calls but only got her answering machine each time. He thought she had just had enough of Alexander Graham Bell.

The next day the phone rang on New Post Road early on a Saturday morning. The hard rain of the night before had turned to a gentle drizzle trickling through the gutters outside the bedroom window, where he slept sandwiched between Susan and a purring Katie. In the distance, a gentle rumble of thunder sounded like a long drumroll.

The head of Bell Security told him that Mrs. Stuckey had been found dead. She had sent the kids to her sister's house so she could rest.

They found her on the deck behind her home after a suspicious neighbor called the police.

Her husband's service revolver was on the floor beside her, one round spent. She had freshened her makeup, fixed her hair, and kept her appointment with death. As some female suicides do, she shot herself in the chest, not the face…the last refuge of temporal beauty they can't bring themselves to mar. How could the morticians ever repair a face so damaged, and what would the mourners say?

A wave of darkness rushed to Michael's shore, and he thought of the randomness of death. She was just a young widow searching for truth. He had met those who say there is no truth, those who say all truth is relative, those who don't know what truth is, those who aren't sure, and those who say that anyone who believes in absolute truth is dangerous.

Jenny was dead. That was truth.

Is there a law? he wondered. *Should there be a law for the person who nudged her over the edge—the dean—or should the woman who killed her husband and now languished in the Hinds County Jail be charged also for the delayed death of Jenny—a double homicide?*

Michael had healed of his physical wounds but hid his emotional scars. He thought of Mark and Jenny, forever frozen in that 1974 wedding picture, all smiles and anticipating fifty to sixty years of wedded bliss. Memphis and Dixie Lee came rushing back.

His increasing bouts of anxiety and depression had worsened, and the nightmares were back in 3-D. Panic attacks had begun to cripple him in sudden bouts of the sweats, a racing heart, and a nameless, faceless fear that could be paralyzing at times. He lost control—what Michael feared most of all.

He was looking for currency in a world that seemed to offer nothing but wooden nickels—an intrinsic value, not the fleeting extrinsic assigned by the world. Driving toward home, he suddenly had the sensation of not knowing if he was stopped or moving.

Desperate to regain perspective, he looked at the cars to his right and still couldn't tell if they were moving or if he was. He looked to his left for fixed points…houses, trees, and such. It seemed the houses were moving as well. It was a metaphor for how he felt. All the fixed points in his life and the culture around him were moving, shifting, changing, and unreliable.

When he arrived home, he reached for the crutch his friendly MD had been giving him—a mellow-yellow Valium to numb the runaway thoughts.

He paced and breathed deeply in vain attempts to slow his racing heart. Finally he turned on his radio, his laxative for the mind to flush away the enveloping melancholy. He drifted off to a tortured sleep where young widows died solitary deaths to join another young woman Michael felt he had failed. Susan moved close to hold his hand and snuggle her soft, warm cheek against the nook of his neck, as Katie the Siamese Geiger counter clicked soothingly at his feet.

As the artificial numbing of the sedatives began to mask his pain, his mind spun the nagging question by Peggy Lee: "Is that all there is, is that all there is? If that's all there is, my friend, then let's keep dancing. Let's…have a ball, if that's all there is."

Then, in his dreams, he saw Jenny bent over Mark's casket on the banks of the Jordan. She turned to look at Michael and whispered, "That's the thing about death. It's just so…final."

CHAPTER EIGHT

*"...the prince of power of the air, the spirit that now
worketh in the children of disobedience."
—Ephesians 2:2*

*"I collared the Holy Ghost in the cellar
and threw him out."—Jean-Paul Sartre*

While Michael struggled with the eternal questions of man—unchanged since the eviction notice was served on the residents of the Garden of Eden—a young, blonde high school principal named Mary Ruth Robinson sat cross-legged at midnight in a circle near the deep old forests of the Savannah River basin in Georgia.

Robinson, her husband Ben, and their friends Carla and Louis Earl Pate were refugees from another of their trendy, libertine parties. They gazed into a roaring fire some two miles from the home of the night's hosts where couples were "swinging" at what was now considered a routine gathering. Partners changed like the songs on the old turntable, which spun odes to "go where you want to go, do what you want to do, with whoever you want to do it with."

The Augusta suburbanites of the club "Self, Self, and More Self" gathered to watch bootleg copies of the trendy play *I Love My Wife*. The actors reassured the audience that their marriages were stronger from acknowledging that the grass isn't always greener, nor the drugs harmless, as was intimated in the show tune "Everybody Today Is Turning On." The local men imitated the stage characters and professed their own love for their wives after engaging in what they said was an exercise in "therapy" of sorts. The play indulged their fantasies but soothed their sensibilities. In the end, the men on stage—after much experimentation—sing the title song, "I Love My Wife," and go home with their own wives.

Mary Ruth's plunge into this twisted world had begun decades earlier. She had been a tortured soul since her youth when a childhood friend was lost to the bottomless depths of an old well he fell into right before her eyes. It seemed the earth had become a living, breathing entity. It just opened up and swallowed him. She watched helplessly as he clutched at clumps of grass and green saplings to halt his slide into the pit. She could still hear the screams of the young boy crying and begging her to save him.

The sinkhole sucked him in like the quicksand of the jungle movies she had watched on her parents' old black-and-white television set. His upper torso was visible to her as his fingers and nails dug trenches in the soft earth, desperate for some handhold. Then only his face and arms could be seen…finally only his hands, until his cries were muffled and then silenced. Mary Ruth had grasped for him, but she couldn't save him. She felt responsible somehow for the freak accident; she believed she had offended God and could never make it right.

She was never quite the same after that childhood trauma. The whipping she suffered—the first of many—reinforced her feelings of shame. The shattered girl began to lean on her physical beauty to compensate for what she believed to be the bad karma she must pay for. She felt slighted by her father in favor of her brother. That fed a feeling of inadequacy and guilt that became tied to her gender and a never-ending quest to please male father figures in her life by whatever means, some that would make Freud blush.

Marriage seemed an escape route. She and her classmate Ben married young, much too young. He was crew-cut clean on the outside, but as troubled as she was on the inside. She was running from something just as he was. It was a union of co-dependents from the beginning. She worked her way through college to become a teacher, as the war of words at home became almost normal to her—something she thought she deserved. To escape, she left for a time to work at an Indian reservation school but found the walls of her prison went wherever she did.

Mary Ruth began to smoke heavily and became well-known to the state troopers, who called her the "blonde racehorse" as she pegged the needles of their radars near Swainsboro in her silver Mercedes convertible. She throttled her car and her lifestyle when she became pregnant, but her initial hope for a change in her marriage faded. When her labor began, she was forced to drive herself to the hospital. Ben lay semi-comatose, passed out from a worsening battle with the bottle.

The parties they attended became increasingly depraved and dangerous. The small groups were businessmen and women by day, church members on Sunday, but libertine enthusiasts on Saturday nights. The private games she and Ben played frequently left her with black eyes. She became a master at concealing her bruises with makeup. The games had grown repetitive and unsatisfying, the fantasies—sadistic and threatening to her life at times.

Ben encouraged her to find new avenues for her love of dance and to turn her training as a ballerina to belly dancing. She complied and became quite proficient at it. He asked her to perform in front of the drunken attendees of Augusta's swinging parties, found in underground newspaper ads: "Married couple seeks married couple." They eventually entered the suburban subculture of debauchery, the "Bob and Carol and Ted and Alice" of their area.

At some parties, she danced at the behest of her husband and the dares of their new friends, who Ben said were like "family." She shook. She shimmied. The women hated her; their husbands longed for her. In scenes reminiscent of Sodom and Gomorrah, the men lunged toward her as her husband dutifully threw them back in mock righteous anger, though he was the one who encouraged it. He fed on the prospect of seeing men lust for his wife and drew a strengthened libido from seeing his fantasies come to life—fantasies that compensated for the handicap of his alcoholism. Mary Ruth told friends that she was a victim, but the truth was more complex.

Ben's friend at Fort Gordon, Army Major Thomas Benjamin, also enjoyed these "harmless" games, and drew Ben, a member of the Marine Reserves, into their ever-sinister manifestations. The events appealed to twisted weekend warriors and sunshine soldiers in private, Central Savannah River area "War Games." Mary Ruth was the hostage combatant Ben and Tom's armies fought over. She was taken prisoner to be interrogated and tortured for information. These contests were thinly veiled excuses to placate the deviant desires of the "generals."

The games ceased to be the harmless indulgences that all the participants knew they never had been. The major showed up at Mary Ruth's home when she was all alone, forced his way in, and raped her. When she told Ben, his only reaction was, "That's not part of the game. He violated our rules."

Then came the night the four partygoers went into the woods after a night of revelry. In a moment of drunken recklessness, they sat in a circle and foolishly began to chant a ritual in hopes of summoning Lucifer to do their bidding.

They began with ancient language from an old book Mary Ruth and her friend Carla had found as the executors of an estate sale at a ramshackle house. Carla, a button-nosed woman with large hips and a tiny mustache, could be as cold as a well digger's grave. Having read some of the text during their inventory, Carla decided that it would be the perfect adjunct for their parties. She had kept it out of the sales inventory over Mary Ruth's objections to use for a special night.

So they slipped away with their husbands from the party to a campsite situated by a small stream running through dense woods. The full moon illuminated the forest, and a white barn owl swooped between the trees like some disembodied spirit. Carla produced the book in her role as the high priestess of the night and began to recite the ancient words to summon Lucifer or his demons. They spoke the Lord's Prayer backwards as the rituals demanded. The pitch and fever of the invocation increased with each utterance and each level of the ritual.

A smothering presence of evil filled the patch of woods where they knelt. *They* thought they were still playing, but this game reached far beyond drunken parties where wives and husbands crossed over to the dark side, where men's decency gave way to the beast in them. This time, they were playing with the fires and forces of hell.

The false imprisonments, the binding and gagging, and the abuse seemed all prelude now—games gone awry, games with eternal consequences. Rituals of depravity had given way to bored people playing with forces beyond their comprehension, reciting trendy incantations, inviting tragedy, and ignoring warnings in the old book itself to "Beware."

The air grew thick, and a sudden weight or heaviness oppressed their souls, leaving their breathing shallow and labored.

They hurried to pick up the Ouija board Carla had brought, and her hands began to move in wide, sweeping, and lyrical movements as she swayed to and fro. Ben and Carla's husband, Louis Earl, watched in fascination—and some fear.

"Why have you called me?" the board spelled out.

It moved rapidly again. "What is it you seek?"

A sudden rancid stench like sulfur, death, and rot filled their nostrils.

"Are you disciples of Faust who wanted the gift?" The foursome was quite scared now, except for Carla, whose hands flew around the board.

Invoking another warning in the old book, the board spoke again.

"There is no shielding in your summons. My approach is unhindered," the words spelled out on the Ouija board as fast as Carla's hands could fly. They all seemed to be able to hear the voice of the board inside their heads.

"Do you renounce Yahweh, Jehovah, and Jesus? Choose now."

All except Mary Ruth nodded. After some hesitation, they said in unison, "Yes, we do renounce them."

Mary Ruth held back, uncertain and terrified. She moved away from the fire and looked all around her in desperation for some refuge. The rest stared at her.

Ben said, "She's on the fence."

"No matter," the board and the voice said, "I own the fence. She's mine."

Louis Earl, Carla's compliant and amiable mate, opened a bag he had brought at Carla's behest and produced a small, squawking chicken that seemed to be awakening from a drug-induced sleep.

"Just another fried chicken dinner," he said sheepishly with a shrug of his shoulders. "No one will miss it."

Mary Ruth loved and rescued abused animals. She felt a sense of approaching horror, as if a new curtain was rising in this theater of nightmares and madness now playing out at the edges of damnation.

Carla, wild-eyed, and cold through and through, had no such sentimentalities about animals. There was no mercy in her. Mary Ruth knew the chicken was to be a sacrifice, and the realization was surreal, unbearable, and unthinkable. She became sick and tried to speak, to say no. Her lips moved, but she was mute and helpless.

Level after level fell away as they descended into the depths of the occult. At level 91 of the ceremony, the ground seemed to tremble, and the night birds that had cooed from their nocturnal perches no longer sang. The wind died, and the trees seemed to croak and moan. Somewhere, some beast—or some entity—seemed to be panting in rapid breaths that alternated between wheezes and hisses. Everything seemed to die—or to hide.

At that moment, Carla raised her knife high above her head in some grotesque imitation of a Boris Karloff movie and said, "To you, oh Father, we give you our sacrifice." With that she cut the chicken's throat and severed its head. The bloody, headless body of the chicken thrashed about and ran over Mary Ruth, soiling her dress. She screamed and clasped her hands over her ears against the echoing squawk of the bird as it was decapitated. She screamed again and again, emitting a dry, rasping, pitiful wail.

The breath of death everlasting was upon them, and there was no way back.

All were panting in heavy, gasping sighs. The others were excited at this new extension of their worldly adventures, but Mary Ruth was traumatized in a way that few ever recover from.

"Ouija board, Ouija board, what shall we call you?" Carla asked.

The board was quiet, and she asked once more, "Who are you?"

Her hands moved involuntarily to spell out language they couldn't read.

"*Fredericus est nomen meum!*"

They all looked at each other, except for Mary Ruth. She couldn't move her gaze from the limp body of the mutilated chicken. Her own glassy eyes and the dizziness of her pounding pulse seemed to bring her to the edge of an abyss where evil lived.

"We don't understand, Ouija. Who are you?" Carla asked again.

The pointer began to move again, slowly at first, then quickly for the last letters.

"My name is Fredrick!"

The board moved again.

"*Michael venturus est.*" It paused and then again in English: "Michael's Michael is coming." They all looked at each other blankly.

"We don't know him, Ouija—Fredrick. What does that mean?"

The board moved again, slowly and methodically, as the group remained transfixed, breathing in rapid, shallow breaths.

"The Archangel's Michael is coming."

The board paused and then spelled out—"She." It stopped.

They all looked at Mary Ruth, and the board began again.

"You shall now be known to us as Lilith."

Mary Ruth was obsessed with tales of Camelot. Longing to be Guinevere, she devoured mythology from ancient cultures in a futile attempt to escape the fragile life she lived. She knew Lilith was a mythological Mesopotamian storm demon associated with turbulent and violent wind, a bearer of disease, illness, and death…a nocturnal female or demon, known as the "beautiful maiden."

Mary Ruth threw her head back to the heavens that shone so brilliantly above her and screamed and screamed: "What have we done? What have I done? Oh Jesus, Jesus, what have I done?"

The board flew out of Carla's hands at the mention of Jesus, and a sudden wind, howling like a banshee, extinguished the fire. Red-hot pellets seemed to rain down from heaven like fire and brimstone, pelting the children of disobedience who thought, only moments before, that Lucifer could be compelled to serve them.

Grasping for each other in the pitch black, some cried, "Jesus, Jesus." Others cried, "Mama, Mama." They saw heaven at a distance from a place of eternal torment, and an overwhelming thirst came upon them. They all suddenly fell silent as the full and final realization of what they had done settled over them. A smothering presence of evil seemed to crowd into their hearts and entrails to devour all of what was or ever would be. That was the moment Mary Ruth's new tenants moved in and began to torment her.

She sat alone, rocking to and fro, holding her hand on her face and murmuring unintelligible words with no meaning. Then the acrid breath came and whispered in her ear a message the others couldn't hear.

"You are mine, Lilith. Prepare. Michael will arrive soon."

That was the moment Mary Ruth understood for the first time… What they reaped from their ode to "free love" wasn't free after all, and it surely wasn't love.

CHAPTER NINE

*"You will never live if you are looking for the
meaning of life."—Albert Camus*

"Well fiddle dee dee!"
—Margaret Mitchell, Gone With the Wind

Since she was a young girl, Susan had been fascinated with "up." She would sit for hours to gaze at the heavens, to watch the planes cross the wild blue yonder, and to marvel at the early rockets from Cape Canaveral and the "One small step for man, one giant leap for mankind." She wanted to know how high heaven was. She believed everything trapped on the terrestrial was only prelude to the secrets hidden beyond the canopy above.

Perhaps it was her illness, but she always seemed to have one foot in the material world and one in the spiritual's haunting allure. She strained toward a place her husband couldn't see to find peace and rest in God. Michael observed that she had unique gifts, some so pronounced that the government wanted to develop them when she had tested high for ESP while a student at Mississippi State. She politely declined and kept her gifts just for their life.

Once as they walked through the woods, she asked him if they could sit for a while under a very old and tall oak.

"Trees touch Heaven," she told him with a faraway look in her eyes. "I think they're like antennas or channels of revelation from beyond. If you sit and listen quietly, you can feel the Holy Spirit where the old earth reaches toward the steep heavens."

He often would find her reading Psalm 111. She took nothing for granted. If Michael tried to hurry up time, she was always trying to arrest it. If he thought it would last forever, she knew life was fleeting with so little time to discover all the riches before the final draft is carved into the granite markers of graveyards dotting the plains since time began. She was a gentle soul who quietly reminded him about her illness, which would eventually cast a pall over their lives. They decided not to have children because she might not survive it.

What concerned her most in their new life in Jackson was Michael's increasing restlessness in the waking hours, which seemed to feed his vivid nightmares. She would often lie awake in the New Post Road home to watch him twist and contort in his sleep, fighting old battles again and again in his dreams.

When he wrestled himself from the nocturnal battles into the light of the waking world, she tried to tell him his mind was just dumping things it wanted to be rid of. But she worried about his lack of deep, restorative sleep, the teeth-grinding that cracked the best mouth guards fashioned by his dentist, and the deeper conflicts that tortured him.

His growing obsession with fighting mock battles against surrogate foes, imaginary enemies, and stand-ins for the real ones from the past contributed to a growing dissatisfaction with his job and disdain for many of his peers.

She overheard him talking to MBN founder and director John Edward Collins.

"These Bell people aren't like us," Michael said in a declaration of contempt.

"What do you mean?" Collins asked.

"It's all money and status. Right and wrong mean next to nothing to them," he answered. Susan shook her head. Peace seemed illusive and unobtainable for a man who sought answers, meaning, and purpose in the very secular world he had so much disdain for.

She gently cautioned him that he couldn't rewrite the past by trying to be the fixer and rescuer of people in distress—particularly women.

"Honey, all women are not fair maidens in need of a knight. All are not damsels in distress needing to be rescued. They aren't Pearl or Dixie, and some are dangerous."

* * *

Turbulence jolted Michael from his dreams—a hodgepodge of Susan's warnings, reruns of the night at the mansion in Jackson, and the hole in life left by Clay's passing. The hum of jet engines and the peculiar cabin smell unique to commercial airliners brought him back to this new reality. He rubbed his eyes as he awakened and thought—*Thank goodness I'm done with corrupt governors.*

Michael peered out the window of his coach seat on the Eastern Airlines flight from Jackson to Atlanta. A woman with blue hair next to him held forth on the state of morals in the country and the Iranian hostage crisis. He nodded politely, nibbled his "free" pack of peanuts, and swished his tiny, plastic cup of water-thin Coke (courtesy of the overworked stewardess, who looked as if her feet were killing her). In the age of politically correct language, he knew they were now flight attendants— just as he wasn't a security manager but an investigative specialist.

Clay's loyal number-two man at MBN Intelligence had sent word before Michael left Jackson that Ace Connelly had died in federal prison in Montgomery, Alabama.

"He had seizures, and before he died, he sat straight up in bed, wild-eyed, sweating and screaming your name repeatedly," Brad said. "The attendants said he moaned, '*Livarsi na petra di la scarpa*—take the stone out of my shoe,' an old Sicilian curse he picked up from his Mafia associates out of New Orleans. Then he began to say, 'Freddie, Freddie, is that you? Oh, no. Oh, no! No!!' They said he collapsed onto his bed, breathed a death rattle of air, and was gone."

Michael thought of Ace and Fredrick, Davidson and Marcello, and all the echoes of the past as he looked at cloud formations that resembled presidents. There to the right was Abraham Lincoln. Over to his left was Teddy Roosevelt. The layers of billowy clouds below the wings of the silver-and-blue 727 obscured the ground below. He knew they must be nearing Atlanta, because the food trays were being collected.

He was scheduled for corporate security training, which came on the heels of working security with the Secret Service for Governor Ronald Reagan's presidential campaign stop at the Neshoba County Fair. He did double duty as Reagan's state criminal justice chairman. He had been offered a slot in Reagan's White House but knew that was impossible, considering Susan's health.

Returning to the reality of mundane assignments was weighing on him. It wasn't his choice to go to Atlanta. No official MBN or Bell contacts with the city had ever been positive for him. It seemed the city had become dysfunctional. Southern hospitality was nowhere to be found, a thing of the past for the once proud Southern-star.

As the descent into Atlanta began, he looked behind the plane to see six or seven jets lined up there. Veteran pilots responded to instructions from air traffic controllers scheduling arrivals and departures. There were also four planes in front of them. The clouds parted, revealing tiny vehicles driven by even-tinier people, scurrying about like ants or Lilliputians waiting to subdue unsuspecting travelers. When he was deplaning, the attendant with the sore feet managed a pained smile. "Thank you for flying Eastern, sir," she said, even as she rubbed one foot with the point of the other.

Inside Hartsfield Airport, he took a long look at the bustling air hub—so many people hurrying to and fro to catch flights to go somewhere, come back again, and then start all over. Business suits, airline crews, tourists, kids home from college, vendors, and police populated the terminals. Conveyers transported people who should be walking. Subway trains sped along in lurching stops and starts that guaranteed chiropractors would never go out of business.

People told him the tired joke repeatedly: "Hartsfield is so big, anywhere you go, you have to first change planes in Atlanta. Even when you die, you change planes in Atlanta. Will that be smoking or non-smoking—going up or going down? Har, har," they laughed uproariously at the umpteenth telling of the joke.

Ha, ha, ha. *Why would anyone want to live here?* he wondered. Then singer James Brown hurried by him in the terminal with a small entourage, headed to some engagement.

Impulsively he yelled to him, "Hey, James! How do you feel?"

Brown flashed a wide smile of white caps against his dark skin and said, "I feel good."

Michael took a taxi to the Ritz. He marveled at the city Sherman had burned. *This is no longer the old South*, he thought, *just another big city—asphalt, concrete, and steel—yet more.*

Like some apocalyptic tale, man's creations seemed to have morphed into living, breathing entities. The leviathans towered above the noise and pungent odors of sewage and car exhausts, jackhammers and sirens. Hustling streetwalkers and government employees had one more awful hot dog, while blaring urban poets proclaimed their new gospel in angry rhyming on street corners of gray and gravel.

Infrastructure reached for the sky like towers of Babylon, replacing the chiseled Scripture on old buildings that were razed to make way for Atlanta's new corporatism. "Blessed is the nation whose God is the Lord" gave way to "We have no king but Caesar." The inhabitants wondered how they'd lost their way, but they didn't wonder too long. Men who had clawed their way to the top of the corporate ladder found when they arrived…nothing.

The conference was long, tedious, and boring. Attendees seemed to follow Oscar Wilde's admonition, 'The first duty is to be as artificial as possible." They not only sought but craved to be in crowds. Seemingly afraid to be alone to confront their mortality and their ghosts, they partied heartily in the hotel until all hours. When forced to part company, they would inevitably phone someone. To be alone was to not be real in the metaphysical sense.

Greetings to the visitors was brought by an attorney who locals said would be governor one day—Henry "Hank" Holcomb. He could have been Hal Davidson, Michael thought, but smoother, smarter, and more ambitious. Holcomb was a big guy—not fat but big-boned. Michael suspected he hid malevolence behind clever politician affability, wide smiles, and bad jokes. Holcomb's wife was present, a dutiful woman who looked adoringly at him.

In stark contrast to Holcomb's wife was an educator from Augusta—Mary Ruth Robinson, a soft-spoken blonde who had been contracted by BellSouth to speak on education projects the foundation was funding. She didn't seem comfortable speaking, but he noticed that men who didn't care about her subject matter complimented her a bit too much.

She watched her audience through the guarded hazel lenses of oval-shaped eyes. Her smile seemed tentative. *When she smiles,* he thought, *her eyes don't. Something's there, hiding behind her eyes: always moving, assessing, something curious and inquisitive but also challenging—creating awareness of who she is.*

She had the air of the wounded birds from his MBN days. There was something about her, something familiar. The more he looked at her, the clearer the images became—Dixie Lee. It flushed up all the buried love and loss of Dixie—the smell, taste, and texture of her. He felt out of sorts, almost out of control of memory and emotion. There was something about the tilt of her head, her blonde hair, and her presence—different yet reminiscent of memory suddenly revitalized. She reminded him of Dixie, but there was something else. He suddenly thought of an ad he had seen for a perfume named *Aliciente*, Spanish for "Temptation."

The last speaker was James Longview, a passionate and energetic motivational speaker who traversed the rhetorical landscape from Lincoln to Covey to Gandhi to Jesus. He advised the attendees to "become the change you seek." Most were nodding off in this final presentation, waiting to rush to the airport for departures to cities all across the South. But not Michael. This speaker, who physically resembled Jimmy Swaggart, held his attention.

As he walked the aisles, Longview's prominent Adam's apple bobbed up and down as he talked. "A man came to a minister and said, 'Pastor, I've given up reading the good book because I can't memorize anything.' The pastor told him just reading would be good for him, but the man said it was hopeless.

"The pastor handed him a wicker basket and asked if he'd fill it with water. The man replied, 'But it won't hold water.' 'Well,' said the pastor, 'just hold it under the tap for ten minutes.' 'It won't hold water no matter how long I hold it there,' the man said. 'Do you have just ten minutes for me?' the pastor asked. The man held the basket under water for ten minutes, returned, and said, 'See, Pastor, it's empty.' 'Yes,' said the pastor, 'but it's a lot cleaner, isn't it?'"

The speaker concluded the story and seemed to hone in on Michael in the closing segment, as if no one was there but the two of them. Michael listened, squirmed a bit, and rose to leave at the end of the conference, unaware that Mary Ruth Robinson was watching him intently.

"Who's that man there?" she asked the local Bell event manager.

"Oh, that's one of our new security managers from Mississippi," he answered.

Watching him as he turned the corner, she couldn't shake a strange feeling. Someone had just "walked across her grave," as Southerners often said.

"What's his name?" a breathless Mary Ruth asked.

"Michael Parker," the manager replied.

Mary Ruth felt lightheaded, her lower lip quivered uncontrollably, and she gasped audibly as her hands began to tremble. That old feeling returned—the hot breath of evil on her neck—and she thought, *Michael's Michael is coming. Michael will be here soon.*

As Michael sat stuck in miles of impatient commuters on I-285, he saw a sign outside a lone, inner-city church. "Oh love that wilt not let me go, I rest my weary soul in thee; I give thee back the life I owe, that in thine ocean depths its flow may richer, fuller be."—George Matheson.

Below it was a footnote he seemed to hear more than read…"There is an angel in the midst of your whirlwinds to come."

CHAPTER TEN

*"I guess a career in the police didn't really
prepare you for this, did it?"—Bob Hunt*

*"Reporters trade in pain. It sells…
Everyone knows that."—Jonathan Maberry*

The gargantuan night bugs chirped incessantly on Michael's all-night surveillance in the Mississippi Delta near Cleveland. The pungent odor of cotton dust hung heavy in the night air and assaulted his irritated sinuses. He considered it had been a successful night of documentation regarding Bell manager Barry Barnes: his coziness with contractors he supervised and the kickbacks they provided to supplement his Bell System paychecks.

When Michael returned to wrap up the case, Barnes would say, "It never seemed so bad until I heard you say it out loud." Word would spread through the company, and momentary deterrence would ensue. Managers would be careful for a while. Then the game…the time-honored dance would begin again.

When he neared the outskirts of Jackson, a bright, citrine sun had just begun to fry Jackson—over easy. The city limits signs shined in the reflection of the morning flare. Michael's heavy eyelids and bloodshot eyes ached for the comfort of his bed as his mobile phone rang. He couldn't quite get over having one of those things in his car. The only one he'd ever seen was an early model Elvis had. Michael used his phone on the road to check on Susan to make sure she wasn't experiencing the insulin reactions that could render her nearly incapable of recovery at times.

The shrill voice of Jackson Police Detective Arthur "Trigger" Warton greeted him when he hit the answer button. Warton was a nervous, balding police veteran with a small, crinkled mouth, who had a habit of nibbling on the knuckle of his right index finger. That wasn't why he was called Trigger, however.

Trigger shot and killed over a dozen men in his career with the Jackson P.D. Some were highly questionable incidents, labeled as executions by civil rights groups. Trigger was not without his supporters across philosophical divides. His instant judgments disabled the cycle of endless appeals in an increasingly unresponsive system. There were no repeat offenses by those he judged. Deterrence? Some argued that in areas where he worked—often neighborhoods no one else would desire to be assigned to—crime had gone down, and perps had moved on to other jurisdictions. After each incident, Trigger would be examined by staff psychologists, who labeled him of sound mind and ready to return to duty.

In a rash of recent convenience store armed robberies, the department turned to Trigger for stakeouts. With Dirty Harry efficiency, he waited for the armed robbers in the back of Quick Stops night after night. When the outlaws finally showed up and approached the midnight shift clerks with guns drawn, Trigger materialized with minimum warning and proceeded to dish out street justice courtesy of the .44 Magnum he carried. He couldn't be as cold as some said, because Michael had heard that his ulcers had ulcers. However, he hadn't yet crawled into the bottle and stayed there as some cops had.

Today the flinty-eyed detective needed Michael's help.

"Hello," Michael said in a sleep-rusty and thick-tongued voice.

"Hey, Michael! You awake?" Trigger asked too loudly.

"I am now. I was out till all hours watching people do what some people do under cover of darkness. You wouldn't know anything about that, would you?" Michael deadpanned.

"Not me," he said. "Say, how're you enjoying your new job with all the red-hot corporate boys?" Trigger teased.

"Oh, I love it," Michael said with too much enthusiasm.

"Michael, you can't lie worth a hoot. How'd you ever make it undercover?" he asked.

"That was sanctioned, good versus evil, don't you know? A free pass on falsehoods, it didn't count. I got to cross my fingers. I was about to add that I do love it—about as much as I enjoy a visit to my proctologist!" Michael laughed.

"You won't do, boy…Anyway, I need your help, and quick, too," the police detective said.

"What's going on?" Michael asked.

"You won't believe it, but a nut wired up on PCP has taken the deputy mayor's wife hostage," he said.

"What? You're kidding!" Michael answered.

"Nope, we're trying to get a fix on where he has her now, and I'm going to need you to help us with communications, call tracing, and all that stuff you security boys do so well."

"No problem. Just let me know when and where," Michael said. "In the meantime, give me all the numbers you think he may call." Before he arrived home, he had the switching centers place all the numbers Trigger had given him on trace to watch for a ransom call.

As he swung by home for breakfast, a flicker of white highlighted an approaching thunderhead near his home. Susan was playing some of the "bubble gum" music Michael detested, and a woman with frosted hair was on television hawking…of all things, Frosted Flakes. By the time he was dressed, Trigger was looking for him again.

"The kidnapper has issued a series of demands to the mayor's office. Just five minutes ago. Can you trace it?" he asked from his office at the Jackson P.D.

"Stand by," Michael said. The trace showed the call came from a number in the inner city, a section of town where even the toughest police veterans didn't venture without backup.

"Trigger, it's coming from 114 Henry Street. We show that as a duplex, but only the one side is occupied. It's listed to a Jerome Kennedy. What's he asking for?"

"It's crazy stuff, Michael. Seems he thinks the deputy mayor had his cats picked up and euthanized. Need you to join us at the command center we'll be setting up near there, just as quick as you can say— "Meow!" The situation may require your constant communication specialties and closed channels for our hostage negotiators."

"Sure, on my way now. I'll bring everything I can think of and get whatever you need," Michael said.

Driving to the command center location to meet Trigger, Michael learned that the media, who monitor police radio bands, had picked up on the news of the abduction and the location of Kennedy's residence.

Better hurry, Jackson P.D., he thought, but the skilled hostage experts were already talking to the kidnapper by phone. They informed Kennedy that he was surrounded, but there was hope as long as the deputy mayor's wife wasn't harmed. The police were fashioning a win-win that could end this thing before it got out of hand.

When Michael pulled up to the command center, Trigger walked over to greet him. The scowl on his face indicated he was not a happy man.

"Michael, those jackals from Channel 5 have gotten Kennedy's number, and in between our calls, just as our hostage team had him talking, they called him asking what his grievances were, promising him air time for an exclusive on Channel 5. We've got to do something now, Michael!" he said with red-faced animation.

Without asking, Michael dialed up the switching center supervisor. "Jonas, kill the dial tone to 114 Henry Street, and do it now!" He looked at Trigger with a raised eyebrow, and he nodded okay.

"It's done, Michael," Jonas said.

Trigger's radio went off, and the dispatcher said the TV station was complaining they were cut off in the middle of a conversation with Kennedy. They were claiming First Amendment privileges and consequences. Trigger's response was not the stuff of Sunday sermons.

"Trigger, I have a reel-to-reel phone system in my trunk with two hundred yards of cable. You can tell him that you have a private phone system the phone company has built just for him, so no one can interrupt his talks with your people. Just leave the phone on his end at his front door, and then it's live when he picks it up," Michael said.

"I knew there was a good reason the phone company hired you! Let's do it!" he said. "Gary," Trigger called to a sergeant. "Help Michael with whatever he needs and get the bullhorn to speak to Kennedy."

Michael and Gary enabled the system and brought it to the "front lines." After a bullhorn message to Kennedy, Michael volunteered to lay the kidnapper's very own private phone at his front door. He laid it on the old wooden porch and backed away quickly.

The negotiations began again in earnest. The give-and-take, offer/counter-offer psychology ensued, and the training of the hostage negotiators became evident. Finally, as a weary sun began to settle over the peach skyline and chimney swifts appeared to dance over it all, Kennedy agreed to let the woman go. Everyone cautiously celebrated and thanked Michael.

The team went up to receive the deputy mayor's wife. A terrified, chunky woman, thickened around the middle by age, finally appeared at the front door and walked robot-like toward the officers. She collapsed into the arms of the police team that quickly whisked her away. A cheer went up from a crowd of onlookers. Michael watched as Trigger and his squad moved to the perimeter of the house, while the negotiators calmly congratulated Kennedy and urged him to come on out to a fine supper and a good end to a bad day. It was all going to work out.

Kennedy appeared at the door, opened the screen, and walked out onto the porch—carrying a rifle. As the bullhorns urged him to lay his weapon on the floor and raise his hands, Michael suddenly saw something in his eyes that he had seen before in his days as a cop—something he had seen in the eyes of the gunman in Tylertown. Michael whispered, "No, don't!"

Kennedy suddenly raised the rifle and pointed it at Trigger, who opened fire, followed by other officers. Shots echoed over the quiet neighborhood, and startled flocks of plump pigeons flushed from their early roost underneath a nearby bridge.

Smoke from the gunfire still wafted over the street as police approached Kennedy, who was now beyond posing a threat to anyone. Somewhere nearby, a wail of grief split the silence. It was surreal. It was numbing. It was nauseating. The trauma and loss of blood had diminished him, and his physical body was retreating by the second. He was once someone's little boy, a kid who fell down when he first tried to walk. He had fallen again, but he wouldn't be getting up this time.

Just as the sun fell from beneath a jagged cloud on the edge of the horizon, a blue van emblazoned with "Channel 5–On Your Side" pulled up next to Michael. The well-coiffed, auburn-haired reporter, who had promised her viewers an exclusive first look at the poor madman, stepped regally from her chariot. She was constantly checking her mirror and fluffing her hair, a good, card-carrying member of the Society of Professional Journalists. A profanity that wasn't attractive lingered on her perfectly reddened lips. She stomped her shiny, black high heels, looking first at the cameraman and then at Michael. "What happened?!" she shrieked.

"Why?" was the better question; it hung heavy in the air. Why did he do it? Was he a mentally ill man who changed his mind, or was he just tired of living? Was it the interference by the media at a crucial time? No one would ever know but Kennedy, and he wouldn't be giving the plastic people at Channel 5 an exclusive.

Michael wondered about the randomness of it all. A man, wired up on a substance created to tranquilize animals, had gone over the edge and past the point of no return, his neural pathways shorted by the drug. Kennedy acted out his most violent and crazed fantasies, and then got his brains blown out by a man Jackson police officers described with fingers circling round their temples to insinuate he was crazy. A man called— Trigger!

As the pouty reporter prepared her most theatrical look for her on-the-scene feed, Michael walked away singing Cohen's lament: "I can't forget. I can't forget, but I don't remember what."

CHAPTER ELEVEN

"He loses sight, by degrees, of common sense…in the petty squabbles, intrigues, feuds, and airs of affected importance to which he has made himself accessory."—William Hazlitt

"Keep stabbing the open wound, won't you?"
—Unknown

Michael's sleep was fitful. Katie slept on his chest all night in a sort of time-honored vigil that dog-lovers believe cats to be incapable of. Susan massaged his neck and back when he came home and fixed him warm tomato soup and a grilled cheese, chased by one of his pills to help him sleep. She lay there beside him, curled up behind his back.

The annoying rattle of the phone, like some angry reptile about to strike, disturbed the tranquility of their South Jackson oasis of pecan trees and flowers. Susan grabbed the phone.

"Yes, sir, he's here," Susan answered.

"It's Mr. Carver," she whispered.

George Carver, general manager of Bell's Security Department, wanted to see Michael first thing at their headquarters in the old Deposit Guaranty building downtown.

Michael staggered from a quick shower, bleary-eyed, with a brain like mush. Susan presented him with a plate full of eggs and bacon. She smiled at Michael and encouraged him with the softness of her hand laid over his. He worried about her increasing number of strange fevers, insulin reactions, and recovery intervals that grew longer with each episode. She dismissed it as nothing and never complained.

She brought him his essential corporate briefcase and car keys. He kissed her and was off again. As he neared the office on Capitol Street, he figured he was in for the latest installment of "How to succeed in Bell by selling your soul." Michael was not a herd animal. The pack was forever trying to make him conform. He'd heard it all before.

"You don't pad your expense account like we do. You make us look bad."

"You work too hard. If you don't stop, they'll expect all of us to work like you do."

"You've been noticed and rewarded. Now it's time to relax."

"You're not at the State anymore. You're in the club. You've nothing to prove."

"Oh, by the by, the results are back from your Rorschach test. Your ink blots don't look like our ink blots. That makes us very nervous. You don't see what we see."

Corporate man was a barroom sage who claimed to know it all. Maybe the savant had known a great deal once, but he'd stagnated and had nothing new left to offer but a grotesque imitation of himself. He had sold his soul to the highest bidder and ceased to grow. Now, such pronouncements were only long drinks at the bar of emptiness to numb his pain as he told all who would listen, "You can never have enough of whatever it is you can never have enough of." He explained the pecking order and how you must stand out by blending in…be "quietly useful" and "aggressively nonthreatening." This was all he knew—the company he had given his life to.

George Carver, the security chief, was a big man with a blunt, happy face and a Bell-blue suit that seemed perpetually wrinkled. Massive, blackish brows arched over a snub nose and a wiry mouth that served up inspirational homilies after each manager meeting such as "Load and shoot" and "Keep on keeping on."

"Hey, come on in, Michael. Great job helping the Jackson police. Sorry it turned out the way it did. Nothing you could do about that. Everything all right? You don't look well," Carver said in rapid-fire delivery.

"I'm fine, Mr. Carver, just a bit tired," Michael replied and thought, *Here it comes.*

"We've had this talk before, but the enemies you've made in Birmingham still ask about you and watch you from a distance. You're the best, but you're always off from the pack—a lone wolf. That makes people nervous. They wonder if you're a team player," he observed.

"How so?" Michael asked with minimal enthusiasm as he feigned a yawn.

"Well, the case where you recommended leniency for the man who got drunk and exposed himself to a woman comes to mind. That irritated people who thought you overstepped. You had a good case for termination, but you undermined it with an opinion you're not supposed to offer," Carver scolded.

"His department head asked me, and I answered him. From all I saw, this seemed to be an aberration linked to a problem with alcohol. I'm glad they didn't fire him. Second chances, forgiveness, you know," Michael said.

"Your case with the operators you caught using or possessing drugs at work. That was a record for the most disciplinary actions in the company—from terminations to suspensions to warnings. *That* was something! But personnel asked you what you thought of corporate security's recommendations. You said they were 'unwarranted over-reactions and a threat to privacy.' Unwarranted overreactions, Michael! You know that didn't go down well in Birmingham. They think that *you* think you're better than all us 'unenlightened' folks," Carver said.

"I bet that was right up there with me skipping the big fish fry with the security boys to take Susan out to dinner," Michael bristled.

"Now, see there? That attitude is just what I'm talking about. You know I try to protect you. Maybe one day you'll tell me what this burr is under your saddle, if you even know yourself. You're all walled up, and it's going to bite you one day," Carver said in a fatherly way.

Carver sighed and his massive shoulders heaved with the rise and fall of his deep breaths. "In any event, some people like you. I really called you in to tell you that you're being promoted and sent to Augusta, Georgia, if you'll accept it. They have the medical facilities I know you want for Susan," he added.

"Augusta? Where's that?" Michael asked. "What will I be doing?"

"Michael, the public likes you even if some in headquarters may not. The company is going to put you in public relations!" he said with a hearty laugh.

"Public relations?!" Michael asked.

"Don't look so shocked. The harder you work, the luckier you get, and I think that almost guarantees your success at anything you do. You're the luckiest man I know," Carver said.

Somewhere Michael heard the voice of the Borg on *Star Trek* saying, "You will be assimilated. Resistance is futile." He had that sick feeling he got as a kid sometimes and thought, *I sure could use a stick of Pearl's peppermint.*

"Oh, one favor before you leave us. Please go by and make an appearance at the retirement party for State Vice-President Edwards tonight," Carver said.

"I think I'm going to be sick," Michael said.

"C'mon now, this will be your last required appearance here. It's important to our budget considerations. So, just for me…show the flag. Besides, after the assist with Jackson P.D., the mayor wrote letters to Edwards calling you a hero. He might even give you a medal."

"Funny, I don't feel like a hero," Michael said.

Carver sighed and shook his head.

* * *

The retirement party for Frank Edwards was in full swing at the Coliseum Ramada Inn when Michael arrived. A cheerful din of voices greeted him, complemented by the tinkling of glasses and silverware.

The waitresses moved efficiently in and out of the crowds of well-wishers, who were feeling no pain. The liquor flowed freely. The quantity of drinks consumed had a direct correlation to the noise level of the gaggle of politicians, lobbyists, Bell managers, and chamber jolly guys. On an adjoining makeshift dance floor with a large, old Wurlitzer jukebox, several inebriated couples were dancing too close and too intimately to a local garage-band hit, "The Baby Bell Blues."

Michael spied Bell lobbyists in the crowd. In addition to supplying whiskey and women to the political types at the party, they were known to take drunk legislators quail hunting at private reserves. The poor quails were farm-raised, hand-fed, and so tame they wouldn't fly when released from their cages; that way, the legislators could have their "sport." He wondered if the lobbyists were corporate clones of Red at the Governor's Mansion.

"Shoo, shoo," one of the lobbyists said, explaining how he tried and tried to get the pet quails to fly so Senator So-and-So could blast them to kingdom come with his 12-gauge automatic shotgun—so he could feel like a *real* man.

"Nothing more than a pile of feathers remained after Billy Bob shot that quail three times! Just *Boom! Boom! Boom!* It's like that movie—Bye, bye, birdie!" a Bell lobbyist joked.

One of the dirty dancers that night was Janis Holley, the wife of a Bell department head. She was notorious for flirting with and pawing strange men in front of her husband at these events. Paul Holley was the butt of many jokes and could do nothing with her.

Janis was plastered to John Weaver, president of Bain Construction, the master contractor for Bell in Mississippi. He was a friend to managers like the one in Cleveland whom Michael had investigated. His employees dug a swimming pool at the home of a Bell executive as Michael watched from the woods. A young woman the exec promoted had taken up residence in an apartment subsidized by the contractor.

Weaver appeared as drunk as Janis was. He spied Michael as he entered the room, and a snarl distorted his party face.

"Well, look what the dogs done drug up!" barked the tall, hollow-chested man in the crumpled seersucker suit. He was so close Michael could identify the Jack Daniels on his breath. Weaver swayed this way and that and looked Michael over with a mocking and challenging eyes—up and down and side-to-side. Michael resisted the temptation to tell him he knew now how women felt when men undressed them visually.

"You security boys have cost me a lot of money. Always meddling in company managers' private agreements that you have no business messing with," he said in a slurred commentary.

"All in a day's work, Mr. Weaver," Michael offered.

At that moment, Janis Holley inserted herself into the conversation, as her husband pretended not to notice from a distance. Reeking of too much booze, the small woman with tangled black hair, a white pasty face, and the reddest lipstick Michael had ever seen, sensed a volatile situation she might exploit for her amusement and her husband's further humiliation.

"I don't know, John," she said. "I like big security men," Janis offered with her hands provocatively positioned on her narrow waist and contrasting hippy-hips beneath a pale-salmon dress.

"Well, you should like my partner, Billy, over there. He's about six-foot-four," Michael offered.

"You don't like me?" she cooed.

"Sure I do, Janis. I was about to suggest we sail the Seven Seas together, swim the deepest oceans, climb the highest mountains, and all that stuff," he earnestly deadpanned.

"Are you making fun of me?" she snapped.

"No, ma'am...not me. You are just as precious as gold dropping from a tree in autumn."

"You mean I'm a thing of beauty...of many colors?" she asked with an arched and finely plucked brow.

"No," he said in a moment of uncharacteristic harshness. "No, I mean you're like a leaf...blown from gutter to gutter."

She flushed a bright, fire-engine red and Weaver's nostrils flared. "Big John, are you going to let this washed-up cop talk to me that way?"

Michael turned and walked away then, something he should have done sooner. He headed for the lobby and his car outside, away from all these people as fast as he could go, but Big John followed him into the rear lobby of the hotel.

"Don't walk away from me, Parker. I'm not through with you!" he bellowed. His eyes were glaring and his jaw was set. Janis seemed to be permanently attached to his coattails.

"You tell him, Big John. Don't let that party-pooper cop talk to us that way," Janis spat shrilly, confirming the rumor that her picture must be in the dictionary next to the word "shrew," along with other unmentionable terms.

"Yeah, come here, Parker," he said, grabbing Michael by the left shoulder. "This ain't Tylertown or Tupelo. You're in the big time now, narc boy, and you ain't got that dead buddy of yours to protect you here."

That ignited some deep and denied pain in Michael. He spun and grabbed the little finger of the contractor's right hand, bent it back and then to the side so far that Janis thought it would break. It was, in fact, the easiest finger to break. He wrenched the hand around by the little finger and forced Weaver to the floor. The drunk man's face was contorted with pain, and his eyes were squeezed shut.

In the midst of his screaming and cursing, there was a small, cracking sound as the bones snapped. Michael wanted to hurt him—and hurt him severely. A rage that lingered deep within was fueling this, and he knew he was on the ragged edge of disaster.

Cancel, cancel, he thought instinctively, an old adage that Pearl had given him when some urges, like a trip to the outhouse or the desire to punch someone, needed to be suppressed.

"Weaver, you don't ever mention my friends or my past again. You wouldn't make a good pimple on their behinds, or for that matter, not even the guys we arrested—you phony little country-club gangster. If you ever see me coming again, you better give me a wide berth. Your finger will take six to eight weeks to heal. I'll be gone from Mississippi by then."

Janis's husband, Paul, arrived then and snapped at her, "Get your things. We're leaving."

"He started it, honey," she nagged. "You gonna take his side against your wife?"

"Shut your mouth, and go to the car. We'll talk about all this and many *other* things when we get home," he barked, in a long-overdue bit of frankness.

A startled, wide-eyed Janis slunk off. Weaver limped to the men's room holding his mangled hand with the finger that pointed the wrong way. Paul Holley managed a weak smile, framed under the saddest eyes Michael had ever seen. "Good luck in your career. I heard you're leaving. And don't worry, nothing will ever be said about this incident tonight."

Michael nodded and walked out into the night. The last smears of purple and pink had been subdued by the gray-blue edge of darkness, even as they were brightened by a million stars trying to break through their hiding place behind the lighted dome of the Capitol.

The night suggested that in the grand scheme of a universe full of laughter and hate and people trying to live and others trying to die—he was not that important. He steadied himself against the roof of his corporate car. His hands were shaking, his heart racing—another of the panic attacks that had begun to plague him. He reached into his glove box for a Valium, the crutch a Rolling Stone's song had dubbed "Mother's little helper."

What's wrong with me? he thought. *There was a time when a creep like that or a woman like her could've never gotten to me.*

Sometimes, as you travel down the road of life, you near crossroads where the past, present, and future all intersect. Suddenly, the veil between the temporal and the hereafter grows so thin you can almost hear the shuffle of angels' feet. He could hear the murmurs now but had no idea what they were saying…something that sounded like forgiving himself for living, for surviving when others had not. All he knew was at times he seemed to have run out of road, and all that was left for this itinerant traveler was to keep walking…all the way to Augusta, he supposed.

As he drove away, the jukebox at the party spun the scratchy 45 rpm behind D6…"Tell it like it is. Let your conscience be your guide…" It was an epilogue of goodbye to all that was…

CHAPTER TWELVE

*"It is better to be hated for what you are than to be
loved for what you are not."—Andre Gide*

*"Heading down the road to Augusta…That
Georgia sun was blood red and going down…"
—Tanya Tucker*

"Welcome to Georgia, Michael Parker," said the border agent in his dreams. "Please sign in here, receive your inoculations and classifications. We see that you're classified as sentimentalist, throwback, romanticist, and ardent believer in a bygone culture. Our records indicate that a Miss Dixie Lee Carter says you are sensitive, empathetic, chivalrous, and even heroic-hearted, but you seek Eden without God, resurrection without the pain of the cross."

The slope-shouldered sentinel paused from scanning the thick file and looked up with the eyes that pierced Michael to his core. "Our records show that you have a hole in your heart. You will find many things here to fill it with, but this is not Eden, Mr. Parker, and there are many crosses. You'll find no cheap grace here. If you are seeking truth, it is over yonder, across the dale, round the next bend, but it is guarded by an army of lies. Our records indicate many things that you are against, Mr. Parker. You're a rebel without pause…but what is it that you are *for*?"

The dream ended with the official stamping of his visa as conditional but one way, and the images would not leave him the next day as he comforted a beloved friend.

"There, there, old girl," Michael whispered to Katie. Her deep motor-like purr sputtered from congestion, and the loving cat-caresses of her eyes were clouded by cataracts.

When he and Susan arrived in Augusta, Katie turned nineteen and seemed to run out of steam. The seal points on her classic wedge face had grayed with age. The bounce had long since gone out of her feline leaps. He dusted her food with Lasix to help with the fluid buildup on her failing kidneys, and they sat in his recliner near the roaring fires she loved. He held and rubbed her to ease the pain of the arthritis that had overtaken her. Michael and Katie had survived so many trials since he found and rescued her from that awful kitty mill.

He finally drove home alone to bury her beneath the umbrella of a giant old oak tree in Parker Grove, where she once frolicked, young and limber, as he fished. It was a long time before he gave up listening for the sounds of her as she came bounding to greet him when he came home each day, slapping his ankle and zooming away in their game of "Tag, you're it." When the world was against him, she still thought he was the best man on the planet.

* * *

He lost himself in a honeycomb of treasures, trials, and temptations in Georgia. As he maneuvered cautiously across the new social and political terrain that seemed like a jigsaw puzzle, he often found himself pausing to look behind him—feeling as if someone was near, following him, but seeing no one. He shivered now and then with the feeling that someone was calling to him. He sometimes heard a faint buzzing, an enchanting melody or distant murmuring, and asked Susan, "What did you say?"

She gave him quizzical glances and answered, "I didn't say anything."

Such indulgences ran contrary to the wisdom of the tenured professors at Augusta State University, where he taught at night as an adjunct instructor. They assured him anything that was not measurable, quantifiable, and validated by the scientific process must be shoveled into the fiery furnace of intellectualism; such fairytale musings must be incinerated. But they had no answer when he inquired about the measurability of their own statements.

His peers at Bell's Atlanta headquarters gave little thought to the tenets of academic musings, but they had the air of habitual disbelief of anything outside the artificial tide pool they swam in. They peppered him with questions in the corporate meetings that he was loath to attend—"Where'd you go to school? What fraternity were you pledged to? Why you working so hard? Who's yo daddy?"

They still labored in the fields of high school or junior high where *who* you were, was who *they*—the "in" crowd—*said* you were.

Michael, who didn't just march to his own drummer, but made the Surfaris' "Wipeout" seem like a sedate cadence, grinned and mockingly answered, "Don't know who my daddy is and can't remember my past. I took a broom and brushed out all of my footprints so I don't know where I'm from and can't find my way back."

"Hmm," the wide-eyed inquisitors and flytrap mouths said to the rustic interloper. "Ain't that something?"

"Well, well," murmured the group's leader, Jason Hemmer the Third. The old quarterback, sandy-blonde hair so heavily sprayed that it appeared to be lacquered, huddled with his team and called an audible. Staring at Michael as if he had just emerged from a spacecraft, he asked, "What people say about you before Bell…Are you still that man?"

"No," Michael answered quickly and quietly. "No, he's gone."

"Hmm," Hemmer muttered, "ain't that something?"

Hemmer, who was most popular in the corporate "who's who" of well-groomed herd animals, revealed the consensus of the group. "We've dubbed you Thomas, our doubting Thomas: the prophet of the pestiferous why and why not, always questioning, questioning—questioning everything that's settled and established."

Michael paused and said, "Hmm, well, I've dubbed you guys what we used to call fence-post turtles in Mississippi."

"Fence-post turtles, what's that?" Hemmer asked with furrowed brow.

Michael replied, "Well, we used to see a turtle on top of a fence post in the country. You knew that turtle on the fence post didn't get up there by himself. He knows he doesn't belong up there. He doesn't know what to do while he's up there. He's elevated beyond his ability to function, and you just gotta wonder, as I do about you boys…What idiot put him up there?"

Hemmer flushed three shades of pink and red and said, "Ain't that something?"

* * *

Over the years to come, his superiors at Bell gave Michael numerous awards that really did not enrich him but ultimately impoverished him at some level. There were moments when he still felt alive and engaged, but they were fleeting and short-lived. As the fixer lost his ability to control Susan's deteriorating health, he couldn't seem to control panic attacks that were debilitating at times. She was in and out of the hospital with long surgeries and extraordinary interventions to slow the advance of her diabetes and the plaque that was occluding her vascular system.

So many of the materialists he now moved among seemed far removed from the warriors he'd known—ones who had given all they had to give. Their noble words and deeds always seemed juxtaposed in his mind against the chatter of those who reduced all of life to the mantra of the '80s—"Don't worry, be happy." They were the models for the modern expression of experts—any corporate suit a hundred miles from home with a briefcase.

One night, as they sat on their deck surrounded by flowers, Susan asked him, "Are you happy? You seem to only want to survive and endure, not enjoy."

"I'm trying to figure out the rules of the game, honey. Don't have a long-term objective. I feel like a castaway speaking a language foreign to the inhabitants of this world. It seems that all they understand is the 'cha-ching' of another deal sealed across the chamber roundtable or amidst the hushed conversations of the Pinnacle Club," he told her.

"Here I am, the former narc who once depended on secrecy. Now I'm known among the patrons of the arts and nonprofit boards. The corporate jet stops here to take me to Washington parties or broadcasts from the U.S. Chamber of Commerce. I'm president of this board and that fund drive and active in political campaigns. It's all a little much.

"Politicians want to be seen with me, but I can't imagine why. It seems a constant battle to remain who I am or become who they want me to be. My core seems crowded now by image over substance. It's too easy to just become an echo of others." He sighed and laid his hand over hers.

She took his hand and said, "I know you're worried about me, but you know I'll be all right, don't you?" He nodded yes, but Susan knew that he was fighting himself and that he was restless and vulnerable.

One bright spot was his friendship with Congressman Charlie Deaton. He was a jolly, Santa Claus-cheeked man who asked him to come to Washington as his chief of staff after Michael had gone against his bosses and the political action committee at BellSouth to support Deaton against the incumbent. The company wasn't happy, but when Deaton won, Michael's influence was all they had. So he was tolerated behind the veneer of fake smiles and rewarded through the grinding of gritted teeth. Some at headquarters told him quietly that he was making enemies who thought he had entirely too much influence for someone of his rank.

Michael thanked the congressman for the offer, but said, "Even the ethically flawed need someone they can trust to guard the piggy bank from the same anointed club members they promote. I think that's my role, and I'd better keep Susan close to our hospitals here. If I had wanted to go to Washington, it would've been with Reagan. Now that he's gone, well…"

He sailed farther and farther from shore on what he deemed the sea of meaninglessness. He cannibalized his core, and his analytical and linear thinking grew into an insular place. Analogies dominated life on his island of isolation and became false before he realized it, obscuring who he was and why he existed. He'd tried so hard to find himself since he left the Bureau that he had lost himself in the process.

Michael doubled down on his plan to insulate himself with more awards for stellar achievements, but he felt that the world he now traveled in surely must be in its twilight and he was but a motherless child, a long way from home. Somewhere there played that distant melody, smothered and muted, yet growing louder as the gravity of the collapsing world tugged at him. *Trying to capture it*, he thought, *is like trying to trap smoke or stack BBs.*

* * *

On the fifteenth anniversary of the day he was warned of the potential ambush in Tupelo, Michael attended the Boys' Club Steak and Burger Dinner at Sacred Heart, a resplendent cultural center with silver spires that seemed to caress the clouds. The vaulted ceilings and ornate stained-glass windows filtered the light in a kaleidoscopic display that spackled the interior and reflected off the reddish marble floors. Three steps up to the altar led to the very spot where former Georgia Coach Vince Dooley was to speak.

As Michael walked to Sacred Heart under the fading tint of dusk, the spider vein spread of lightning silhouetted distant thunderclouds. An amalgamation of odors drifted to him: flowers in bloom under the old pin oak trees lining Broad Street; the unique smells of the polluted, muddy-brown Savannah River; and the petrochemical toxins that belched from the smokestacks of the local chemical plants, yellowing the air.

All was well, though, because the azaleas and dogwoods out on the Augusta National Golf Course had bloomed in time for the Masters Golf Tournament—the things that mattered in "Golf Town USA."

At Michael's table were the local newspaper editor, Bill Cook, and two state legislators, Ricky Garcia and Joey Tomlin. In his columns, Cook, a man with a lantern jaw and a penchant for garish sports jackets, ignored those toxic plumes rising from the plants, just as he did the failings of his political allies and those who bought his food and spirits at the Pinnacle Club. He often told Michael, "The news is what we say it is."

Even at the dinner, he couldn't leave his acerbic commentary behind. "I think he was overrated as a coach," Cook commented with his permanent smirk, and the two legislators nodded in agreement, heads bobbing like the bobble-head doggies in auto rear windows. They talked through the national anthem with characteristic juvenile antics.

The razor-tongued editor wasn't from the South but was a native New Yorker, the descendant of a long line of Copperheads who supported the South in the Civil War. Hired directly from the UGA School of Journalism as a reporter, he moved rapidly to editor. He was a professing conservative, albeit the kind that gives all a bad name. He was a pragmatic and ruthless self-promoter who enjoyed power and the exercise of that power over people who feared his poison pen.

People walked on eggshells around him. It was only a matter of time before one of the smiling victims would find a way to get even for his needless cruelties or for his advances to their wives and girlfriends—a terminal adolescence his twisted humor failed to cover.

Michael had tried to make common cause with him when he still believed that the editor might be someone who actually cared about good public policy, only to discover that his rhetoric didn't match his words. He told Susan that Cook had beheaded so many people in his columns that Broad Street was littered with rolling heads like stray balls in a bowling alley.

When he began to see Cook give protection to people who deserved none and attack others without cause, he asked him one day over another of the two-martini lunches that had become three or four for the editor, "How do you respond to those who say you practice yellow journalism?" Cook replied, "Not true! Green is the only color that moves me."

Cook's legislator sycophants, Garcia and Tomlin, were in his circle of protection, and Michael once overheard their private conversation outside the House chambers in Atlanta.

Garcia said, "Joey, I need you to vote for my bill."

Brow creased in mock seriousness, the short man replied, "But Ricky, I haven't read your bill. I don't know what's in it."

Garcia said, "Boy, does it matter as long as I support yours?"

After a pregnant pause, the two laughed uproariously at their little ritual. They slapped each other on the back and returned to the chambers to vote in the style that had become the custom in Atlanta. At a distance, they might fake the public servant image for the casual observer, but Michael had gotten too close to their stage. The smell of alcohol, the ugliness of their dirty deeds, and the grubbiness of their soiled and tepid lives had spoiled the illusion. They appeared to be amiable, good ole boys, but they weren't to be crossed.

It wasn't these perpetual juveniles Coach Dooley had come to challenge, but the boys from the inner city. He spoke eloquently of Herschel Walker, the great running back on Georgia's national championship team, and the many obstacles he had overcome in life. Just as Dooley was reaching the apex of his speech, the long folding table to his right collapsed; elderly men and priests fell backwards, only the soles of their shoes visible to the audience. The sounds of shattering glass, crashing china, and clattering, bouncing silverware reverberated again and again within the cavernous echo of the old church.

Michael rose to help the men who had fallen. Other attendees scurried to assist and caterers swept the glass shards and pieces of china from the corners of the old cathedral.

Dooley looked stunned, but when it seemed that no one was seriously hurt and the table had been righted, he looked at the crowd and said, "Father Tom told me that he would send me a sign if I was running too long, but I thought it would be more subtle than this."

It was a great recovery, and everyone laughed. The editor and his amigos laughed so hard the band of fat around Garcia's waist jiggled like a bowl of Jell-O. While Dooley may have found *his* sign in Augusta, no cartoon light bulb had appeared over Michael's head.

He was still looking for the marker or hieroglyph that pointed his compass to true north.

CHAPTER THIRTEEN

*"Has God actually said that you shall eat of
no tree in the Garden?"—Genesis 3:1*

*"You walk on the wild side. Odds against goin' to
heaven, six-to-one."—Brook Benton*

While Michael tried to find his way and read the signs along the back roads of his new life, his fellow refugee from Mississippi, Billy Joe Estes, was not concerning himself with the finer points of philosophy. No sir, he was a carnal man who lived in the moment and documented it all for his bosses in copious notes written in his childish scrawl.

"Time's a-wasting," he always said.

His days were filled with the usual challenges in the alcohol-soaked village and Kabuki theater of Atlanta, where too many of the boys under the gold dome fancied themselves supreme beings in various stages of pickling.

Billy Joe was the fix-it man in the city of one-way roads, where Peachtree Street had no beginning and no end. If some legislator or staffer let the nose candy overtake them, he was their man. If someone was making trouble for a legislator's indiscretions, he was the bag man with the crisp, new bills. He endured and applauded endless speeches by blowhards with voices like rusty, shaky hinges on an old door. He entertained widows with sour, rotten-egg breath to find money for the campaigns of the Speaker's favorite candidates.

He didn't tell his benefactors everything he did. Ace Connelly didn't want to know it all when he was alive, and neither did those in politics—plausible deniability was the name of the game. He got punished now and then when things didn't go right, but the word around Atlanta was that Billy Joe didn't say nothing to nobody about nothing. He never snitched.

Billy Joe also managed the wounded birds discarded by the political practitioners of emotional usury—the young sparrows with the broken hearts and hollow eyes, the cracked lips, and the smell of lives wasted. He wondered what the ones he protected had done to them—but he didn't wonder too long. In a land of guilty and grimy pleasures, he just poured some more Planters peanuts into his Coke to remind him of home and Mississippi, where old times are not forgotten.

Now and then, he was rewarded with more than money. Big Jim, the Speaker of the House and Czar of Atlanta, had ruddy cheeks, jowls that quivered when he talked, and pungent cigar smoke that would gag a moose. He told Billy Joe, "Son, I'm glad you're here. You gotta be someplace, and I'm glad you're here. Mississippi was no longer the place for you," he said.

"When you open an oyster and there's no pearl in it, you don't throw more sea and sand in it, shake it all around, and hope to make one. No sir, you move on and cut your losses, boy," Big Jim opined.

That was high praise, almost father to son the way Billy Joe saw it. Big Jim told him one night after a few suds, "Boy, this is a dirty business, but somebody's gotta do it, and I guess we're as good as any. We live large, boy, but we don't steal. We're just compensated for the long hours of doing good things for the people of the great state of Georgia. We are who we are. Atlanta politics is just show business for us homely folks.

"Innocent? No, we ain't innocent, I suppose. We're just part of that stuff they call Karma—merchants, travelers in our world, and high-livers merely getting what is coming to us. We only want our snouts in the trough for our rightful dues.

"Sure there's gonna be some collateral damage, but if we don't do it, Billy Joe, someone else will, and just think what those rotten, lousy, no-good so-and-so's might be doing if it weren't for us."

Billy Joe loved it when Big Jim shared with him, making everything so clear about how the victors get the spoils. *And aren't we the victors?* he reckoned. He craved the validation, and viewed the old Speaker as a father figure or a beloved commander and himself but a centurion in his army. They were almost like the Roman Empire that Ace Connelly used to tell him about.

The Speaker was wound up tonight. He constructed large, sweeping arcs in the air with his big hands and went on and on about the guy who would almost certainly soon be governor.

"He dreams big, boy. We could all get well under him. He doesn't just want to be guvnah. He wants to be king or some kind of god of Georgia. I met with him and his inner circle, and they have ambitions for things that we've never even thought of. Some folks say that he might be president one day.

"They talk about taking over every state agency and overriding the constitutional officers, and pushing aside anyone who won't go along. They want everything—I mean everything! Roads, bridges, ports, the courts, education, police, and prisons…all of it—maybe even us, the legislature. That's where we got to watch him, protect ourselves, and negotiate. We also got to shake the tree sometimes and see what and who falls out. There's a place for you, a future for ambitious young men," the Speaker said in a conspiratorial whisper.

He paused and looked Billy Joe squarely in the eyes and blew cigar smoke in his face. "Boy, are you gonna let anyone get in our way? You gonna let some publican or some white knight ride in and spoil our future and soil our ground? Or you gonna follow our golden rule? You know, do unto them before they do unto us! You gonna wait in line for the leftovers from any of these reformers?"

"No, sir. I promised myself when I left the military that I'd never stand in line again," Billy Joe pledged.

The Speaker smiled and nodded. As he rose to leave, Billy Joe asked him, "Mr. Speaker, do you think God is on our side?"

"Oh, absolutely, son!" he said with certitude. "It's 'Render unto Caesar,' and aren't we the agents of Caesar? Church people are told to obey their leaders, and that's us. The people today listen with their eyes and think with their feelings. So all we got to do, son, is to put on a good show of pomp and circumstance for 'em, and play their emotions like a fiddle until they beg us to take more of their taxes and their local control. Oh, and we mustn't forget the dog whistles now and then," he said.

"What's that?" Billy Joe asked as he leaned forward, elbows on his kneecaps.

"That's the code words in our speeches for our base—those loyalists in municipal and county governments who need to be assured that the spoils of the system will always flow, no matter what we might have to say for the masses. It's also for those cooperating individuals who perform services above and beyond the call of duty—union chiefs, enforcers, lawyers, organizers, and good ole boys and girls who need to know we're looking out for 'em."

"But why do you call the code words 'dog whistles'?" Billy Joe asked.

"Because, son. Those bowwow tail-waggers are a politician's best friends, and our whistle-toots can only be heard by our mutts who come a-running."

Billy Joe looked uncertain, so the Speaker leaned back, took a deep draw on his rancid cigar, and added, "Now, I know that might sound a bit harsh. So let me put it this way. We're just the descendants of Adam called to tend the garden, to tend to unruly children, to get rid of the weeds—the freeloaders who don't cooperate with the gardeners. Now and then, we might have to do some serious pruning to enrich the soil of the garden with the blood of our political enemies."

He paused and tapped the ashes of his cigar into a garbage can bearing the seal of the State of Georgia. "Don't look so glum, boy. Why, we hired a House chaplain to read from his penitential every day and certify that we're actually doing God's work. We're just part of the four S's that folks worship today—self, sex, stuff, and state."

CHAPTER FOURTEEN

"I arise…torn between a desire to improve the world and a desire to enjoy [it]. This makes it hard to plan the day."—E.B. White

"They…clawed the money off of his table—hand over fist."—Seba Smith, The Life and Writings of Major Jack Downing

A tinny voice, muffled by static and the increasing cabin pressure, said, "Ladies and gentlemen, the captain is now beginning his final approach into Reagan International Airport. Please buckle your seatbelts and remain seated until we have landed and turned off the seatbelt sign."

"Sir, please buckle up. We are making our final approach to the airport," said the pretty airline attendant with crisp efficiency as she nudged Michael from the book he was reading.

He *was* buckled up, in the sense that he was caught up in memory as he peered out from his window seat on the Delta Airlines flight. The rippling red, white, and blue flag over the dome of the Capitol Building in Washington seemed to wave at all the silver birds in the lucent sky.

He'd heard all the speeches about enemies—both real and imagined—around the globe, but looking down, he suspected that there was more danger to liberty and to the Constitution within a ten-mile radius of the arcaded passages of the Congress and the White House than in all of the Capitols of the world. The organic coffee houses below were packed with the courtiers of the incestuous commingling of press, government, and Wall Street players who thought it all a game.

The self-congratulatory herd undermined what was left of it all. As they lived on their parents' trust funds, pretended to be great public servants, and quoted from their dog-eared copies of *Das Kapital*, they inhaled another latte at Starbucks, preached that big was not bad, and giggled, "Why, we're all good Socialist Capitalists—aren't we?"

These trips to see elected officials in Washington always stirred memories of Michael's first trip to the nation's capital. It was one week after graduating from high school, and he had ridden the train into the old Union Station, heading to work for the FBI. "Summer in the City" by the Lovin' Spoonful was playing when he arrived, and a blonde beauty named Dixie Lee was waiting there to change his life.

The second time he visited D.C., the Mississippi Bureau of Narcotics decided he should attend the DEA Academy. When he landed at what was then Washington National Airport, he walked through the terminal to the music of Steppenwolf's "Born to be Wild" as it blared through a vendor's sound system.

"You know that song was written about me?" he told agents with him.

"No, it's true," he said to disbelieving looks.

He smiled. "The original title was—'Born to be Mild.'"

"Now we *could* believe that," they all agreed.

While Michael attended the Academy, he lived with other agents in an apartment near the DEA headquarters. He often walked to a small community grocery store that had not been driven from the once-tranquil Washington residential neighborhood by crime.

On one such bright day, the cherry trees were in bloom and the mockingbirds sang odes to life from their perches amidst the white and pink flowers. Michael thought that life was good and despite the challenges that the old city faced, there were still moments of beauty to be harvested. If you squinted just right and let the combination of flower fragrance and song sweep you along, the reality of ugliness could be displaced by the friendly ghosts of yesterday.

Then he saw them up ahead on the edge of the sidewalk that he was on.

The gang of feral, young males sat on a low brick wall that bordered what once was a fine old home in inner-city Washington. When those bricks were laid, neighbors knew neighbors, and they could walk these streets on gentle summer afternoons or stroll to the lawn of the Capitol to hear summer concerts, as Michael had when he came to work for the FBI.

Now that was impossible because of the crumbling societal infrastructure which far exceeded the decay of bricks and mortar. These boys with the angry eyes were sired in a sea of poverty and drugs, skipping childhood to become creatures of the streets—predators that drove the elderly to chain their doors and hide behind deadbolts and barred windows. This lost generation's identity was no longer forged within home and hearth by loving parents. That was a foreign concept to the orphans of America's Capitol, who knew only the family of the gang.

"Hey, man, wonder what he's got in those sacks," the tall, wiry, alpha male said. Steam rose from the summer baking of the asphalt, and his image seemed to fade in and out, wrinkling in the distortion of the air. A police siren wailed in the distance, a stray dog barked, and a screen door slammed shut after a call to children to "Come in this house!"

"Yeah, man. Let's get 'em," said pack member number two, his flattened nostrils flaring. Michael caught a flash of an image in the edge of his pocket that looked suspiciously like the outline of the cheap .32-caliber automatics so favored by enterprising gang members.

He'd seen it all before. He moved to cross the street to avoid close contact with them, even as he shifted the grocery sacks to the crook of his left arm and watched them in his peripheral vision.

"Hey, hold up, pretty boy. We want those sacks. Think about living—think about dying before you mess with us," said the leader with the shaved head and high cheekbones. They rose from their perches like vultures that had just seen fresh road kill ripening in the summer heat.

At that moment, Michael pulled back his navy blazer to expose the long-barreled, .357 Magnum revolver with oversized grips that rested on his right hip like a bazooka. The gun held six hollow-point rounds that would go in small but exit the back in a mushroomed effect. DEA attendees were authorized to carry in D.C. because crime was so bad, and any extra cops on the street had to be a deterrent, the authorities figured. So it was today.

"I did think about it," Michael said without making direct eye contact, releasing the snap on his belt holster and wrapping his hand around the giant grips of the Magnum.

Six posteriors tightened and froze in midrise from their red-brick bleachers, then retreated in unison to their previous perches but with new respect for their intended victim.

"Geez, did you see the size of that gun?" one muttered to the nodding affirmations of the rest of the pack, a cartoonish image that momentarily masked the deadliness of the game.

Michael smiled and thought, *Yes, when you encounter another shopper who appears hapless and helpless, you might pause and wonder—what's he packing under that blazer? And some say that guns don't deter crime. What was it that the sociologist instructor told us last week in class? Oh yeah. "Enforce with love, gentlemen."*

But these punks were only petty street thieves and hoodlums. The real bandits practiced their legal larceny under the guarded eaves of Capitol Hill, where earmarks did not refer to the scars of steel studs in pink and pendulous earlobes.

* * *

Michael walked down the halls of Congress and passed well-known faces in the breezeways. Senator Tom Williams, a balding man bound to a wheelchair from an injury in Vietnam, was the very one he had warned young female aides about. Michael told them to pass up the elevator if Senator Williams was on board or risk his standard grope and pinch when the doors closed.

"But…he's in a wheelchair! He's disabled," they protested.

"That doesn't restrict his hands or mute his vulgar tongue," Michael replied. "At a charity function hosted by BellSouth where he was the keynote speaker, he propositioned the genteel chairwoman—at the head table, no less. At a chamber function in Augusta, he asked the mayor's wife if she would like to get to know him—intimately."

Michael finally arrived at the office of the new congressman he had high hopes for. Just as he reached for the door, it opened and out walked Majority Leader Tom DeLay. With him, a man dressed in a mohair suit with a flamboyant godfather-style hat to match his demeanor. DeLay nodded, and his companion looked at Michael the way big cats in the jungle look at potential prey or sources of amusement. *K Street, not Main Street*, Michael thought.

"Hello, Michael," the beaming, new redheaded staffer for Congressman Tom Bassett said. "Welcome to Capitol Hill!"

The office was bustling with eager, young interns and staffers, many battling the scales from too many free lobbyist buffets and cocktails—the candy-apple, cotton-candy youth that typified most Congressional staffers. Most were thrilled to work for Bassett, a lanky, Midwestern reformer who looked like Jimmy Stewart.

"Oh, I thought you guys were already referring to it as Capitol Hell!" Michael said with a grin.

The young man, with peach fuzz for a beard, looked all around and confided, "Some days, I think that's exactly what it is. But hey, what do you think of the digs we drew for our office? Pretty impressive and just remodeled. We feel quite lucky."

"I'm surprised that a freshman warrants such treatment," Michael said.

"Yes, we were a bit surprised ourselves," the eager young staffer replied.

"Who was that with the majority leader?" Michael asked.

"Oh, that was Jack Abramoff, a big-time lobbyist, a wheeler-dealer. He once worked with Norquist and Reed at the College Republicans and knows everyone who is anyone in D.C. He could sell ice to an Eskimo. He was here with DeLay to visit with Congressman Bassett. The deputy whip is still in with the congressman now," the staffer replied.

Michael was shown to the empty office of the chief of staff. As he waited, he realized that the adjoining door to the congressman's office was ajar. He heard a mechanically jolly voice that pierced the solemn atmosphere of the discreet suite—a voice that he recognized as Representative Carl Brea, the deputy whip, who said, "Tom, it's so good to have you with us. As a freshman, you're going have a good deal of pressure on you, and we want to help." Michael thought, *Words you should fear most—"I'm from the government, and I'm here to help you."*

Brea's singsong voice waxed philosophical. "This running every two years is a terrible burden. You must campaign constantly, and we know that a principled public servant like you came to Washington to get things done, not to be running around raising money all the time. So we're going to relieve you of that burden."

Michael felt like a voyeur, an eavesdropper, but thought, *Uh-oh. Run, Tom, run.*

Brea, a round and red-faced man, was as big as a house, with a mouthful of perfect teeth that gleamed under the fluorescent lights just as his dentist had promised. He droned on like someone used to mounting filibusters. The tones and the rote recitation were delivered by a man who had made this speech many times before.

"I hope you find this new office to your liking, Tom. We jumped you over so many to get this prized location. Don't want the folks back home to come up and find their boy in anything less than the best, you know. I'll help you hit the ground running now that you're here. We'll set you up with all the right people: invitations to upper-tier social gatherings along the Potomac with those who have loads of money and positively love congressmen. They want to help you. *We* want to help you," he said, caressing the words of mock sincerity that dripped from his lips.

"Now, the leadership doesn't want a thing from you except to know that we can count on you on the tough votes, the votes when we really need you. Oh, we understand that all politics is local, Tom, and you have to make some pretense of listening to the common man in your district now and then on these hot-button issues that stir the masses. That was what you called yourself in the campaign, wasn't it—a 'man of the people'?" he said with a sneer of thinly veiled contempt.

"Now here's how it works. When your district is against us on something that the lobbyists on K Street want, we'll allow you to vote against us…if we don't need you. You can pound your chest and say you fought gallantly because you're with the people back home against these professional politicians in Washington…You know, all that nonsense."

Brea leaned over Bassett's desk with a sudden sharpness as keen as a knife. "But when we need you, we need you. If you are the 218th vote for passage of a bill that the Speaker wants, then we expect you to step up and vote with your D.C. team. More money will come to your campaign treasury to help with any fallout back home, and we'll give you statements our gifted stable of writers produce to convince the yokels how you really voted in their best interest and to remind them of all you've done for them. If that isn't enough, why, we always have your back.

"Those ratings issued by our friends at the Conservative Council? Why, they're written up by former members of Congress, and they only rate you on the votes we send them. So it's all fixed, you understand. You can vote against your conservative constituency and still get a one hundred percent rating to tout back home. All the hard votes are excluded from the ranking. The votes they track are mostly for the flag, the troops, for Mom and apple pie, you know—nothing that means anything. It's all a game. Heck, the other side does the same thing with their rating groups to appease the lefties always nagging at them, just like our wing nuts. It's a game, man—just a game. The real decisions are much too important to be left to the *little people*."

Michael could hear the background noise outside—the clacking of keyboards, the ringing of the phones, the hum of official Washington's image, but *this* was the real face of D.C.; these scammers and muggers made the gang he had encountered look like cherub-faced choir boys.

"So you see how it is. We'll eventually work you into positions on the leadership team. Why, one day, you might have my job." Brea laughed so hard that his belly was barely restrained by his belt, and his suspenders bounced and shook long after he ceased to laugh, like aftershocks of an earthquake.

Then Brea reverted to character, the only thing he knew. When all you know is the hammer, then everyone who might get in your way looks like a nail.

"But, freshman—and that's all you are, a freshman with no future if you don't play ball with us—if you decide to be a maverick, you will get no money for re-election. In fact, we'll bankroll an opponent against you in the primary. You'll get no leadership positions and no committee and subcommittee assignments worth spit. You'll be relegated to the short life of an unknown back-bencher that no one has ever heard of and no one will remember—a nobody, a loser—a one-termer, two at most."

The new congressman looked stunned and diminished. Beads of sweat had formed on his upper lip. The brutality of Brea's dialogue was bruising and sobering to an idealist. Brea continued, "Why, any hopes of getting all that good ole pork for your district—or seeing your name on bridges, highways, and post office buildings that makes you practically immortal…you can forget all of that if you want to go your own way. You've got to decide if you want to be a winner or a bum. The train of champions is leaving the station. You better get on board now, or get left behind with the rest of the pathetic little people who think they are somebody. The only principle that matters is the principal in your House Bank account."

He was a master—the caress of the soft glove, the stinging slap of the backhand. He leaned back and clasped his hands like a country deacon about to lead the congregation in prayer. He paused to let it all sink in and said, "It's the trade-off here in the club that so many naïve newcomers don't understand, but it's not so bad, really. You just look at it as part of the deal to get to do much of what you say you're for—all those high-minded things you spoke so eloquently of in your campaign. It's all for the greater good, you know. We know you're a reasonable man, a practical man. That's why we picked you, why the Speaker came down to campaign for you, and the Congressional Campaign Committee—along with some other key PACs we control—sent you the money that made the difference in your close race."

He paused again, and his eyes narrowed.

"You didn't think that was by accident, did you? You didn't think it was because you were anything special, or your Reaganesque speeches just moved us to open our purse strings? You didn't think that you were better than the rest of us—did you? You didn't think that it was all free—did you? Nothing, and I mean nothing in life is free, Tom—including this fine office we picked to give you a preview of the limitless bounties of our generosity."

The deputy whip rose and said, "Don't look so glum, my friend. If the people ever reject you, why, brother, that rejected stone will become the cornerstone of our wall around this old capital city. Why, it's practically Biblical. You'll be building your career, not on the sands of idealism, but on the rock of the way that it's always been and always will be.

"We'll protect you, and if you are ever defeated, a cushy job as a lobbyist always awaits you—courtesy of our corporate friends who value team players. I don't think we misjudged you. I know we can count on your loyalty, can't we?

"Hmm?" he stated more than questioned, spreading out his hands high and wide as if making a giant banner. "This little plot of ground on Capitol Hill can be all you ever hoped to know of heaven if you go along and get along, or all you never wanted to know of hell if you don't play ball with us." He paused.

"Tom Bassett Federal Building—has a certain ring to it, doesn't it?"

He moved around the desk, hands extended and palms up, to embrace what was left of the new congressman as the imagery and visions of Jimmy Stewart in *Mr. Smith Goes to Washington* were now but a shattered dream. Brea privately told friends that he really didn't enjoy the brutalizing of these Boy Scouts who came to Congress, but it was "necessary." In private, he stored away these sessions in the library of his mind, trophy shrunken heads to be taken out and shared over cocktails as humorous anecdotes with those in his tribe of cannibals.

The cowed congressman, eyes affixed to the new red carpet of his office, embraced him reverently in an act of submission and unity. The gatekeeper offered him a taste of the forbidden fruit in Washington. All that was missing was the hissing of the serpent promising that he would be like God, knowing good and evil, and the Mafia symbolism of the kissing of the ring with the utterance of—"Godfather, Godfather."

Carlos Marcello would be proud, Michael thought.

Then the door which he had borne silent witness through was slowly closed by Brea's aide—a scene right out of the closing moments in *The Godfather*, symbolizing the selling of souls, pledging of fortunes, and common cause until death do them part.

Shortly after Clay had died, a plain brown package addressed in his handwriting arrived at Michael's private post office box. It was a last purging of files at the MBN that weren't quite official: raw intelligence that Clay did not want to fall into the wrong hands after his death. As he witnessed the scene in the congressman's office, Michael thought of those files and transcripts of wiretaps he hadn't known existed until he read them late that night—New Orleans mobsters in Jackson, not all of Sicilian descent, reciting Sicilian proverbs as they met with state politicians over Italian dishes at the Jackson Country Club.

"*Li ricchi cchiù chi nn'hannu, cchiù nni vonnu,*" one whispered to the lieutenant governor. "The more we have, the more we want."

His companion nodded and told the governor, "*Lu pintimentu lava lu piccatu.* Repentance washes away all sin."

As Michael quietly slipped out rather than face the emasculated congressman, the hallway was alive with the creatures of government rushing here and there, who no longer knew anyone but their own kind and thought everything was all about them. Their poseur heels clicked on the marbled floors. Snatches of conversations from aides to their bosses echoed against the monuments of opulence—who needs to be called, requests to speak with CNN on the new farm legislation, and what time the Speaker expected to call votes on bills so "vital" to the Republic.

He took a deep breath. His lips felt chapped, and his breath smelled sour. *No, this is not Capitol Hell,* he thought. He didn't feel the heat but the emptiness, the barren and frozen landscapes of hardened hearts here in Siberia, USA, where spring never comes, and all exists in a perpetual winter of despair.

He thought of the old story about the man who always took his parrot with him to some of the seedier nightspots in Washington. Later, when he and his bird visited Congress for an exhibition, the parrot began to chatter as they turned down each corridor, encountering more and more congressmen. "Road-house," he squawked.

"No," the man said, "this is Congress."

"Juke joint," the parrot replied.

"No, this is Congress," the man countered.

"Honky-tonk," the bird insisted.

"No, no," the exasperated man repeated. "I told you. We're in Congress now."

The parrot paused, looked all around, and said…"Same people."

CHAPTER FIFTEEN

*"Ninety percent of politicians give the other
ten percent a bad name."—Henry Kissinger*

*"Truth…is often protected by a bodyguard of lies."
—Winston Churchill*

As Michael walked toward the Senate, he ran into a silver-haired senator who was once a member of the KKK. He was trembling a bit from what Michael guessed to be early Parkinson's disease. He was walking his little dog, Billy, on a leash…in the U.S. Capitol.

Michael's mind checker-jumped from that to memories of Herman Walton, the grand dragon of the White Knights of the Klan, a branch back home in Tupelo. Walton, a nervous and mousy man with a receding hairline, drove around town in a car with a sawed-off double-barreled shotgun on the dash. If he was kind enough to open his trunk, you would find every manner of semi-automatic weapon and machine guns bolted to racks and the underside of the trunk lid. The police in Tupelo looked the other way in those days because of his Klan status.

Before Carlos Marcello ever visited Governor Davidson or thought of killing Bobby Kennedy, Herman heard Kennedy was coming to Ole Miss in 1968 and declared, "I'm going to kill him." Anyone who knew Herman knew that was no idle threat. He loaded up for Oxford, but Charlie Patterson, an FBI informant who hung out in Herman's store, tipped off the Secret Service, and Walton was intercepted on campus.

His guns were taken, but he was released. Why he wasn't detained, no one knew. When asked by fans if he killed this or that person, his dry answer was always the same: "They're dead, ain't they?" He continued on his path until he lost everything. He was seen wandering the streets, homeless and alone, until he keeled over one day and was buried in a pauper's grave.

Memories of old Mississippi flushed up as Michael tracked down his friend Senator Paul Dale, whom he considered the best of the best at that level. Dale had been to Augusta recently, and Charlton Heston had flown in to campaign for him. Michael and "Moses" had their picture made together. Michael's mother and the folks back in Mississippi were thrilled.

Lost in yesterday, Michael ran into the senator walking briskly through the Senate chambers, followed by his aide. Dale brightened when he saw Michael, but did not slow a bit.

"What news do you have from home? Walk and talk, Michael. Walk and talk," the small, bespectacled man said. He had the bookish, green-eyeshade look of a man straight out of central casting as an accountant or undertaker, but looks were deceiving. Dale was a smart man, a workaholic always on planes, boats, and trains raising money for candidates.

"Michael, I'm glad you came by," the senator said as he practically sprinted through the halls of the Senate with his harried, pimply-faced aide in tow.

"Texas Governor George W. Bush is coming to Augusta to help me raise money for my own campaign treasury. I must tend to my own campaign coffers now and then," Dale said in a voice that sounded helium-fueled.

"I know. How can I help?" Michael asked.

"Bush is going to be our next president. He is riding high out of his terms as governor of Texas and the success of the 'Texas Miracle.' They're doing great things to reform education, particularly in the Houston area, where Rod Paige is firing administrators who don't improve test results and dropout rates," the senator said.

Michael had been chamber education chairman for many years, chaired superintendent searches, and served on a national panel to set education standards. He was an education reform junkie. He knew of the so-called Texas Miracle and was highly skeptical of the overnight results they seemed to be touting. There were already rumblings of test scores being changed to save teacher and administrator jobs, altering student answers on tests, and manipulation of data to exclude and reclassify students to boost graduation and dropout statistics. He also knew that the senator was close to the Bush family.

"Paul, I'm not so sure about those miracles they're bragging about. Those kinds of numbers and turnarounds just don't happen overnight unless you fudge the data. Anyway, shouldn't that be a state prerogative, not another top-down directive from Washington?" he asked as they passed through the hallowed institution where dramas and betrayals were found down each hallway, quiet madness around each corner.

The senator looked surprised and perplexed. "What? No, no, it's wonderful! And he can do for the nation what they're doing out there. They're going to call it No Child Left Behind. Isn't that a great title? Don't worry, Michael. This will be a proper application," he said confidently.

"Back to business at hand," he said. "Can you set something up for us—a fundraiser? Get a nice home where we might hold a reception, call some of our supporters, get some pledges and invite them to come by for a little party for the next president. Let's have some pictures and some fellowship. Can you do that for me?" the senator asked, a bit out of breath and so pale as to appear brittle and bloodless for a moment. Still, Michael and Dale's aide struggled to keep up with his frantic pace.

"No problem," Michael said, but he was concerned about the senator's pasty-white color.

"Paul, you aren't pushing yourself too hard, are you?" Michael asked.

"No, Michael. I'm fine," he sighed. "Never enough hours in the day, it seems, and now I'm criss-crossing the country to raise money for the Senatorial Election Committee. Thank you for helping me. Keep me apprised of your progress." And he was gone.

So Michael left Washington and returned to Augusta to arrange an intimate fundraiser for his friend and the friend of his friend—the odds-on favorite to become president.

* * *

The stately old mansion in Augusta, owned and renovated by Dr. Elizabeth Proctor, provided the perfect backdrop for Senator Dale's fundraiser. A rotund lady with an overbite, she was a respected surgeon at the Medical College of Georgia.

"Oh, it's so wonderful, isn't it?" the pneumatic physician and queen of the Augusta Social Club cooed. "We have the sen-ah-tor and maybe the future Prez-e-dent right here in my home! Imagine that! Thank you for asking us to host this historic event."

Michael lured as many folks there as he could muster on short notice, and they were all attentive and generous when the senator arrived with the presumed nominee for president.

Michael had some time with the man who was making education reform central to his campaign for the White House, and encouraged the Texan to remember Mary Ruth Robinson, who had been elected state superintendent of schools in Georgia.

"She's a reformer, Governor," he said earnestly. "She's already shelved the disaster that was whole language and reinstituted phonics. She's the only Republican in Atlanta, and she's having a tough time there with a State Board of Education appointed by the establishment."

"What's her name again?" the personable governor asked as he smiled so wide that it made his eyes crinkle around the corners. He had an interesting cadence to his voice. Michael wondered for a moment if it was affected but decided it was real.

"Robinson, Mary Ruth Robinson," Michael repeated. He thought that the governor was a charming and likeable fellow but perhaps not the sharpest blade in the drawer.

"I hear that y'all had some success with test scores and dropouts in the Houston school district, and you are going to make this a centerpiece of your education platform," Michael ventured in a casual and complimentary manner.

Bush was being summoned to a photo op with a donor for the senator and gave a parting, "Yes, yes. Rod Paige and his people have increased the graduation rate, cut dropouts, and boosted test scores almost overnight. All Texans are proud of what they've accomplished, and we hope to bring that success to Washington. They need some fresh air up there, don't they? Ah, we'll talk more later, gotta go over here for a bit. Thanks for all you do. I know that Paul and I can count on you."

Bill Cook was there and ambled over in a loud sports jacket and a gunmetal-blue tie.

"What were you and the governor talking about?" he inquired, ever the curious journalist and hatchet man for his publisher—always trolling for opportunities to sponge off his fellow travelers.

"Oh, about education reform and helping Mary Ruth if he gets elected," Michael shrugged.

Visibly disappointed and thoroughly disgusted, he scowled as he asked, "Why must you always be on these crusades about things that don't amount to a hill of beans? You didn't ask him about opportunities for us in his administration? We must always leverage these moments that our contacts provide us, not waste them. No party invitations or freebies for your editor?"

"No, that didn't come up," Michael said. He sometimes thought the editor had ice water in his veins and was mean down to his toenails. He noted Cook's increasing intake of alcohol at these events. *But who am I to judge?* he thought. *I take meds to calm these panic attacks, but that's from my doctor. It's all right,* he reassured himself.

"You live vicariously through me, you know? You want to be me," Cook said.

"No, if I wanted to channel you, Bill, I'd just make like an old rooster weather vane on top of a Mississippi barn and spin every time the smell of money was on the breeze," Michael jabbed. *Old rooster fits Cook,* he thought.

Michael watched the party and the networking from an emotional distance. He considered that he had always been apart from the whole—from the games, the parades, and charades—but he sensed that the distance was increasing. He thought he might die of hypothermia if he moved any farther away, but he feared incineration if he moved an inch closer to the sun of their universe.

All the hugs and kisses by party people were metaphors for the larger bestowing of casual affection and commitment, with the implied assurance that such would never require explanation or ethical challenge—only the equity of access. The happy citizens were off over there somewhere warming themselves by the superficial flames of their fires. Michael watched the trivial chatter, all second-hand to him, too distant to ever realize any comfort from their communion. He was just off from the main, living without being alive in their world. For a moment, he wished he could hop out of himself and into the skin of one of these outwardly happy people. In the midst of their laughter and joviality, he was alone. They didn't know him, couldn't see him, and had no clue how desperate he was to figure out how it had all gone wrong.

When the party became too much, he wandered outside and readied his Nikon camera to take the senator's requested parting pictures of the president-to-be and his merry supporters. He watched a long, narrow, flowing cirrus cloud called a mare's-tail, and sang to himself as he often did when he felt isolated: *I'm just an old chunk of coal, but I'm gonna be a diamond someday.*

Mosquitoes buzzed in his ears. Humidity left the air thick, requiring gasps for breath, and somewhere, the giant metronome above was ticking left and right, right and left…*tick, tick, tick,* and the rhythm was interrupted by a solo vocal, "It's later than you think."

CHAPTER SIXTEEN

*"The greatest evil…is conceived and ordered
(moved, seconded, carried and minuted) in clean,
carpeted, warmed and well-lighted offices, by quiet
men with white collars and cut fingernails and
smooth-shaven cheeks who do not need to raise
their voices."*—C.S. Lewis

*"If you are going to sin, sin against God, not the
bureaucracy. God will forgive you, but the
bureaucracy won't."*—Hyman Rickover

Mary Ruth Robinson—the itinerant politician of the shiny golden tresses, scarlet-red dresses, and ivory skin that seemed to glow from within—had lost a local election, but she was swept to power by the landslide election of her party in Washington. Official Atlanta had already labeled her "a blonde bimbo from Augusta who couldn't add two plus two and wasn't fit to tie the shoelaces" of the patrician she defeated.

She arrived without fanfare in the city advertised by local government as a healthy habitat for humans, although it was actually considered "noncompliant" by EPA standards. Clean Air Act regulations were routinely waived despite the presence of a gazillion particles of carbon monoxide, nitrogen and sulfur dioxide, and lead per cubic centimeter of air. No matter that clothes left on balconies to dry were bleached yellow and green over the course of a single day. No matter that the birds were dying and the water had that funky smell of death.

Her apartment high above Peachtree Boulevard was more sepulcher than home, and her agency was more commune than citizen-friendly community: a self-contained universe where the Protestant work ethic was passé and capitalism was a foreign concept. It was an artificial world where worker bees hurried to and fro pretending to be busy, pretending to matter, and measuring their pretenses in complicated charts rigged to show that they were indispensable.

In a harbinger of muggings to come by the professional bureaucrats in Atlanta, the inner city "Welcome Wagon" came not to give but to take from Mary Ruth Robinson.

"Give me your purse, your money, and all your credit cards, and I won't hurt you!" the would-be teenaged bandit at the I-85 Exxon station demanded as the new state school superintendent fueled her car on her first day in Atlanta.

"Why would I want to do that?" she asked with a blank stare as patrons at other pumps pretended not to see the familiar scene unfolding.

"What? Are you crazy? Give me that purse now!" the incredulous robber screamed as he waved his .22-caliber Saturday night special at her.

"All right then," she shrugged as she reached for the red purse matching her dress.

She opened her purse and produced the heavy .38-caliber Smith & Wesson she always carried. She gripped it with both hands and pointed it at the ten ring of the target before her.

"Now you go on, get out of here. Shoo!" she ordered the man, whose eyes went wide. Mary Ruth was a veteran of many firing ranges and a family that was always armed to the teeth.

After the mugger fled the scene, as police reports would say, she calmly put the gasoline nozzle back on the pump handle. As a crowd of commuters applauded, she waved and drove off to face the bandits at the Department of Education, where more would-be muggers awaited.

* * *

The deeply-bitten fingernails were seen everywhere at first, but the initial panic in the ranks at the Georgia Department of Education over the loss of the last superintendent had subsided. A confidence had overtaken career bureaucrats, who were certain they could be cordially condescending to this interloper who needed them far more than they needed her.

The pros at the Department of Education were betting that a naïve girl from Millen, Georgia, suddenly thrust into the big casino of politics, didn't really know that the game is rigged and the deck stacked—that you have to make the smart plays, calculate your odds for a brief time on the political stage, take your winnings, and get out before you are crushed.

The house controls the rules, and sooner or later, the house will take all that you have. The percentages are with the system, and people who play by house rules, but the only rule in Atlanta was—there are no rules.

Some called her Pollyanna, certain that Atlanta politics would consume her. In their own play on this nickname, combined with her prim-and-proper method of governing, the Speaker and Billy Joe began to call her Polly Polity: the naïve girl who came to play in a man's world. Misogyny, never the exclusive domain of any one political party, was rampant in Atlanta.

"Madam Superintendent, your section chiefs are here to brief you on what you need to understand about the department and state government," the prune-faced guardian of the Georgia Department of Education announced with an unspoken subtext—"We are indispensable and you can't make it without us."

When the bureaucrats and number-crunchers marched into her office to brief her on the volumes of rules applying to federal grants and their interpretations, they mentioned an obscure term in the Title One binder, which they knew would make her limited little hazel eyes glaze over.

Mary Ruth said, "I think that must be a part of the Baader-Meinhof Phenomenon."

"What's that?" the crisp pastel men in their crisp pastel suits asked as they glanced at each other. They looked perplexed.

The reflected sun from the mirror in her office cast a honeyed hue to her face and accented her lilac dress and pearl necklace. She had the slightest trace of amusement. "I'm sure you know what I mean. I have seen that phrase invoked so many times in my research that I thought of that phenomenon where you see some obscure term and then see it over and over for days. You know, fellas, I think this department is just butt-deep in Baader-Meinhof!"

Like the robber at the gas station, they gave her a second appraisal and fled the scene.

* * *

The *Atlanta Journal-Constitution* was out to punish Robinson from day one and to right the "wrong" committed by voters who elected her.

The media ignored all the evidence of systemic corruption; instead, they concentrated on every Robinson idiosyncrasy, any supposed flaws and foibles, hang-ups and superstitions. They also developed an obsession with her style of dress and grooming.

She added fuel to their fire when she surveyed the department's payroll and found employees who had been rewarded for skullduggery, over the years, by a grateful political machine. Some had been on the payroll for twenty years and were eligible for retirement, though they had never shown up for work or "hit a lick at a snake," as people in the South liked to say.

Mary Ruth found one man who hadn't shown up for work in over twenty-five years, but the checks went out to him like clockwork. She called and invited him to report for duty. His response was, "Come to work? I signed on for a check, not a job!"

As the new gunslinger in town, all she could legally do was to force him and others like him into retirement, making way for actual employees. The political graft which the taxpayers had subsidized continued in the retirement checks for the political machine's loyalists. Even that tinkering with their private slush fund and payoff gravy infuriated the old guard.

In the midst of a personnel meeting, Mary Ruth found a current anomaly. "What's this?" she exclaimed as she reviewed one particular personnel file.

"We thought you knew," the personnel department manager said with a shrug of his shoulders. "It's just the way it is, the way it's always been."

Ricky Garcia, the rotund Republican legislator from Augusta, had an eighteen-year-old girlfriend named Doris on the department payroll—a dumping ground for friends and paramours of *both* political parties.

The new superintendent confronted her about dragging in late or not coming to work at all. "Doris, you've missed eight days this month, and your record of tardiness is abysmal," Mary Ruth told the young woman with the mini-skirts, beehive hair, and apparent stock in Revlon.

Doris smacked her gum and tilted her head to the side with a quizzical "What?" look. "I'm with Representative Garcia. He's important.

That's the way it is. You can't tell me what to do, and you can't fire me. I do what he says, not you," she replied without missing a beat.

"Doris, I don't think you understand. This isn't a game. This isn't a hotel, some convenience for Ricky Garcia's amorous proclivities with guest towels and mints on the pillow. You have a choice—work or leave." The muscles in the young woman's jaws tightened and her eyes, bloodshot from too many late nights, went wide as saucers.

Garcia was furious when he heard the news. "Who does Mary Ruth think she is? I'll show her who she's messing with."

So Doris stayed out again partying with Garcia and didn't show for work. Her name was removed from admittance to the building, and when she did show up, she was terminated.

That sent her flying and crying to Garcia, who threatened Robinson. He was backed by Bill Cook, who partied in the same circles and depended on the free flow of Garcia's beverage dispensers. Cook threatened to abandon Mary Ruth, who needed outstate media support to counter the Atlanta paper, but she was unmoved. The new kid on the block was making enemies.

Before Governor James Robert "Jim Bob" Tucker left office, he rammed a bill through the legislature that gave Mary Ruth four deputies to help her run the department. He dismissed the incumbent Board of Education and hand-picked a group that actually cared about education. It ended the squabbling, but everyone knew that the next governor would not be so generous, especially if it was Henry "Hank" Holcomb.

In the midst of it all, Mary Ruth Robinson searched for allies. Michael's phone rang in his Augusta office one afternoon as he stared out his window at a buttermilk sky.

"Michael, this is Mary Ruth," she said. "Are you keeping your editor and those wild children in the Augusta delegation in line?"

"That's like trying to herd cats, Mary Ruth," he answered with a chuckle.

"I have an offer for you," she said. "I need someone who knows business and education. You have a good reputation, and everyone knows that you are a reform advocate. I want you to be on my business advisory committee."

When Michael first met Mary Ruth, he became an ally of the reformer. She offered a distraction from the doldrums of sameness he found himself in and represented a greater battle to join. Her quest to confront the status quo had all the elements he craved—David against Goliath and echoes of his battles of yesteryear.

He remembered her from the speech in Atlanta when he was visiting there from Jackson. Susan asked him what he thought of her.

"I think I missed a great deal in my initial assessment," he said. "She's a study in contrasts, a chameleon ever-evolving, even as you watch…shifting, changing, and morphing from this to that. The only question I have: Is it accidental, a result of her insecurities, or a cold calculation? I don't know."

"Why do you think that?" Susan asked.

"Well, she sometimes seems like a bouffant little girl, a dilettante who wears that fixed smile dogs wear when they have been kicked too much. The nails seem too pink and shiny. The false eyelashes and the poses and pouty innocence seem too rehearsed. You know, I wonder if it all wasn't honed in front of the mirror one time too many, a careful and calculated con or defense.

"I don't know," he sighed. "I know that's not scientific, but she seems to wear so many masks. At times, she looks at people she meets with tender, wet eyes, as if she's never met anyone more charming. At other times, she appears capable of cutting an opponent off at the knees with invectives that could peel paint off the walls."

He looked at Susan. "You may be the exception, but I don't think that women like her, because they feel threatened by her. I suspect that under that exterior may be hardness from abuse. I want to believe that her crusade is real, yet there's something that seems haunted and hollow."

"What're you going to do about her offer?" Susan asked.

"Oh, I think I'll take it and watch and see. You know I love underdogs everyone picks on, and she certainly qualifies. Besides, I heard the story about the mugging," he laughed.

It was a match made, if not in heaven, in the land of aging knights who longed for battle. But with whom? Michael was tired of it all: tired of them—whoever "them" were—getting away with it—whatever "it" was.

This might be a respite from the dolor of sameness, the dull-as-dishwater chatter of banal people, and the pseudo-important fields of nonsense he felt consigned to.

The lonely reformer often called him in Augusta to talk for hours at night, seeking advice and friendship. Some suggested to Susan that Mary Ruth was always drawn to strong men, and this was an unwise friendship. Susan would have none of it.

When Michael was not available, Mary Ruth would talk to Susan just as she talked to him. She once confided, "If I owned both Atlanta and Hell, I think I'd choose to live in Hell and rent out Atlanta."

She expressed in those late-night talks that she felt like Alice in Wonderland as she surveyed the unforgiving world that she had opted for. "Susan, I'm like Alice up here—lost and in search of directions on which way to go, only to be told that if I don't know where I'm going, then it doesn't matter how I get there! In my dreams, when I'm alone in my apartment, I seem caught in a never-ending loop where I'm Alice talking to the cat in Wonderland."

"But I don't want to go among mad people," Alice remarked.

"Oh, you can't help that," said the Cat. "We're all mad here. I'm mad. You're mad."

"How do you know I'm mad?" said Alice.

"You must be," said the Cat, "or you wouldn't have come here."

CHAPTER SEVENTEEN

"Corruption's like a ball of snow; once it's set a-rolling, it must increase."—Charles C. Colton

"Life can only be understood backwards; but it must be lived forwards."—Soren Kierkegaard

Some politicians see the graft at the top and come to believe in a sort of "trickle-down ticket" that allows them to belly up to the buffet with the rest of the piglets for their portion of goodies. Even as the world begins to sink under the weight of "I scratch your back, you scratch mine," they decry the loss of innocence in their speeches while choosing tyranny over the chaos of reform. They embrace the hedonism of the ruling class rather than see their merry-go-round of pleasures come to an end. They jam the front pews of churches on Sunday but reduce Jesus to whatever modern image suits their philosophical bent, to be invoked only when it suits their interests.

Such was the case with Ricky Garcia, an incumbent state representative who lived large at the taxpayers' expense. He was overweight, out of shape, and had a gut that would have suggested imminent childbirth on a woman. A hunger for women, whiskey, $100 haircuts, and Dior suits marked a style all his own. His wife was noted for the shiny black eyes she received from "accidents"...his paramours for their shiny new toys, rewards for their "companionship."

The fast-talking politician with his nervous energy and machine-gun-like delivery was often compared to Joe Pesci in *Goodfellas*. Asked by an angry constituent if he wasn't just a prostitute, Garcia replied, "No, there are some things even a prostitute won't do for money. There's nothing I won't do."

He lobbied for statehood for Puerto Rico, which did not endear him to many of his supporters, but he was quick to snap at them with invectives punctuated by profanity.

"Don't bring that up, Bocephus. They aren't going to get it anyway, and that bought a new piano for my daughter." Though of different political parties, he and his associate, Representative Joey Tomlin, were informants for Big Jim, the Speaker of the House in Georgia. Garcia bad-mouthed everyone who challenged him and used the powerful Speaker as his shield.

Like his corpulent friend, Tomlin's indulgences of the bottle became progressively worse over time. Garcia entertained his friends with stories of running through DUI taskforce roadblocks with Joey Tomlin. Both were so drunk they could barely stand, but legislative immunity put them beyond the reach of the law while in session.

"I had it all straightened out with the officers," Garcia said. "I told them that I was a legislator in session. Then little ole skull drunk Joey lurched from the car, clothes askew, staggering and muttering at the police until he slumped against the car and slid to the ground, stoned out of his mind. 'Who's that?' the cops asked. 'Oh, that's just my idiot cousin, and I'm taking him back to the home,'" Garcia said.

The narrative was invariably followed with his famous imitation of a stumbling, falling-down drunk, Representative Joey Tomlin. The hanger-on sycophants would cackle with abandon as if they'd never heard it before. Encouraged, he would embellish it and repeat it again and again at beer fests and meetings with other politicians.

Ha, ha. Not funny, Michael thought. *Not funny at all.* Michael only saw visions of innocent people maimed or killed by the indulgences of these men who felt above the law.

Tomlin had a boyish countenance complete with a Buster Brown haircut and cherub-like face, and he enjoyed a squeaky-clean reputation. His constituents were blissfully unaware of both his penchant for hard drinking and his unfortunate habit of running into power and telephone poles when he was driving drunk. BellSouth construction managers joked that if they could just direct his assaults to targets of their choice, they could expedite the replacement of old pole lines that the budget would not currently support. Then Michael and his Audubon friends could have the damaged ones they coveted for nesting habitats for birds.

It was a miracle that he had not killed someone while driving in an inebriated condition. As it was, the Augusta editor protected him and his running buddy, Garcia—he had labeled them "The Two Amigos." Tomlin's constituents loved him; they were oblivious.

Michael was in Garcia's office and heard him take a call from a man to whom Garcia owed money—one of many creditors he routinely stiffed.

"Ricky, this is James. How're you doing?" the caller and local Republican Party chair said. "Look, I was wondering when you're going to send me the money you owe me on your office rent?"

"You piece of garbage. What do you mean bothering me? Don't you know who I am?" Garcia snapped.

"But Ricky, I got bills, too," the man protested.

"I don't want to hear it. Don't you ever call me here again! Do you hear me, fat boy?" Garcia said with a sneer.

"Ricky…aw, that's not necessary," the man said in an injured tone.

"Shut your trap! You *should* be grateful that I make deals that help everyone in this town, but you're not, are you, Porky? No, you just want to whine, whine, whine, you swine. I'll put you out of business if you ever call me again! Do you hear me, lard butt? Oink, oink!" Garcia screamed.

When he hung up the phone, he was red-faced and out of breath. He slicked back his hair, mopped his brow as he recovered from the exertion of his tirade, then he said with a smirk, "I had him begging, groveling before I hung up. That's how you handle 'em, boy. Grind 'em under your heel. No mercy," he told Michael and others present.

Michael wasn't laughing. He abruptly left Garcia's office and walked to his company car, where he leaned over and took deep breaths to try to keep from retching.

* * *

The next week, Michael was invited to a dinner in Atlanta, because insiders feared that the Boy Scout was about to wander off the reserve. Bill Cook and Representative Joey Tomlin were at the table, along with a political operative named Patty Patterson from Atlanta and James Colton, a state senator from Columbia County.

Garcia waltzed in with a nubile young girl of questionable legal age; she looked like Raggedy Ann with her red hair and freckles. She was the daughter of Garcia's friend, who had asked him to tutor her in the ways of Atlanta. The body language between the legislator and the girl left little to the imagination, and was punctuated by the hard liquor that Garcia was buying her, shot after shot. Michael didn't think that her father would be too happy if he knew how Garcia was "tutoring" his little girl.

Garcia turned to Michael with an accusatory tone and asked, "What's wrong with you lately? Something's going on with you. You've changed. I think you've must be sleeping with Marcie, that lady at the chamber." This was the first time he had dared to go after Michael.

Michael put his finger in Garcia's face and said, "Shut your mouth, Ricky. I don't do that. *You* may do that, but I better not hear that you are spreading it around that *I* do. You hear me?"

"Yeah, boy. Yeah," a wide-eyed and startled Garcia said.

As he said this, Tomlin, who once professed that he wanted to grow up and be just like Michael, glared at him over a glass of whiskey, stoned out of his mind and seething with anger. Michael thought at that moment that he had seen that look before...at Horn Lake with the two assassins. But that was only business with those guys. This was very personal.

When Patty rose to leave, the group asked if she needed an escort. She looked at them and said, "Michael is the only one here I would trust to accompany me." Her remark punctuated the divide of mistrust now evident between Michael and the rest of the group.

Michael walked her out and then left for a company conference at Chateau Elan. The luxury inn and winery, situated north of Atlanta in Braselton, was a favored location for conferences, golf, and the finer things of life that many corporate managers coveted.

That night the phone in his room rang as he read *The Winds of War* and consumed hot Krispy Kreme doughnuts, his favorite indulgence.

"Hi, Michael, it's Dawn Rogers," the voice said. Dawn was a long-bodied woman with a mop of black curls. She had brooding eyes almost as black as her hair. Michael knew her father and had helped her find a job in Augusta. She was a troubled young woman who wasn't the brightest bulb in the lamp and lacked self-confidence—the kind of "disposable" person to be used and abused by the folks he had just dined with. They tossed her the scraps from their tables and used her in the most demeaning ways as a "party hostess," reminding her of how much she owed them and how quickly it could all end if she didn't play along.

"Hi," Dawn said with a low, whispery voice. "I heard you were at Chateau Elan, and I thought I might drive up tonight to have dinner with you if you aren't busy," she said.

After what happened at the dinner, all of Michael's alarms were going off. They were trying to reel him back in with a setup.

"Dawn, I don't think that would be a good idea. People might get the wrong idea," Michael said.

"I didn't say I was coming up there for anything like that!" she said indignantly. He could hear her snuffling and knew he had hurt her feelings.

"I know, Dawn. I'm only trying to protect you. There are a lot of wagging tongues here, and if they saw me with a pretty young woman— young enough to be my daughter, the talk would start," he said.

"Oh, okay," she said in a little-girl voice. "I was just lonely and wanted to talk. Promise."

"I know. By the way, how'd you know I was here?" he asked.

"Oh, one of the guys called me tonight and told me you were at this fancy place and feeling kind of down like me. They thought you could use some company. That's all," she said.

With that, the woman-girl with the baby-faced blandness was gone. To the abusers, she was just a throw-away girl in a throw-away world, and the moon hid its face behind the clouds over the battlements and prominences of the French resort, as if to say, "I resign."

* * *

When Michael returned to Augusta, he got a visit from a petite, curly-haired blonde named Shirley Bannuck, a homemaker and ambitious political up-and-comer who supported Mary Ruth. She had bright, energetic, blue eyes and a wide mouth that almost diminished the rest of her face when she smiled.

"Michael, are you busy? I need to talk to you," Shirley said.

"Sure! Have a seat, Shirley," he said.

"Michael, I think I'm going to pass on the local Board of Education seat that's coming open. I'm going to run for Ricky Garcia's seat. What do you think?" she asked.

"Are you prepared for the attacks that'll come against you? You know that Ricky doesn't play nice. It will be savage, brutal. And Cook will come after you as well. The paper will no longer be your friend as they have pretended to be," Michael warned her.

"I know. Charlie…Congressman Deaton is going to back me quietly," she said. "He told me to come see you and ask if you will help."

Michael knew he was crawling out on a thin limb—that there would be consequences at BellSouth, where some executives and most lobbyists cared only about power and money.

Nevertheless, he said, "I'll put the word out that I'm on board, and you can tell Charlie that I'll raise money for you."

Why did I do that? he wondered. *Garcia keeps his seat by fear and intimidation. Anyone who dares to run against him receives threatening calls from him or his emissaries. The challenger is told, "You're going to lose your job. Your boss has contracts with the state and those will stop, and we'll get your boss to fire you. Police have given us old records of your drunk driving and domestic disturbances from twenty years ago. By the time Bill Cook gets through with you, it'll seem as fresh as yesterday. You'll lose, and your life will be ruined." He rarely even has anyone run against him. Oh yeah…that's why I'm doing it,* Michael thought.

The part about the editor stuck in Michael's craw as well. His company's alliance with the paper, intended to encourage positive stories on BellSouth, had soured when Michael began to see the local political mafia for who they really were. Garcia carried the water for the media conglomerate and delivered subsidies for local business projects owned by the paper. He was little more than their bag boy.

What sealed the deal, though, was the night that Michael and Susan attended a party where Bill Cook was greeting guests at the door. Susan's ankles were always collapsing. She stumbled going in the door when her ankle gave way. Cook grabbed her, ostensibly to support her, but tried to kiss her on the mouth. She turned her head, and he caught her on the corner of her lips. He had the glazed look of a very twisted man in his alcohol-pickled eyes. Susan told Michael later that night. That was the end for him, no matter the cost.

A clandestine meeting was arranged at a private club on Lake Thurmond with Congressman Deaton, who was distressed over Garcia's actions. Ring-billed gulls swept by the deck as the congressman arrived, and a brisk wind was whipping up some whitecaps on the blue water.

Deaton's voice had a hard edge to it as he began to talk to Michael. He plucked at his signature red suspenders that matched his Liberty Bell tie. His staffers were zipped up like clams.

"Michael, we've got to do something about Ricky. He's hurting and embarrassing all of us...me included. He's always poking around in things we're trying to do and perverting it for his own political grandstanding and greed. The U.S. House leadership just visited us here, and Garcia was drunk and clumsy. He tried to ingratiate himself with them, but they just asked, 'Who's the sleaze?'"

"I understand, Charlie. I can raise money for Shirley and put out the word that I'm backing her. I'll unofficially manage the campaign if that'll help," Michael offered.

"That's great, Michael. By the way, how'd your mama like the speech I gave on the House floor? The one about your fight to protect the nonprofit you chair from the attack of those skunks at OSHA?" he asked with an almost jolly expression on his face.

"She saw it on C-SPAN and was impressed that her son merited such attention—though she's not exactly sure why!" Michael said. Everyone laughed.

"What help can you give us in this campaign?" Michael asked.

Deaton's game face reappeared. "My staff will poll constantly to tell you where you are, where you need work, and when to run your commercials. We have a firm that will make the commercials at a favorable rate and serve at your beck and call. Certain mailing lists will be made available, and some donors will be waiting for your solicitation," the congressman said.

"That's great, Charlie! I think this can be done," Michael said.

"I know you can do it. You *do* understand that—for political reasons—I can't go openly against him *or* let the newspaper know that I'm backing their boy's challenger, right? But we want to encourage the voters to retire Ricky," Deaton said as he leaned forward to shake Michael's hand. It sounded a bit like the old *Mission Impossible* show where Mr. Phelps was told that if he and his team were caught, the director would deny all knowledge.

And so it began—the white knight to the rescue, Paladin rides again.

* * *

Michael began to make calls. Randy Patra, the top retinal eye surgeon in the South, had saved Susan's eyesight from diabetic retinopathy. A soft-spoken intellectual with a heart of gold, he quietly donated a suite of offices in his medical building for the campaign for its headquarters.

Dr. Greg Richey and all of the local ophthalmologists referred their patients to Patra as the best chance to save the eyesight of those with retina issues. The problem was—they backed Garcia. Richey, known for his all-night alcohol-soaked parties, was the leader of this group of doctors. He called Patra when they learned of his donation.

"Randy, you need to withdraw this offer of a headquarters for Ricky's challenger, or there'll be consequences," Richey demanded in a spitting, spurting, and rambling indictment of Patra's decision.

"What do you mean by 'consequences'? I don't understand," Patra asked.

"We'll stop sending you referrals if you help Michael Parker's candidate," Richey told Patra, who was known for his kindness and love of his patients.

The stunned surgeon, who had entered medicine because of his own father's illness, exclaimed, "You'd use your patients as bargaining chips in a political race and subject them to blindness for this…for this?! What about our Hippocratic oath?"

Richey responded, "We're the bulldozer operators who see obstacles. We crush and bury them—no mercy, no scruples, no looking back. You're in our way."

Michael was surprised by little, but condemning patients to a possible life of blindness simply to gain political power was a new low—even for Garcia and his allies. It was unconscionable. Patra stood firm, and Michael doubled down.

Then there was ringing of the midnight phone call, which is never good news.

As Michael cleared the cobwebs from his mind, Ricky Garcia's unchained cadence, which seemed absent any commas and periods, commenced, "Michael, this is Ricky. I hear Shirley is going to qualify to run against me. I hear you're in her camp. If she runs, Michael, I'm going to destroy her. You hear me, boy? I'm going to destroy her!"

Silence…There was only Ricky's heavy breathing, like a runner out of air.

"Are you there, Michael? You hear what I'm saying? I'm going to break up her marriage! I'm going to destroy her family! I'm going to run her out of the state! She won't be able to live here when I'm through with her! Do you hear me? I'm not a man to be messed with. I'm going to destroy her, destroy her, DESTROY her!!" Garcia screamed like a madman. It was chilling and surreal.

He was breathing hard…gasping for oxygen in a rage of major proportions.

"The doctors are with me, Michael. You know that. I got their money, their power, and don't you think that you can go out and get some laser-boy surgeon to back you and think that's going to mean spit. You hear me? We're gonna bury her!"

Silence…

"Are you there, Michael?" Like the boxer from long ago facing the opponent who punched and flailed until he had no more, Michael waited him out.

"Yeah, I'm here, Ricky. Don't you ever call me at my home and threaten me again. Don't ever have your friends threaten my friends. You want to play? Then, let's play," Michael calmly replied as he hung up.

Garcia's call was followed the next day by one from another angry man—Bill Cook.

"What do you think you're doing? We've been very good to you with editorials for your company. We've supported your positions and made you look good. You're the toast of the town, and *we* had a lot to do with that. You've got to stay out of this race," the editor chided him.

"Thanks for your concern. I'll keep my head down while I'm doing what I have to do," Michael responded.

"What?! You'd better do more than keep your head down! You'll regret it if you go against us!" the editor fumed.

"Is that a threat?" Michael asked.

"No, that's a promise…a friendly warning for someone we—ah, care so much about… someone we wouldn't want to see make a decision he'll regret. We're going to demolish this little pixie you're backing," he said, with all the sincerity of a pit viper.

"Well, Bill," Michael said, "I suggest that you pluck and debone that bird."

"What do you mean?" the editor asked.

"I think that crow you're going to eat when you lose will go down easier that way," Michael said as he hung up.

Cook called Shirley that night on the way to qualify. He cursed her and told her all he would do to her if she didn't turn her car around, go home, and forget this foolishness. He cursed her in a way that would make sailors blush when she refused to comply.

So Michael was in—all the way in. When word spread that he was secretly managing the campaign, checkbooks opened for Shirley. Shirley qualified, and the newspaper attacks began, as well as commercials comparing her to a shrill, barking poodle. Some quiet calls came from well-wishers asking Michael if he knew what he was doing. "You've got standing with the 'in' crowd, and you're well liked. Why risk it *all*?" they asked.

As Michael had predicted, the attacks soon began. Fliers on pink paper began to anonymously appear in the district, claiming Shirley was supportive of a radical gay agenda. It wasn't true, but that was the stock in trade of smash-mouth Augusta politics and cutthroats who had no record to run on.

As the battle intensified, calls were made to Michael's employers. Then came an offer that led Michael to bend the rules once again. He had taken a tiny step toward the edge by accepting free polling services and such from Congressman Deaton, but when a wealthy insurance owner approached him, he went on down the road.

Jim Chestnut sat on the patio of his home outside Augusta. He was sipping a tall glass of tea when Michael arrived. His craggy face bore a stern look, one that seemed to match the short, white brush-cut of hair and the mood of the moment.

"Thanks for coming, Michael," he said as he rose and extended his hand.

"You know, when I was coming up in life, I did a lot of really bad jobs and took a lot of abuse. When I was emptying bed pans at the State Hospital, I swore that one day I wouldn't ever be forced to take that kind of treatment again. Do you understand?" he asked quietly.

"I do," Michael said.

"Then I made it big by hard work and playing by the rules. I have money and enjoy making more, and the good life is…well, good. I approached the establishment—the professional politicians—about getting my insurance services on the state government master list, so employees can choose it if they wish. All I wanted was a chance to compete fairly in this closed state. So they told me…put a little money here, a little money there…grease the skids, you know. 'Good faith' money would encourage the assistance of those who could help me in getting a fair chance to compete with companies that have been paying off state officials for years," he said with a sigh.

"Ricky Garcia said that he'd take care of it all. He arranged for me to meet with the committee that could approve me. Everyone's happy, the fix is in. I didn't feel good about having to go that route, but otherwise, I didn't have a chance, and the incumbent providers would just go on and on forever. No competition…We might as well live in the Soviet Union."

He sighed again and was quiet for what seemed like a long time.

"So Ricky said I should give him some more money, and he'd take me to the committee, take me right in the room to the people who'd sign off on it all. So, I did. I met him and he said, 'Right this way, Jim.'

"He took me down a long hall in the Capitol and just before we went in where they all were, he said, 'It's all set, but I've got another appointment, and I'm gonna have to leave you now. Don't worry! Everything's fine. Just go on in.'"

Chestnut took a long drink of tea, shook his head, and bit his lips. Michael saw that his right hand had clenched into a fist.

"Michael, I went in the room, and there they sat all around the table…these stuffed shirts who looked at me as if I was nobody. I said, 'Excuse me, but Ricky told me to come in and talk about my products getting on the approved lists for state employees.'

"They looked at me and looked at each other. Kinda amused, you know? Then, the guy at the head of the table said…and I'll never forget it, 'Mister, you see that table there? You got as much chance of getting on the state list as it does to sprout wings and fly out that window.'"

He paused again, and Michael could tell that he was back there, reliving it all.

"Michael, as I was leaving, they laughed at me…*laughed at me!* Just like I was back emptying bed pans again," he said with a sudden catch in his voice. He had been shamed.

He straightened up in his chair and said, "I have some money I want to go into Shirley's campaign under many names. I can't afford for them to see that it's from me, and it's more than I could legally contribute anyway. Can that be done?"

Michael nodded yes, and told him what he had told Sonny, an old club owner, one night near Memphis so long ago. As they made arrangements to take down a larger and more corrupt operator who was squeezing Sonny out of the business, Michael had said, "Let me be the instrument of your revenge."

"Is that wrong for us to do, Michael?" he asked.

Michael said, "It is only an artificial right and wrong, created by men in Washington and Atlanta to protect incumbents who get donations by extortion. These rules were enacted under the guise of fair play when, in fact, it is about eliminating fair play. The corruption goes on and on unless there is a chance of electing reformers. Do you really think the

Founding Fathers wanted people jailed or fined for giving money to a candidate? These laws are made by incumbents to protect incumbents."

Chestnut didn't seem convinced, so Michael continued.

"Say that you're against abortion, and an incumbent is taking money from the abortion industry, making it possible to abort babies— even partial birth abortions. He threatens anyone who goes on a public contributor list against him, telling them he will have them fired, and their boss will lose all government contracts if they support his upstart challenger.

"You contribute the legal limit to your candidate anyway and put your name down because you want to follow the law, but the incumbent wins because he has every political action committee pooling money in bundles like you can't imagine, and every corporation that he takes care of forces their employees to give the max or lose their jobs.

"The incumbent comes after you and your employer. You lose your job. Your kids go hungry. Your employer loses his government contracts. He has to lay off a thousand people who can't feed their kids. Local economies go south. Working-class people go on welfare for the first time in their lives. Homes are seized because mortgage payments can't be met.

"Your kids can no longer attend the good schools because you have to move. They don't see their parents because you have to take two or three jobs to make up for the good jobs you lost. With absentee parents, your kids become involved in drugs and theft and go to jail. Tithing to your church bottoms out because people are out of work. Mission work for the needy can no longer be continued. People have to move their elderly parents in with them because they can't afford to subsidize their care. It's suddenly a struggle to make it. The nice university you envisioned for your kids becomes the local community college. Divorces result from the stress, maybe suicides, too. And the babies you were worried about? They continue to be aborted.

"Why? Because you filled out a form and followed the rules written by the same guy who set all this in motion? You think they pass these rules because they care about liberty and the good ole United States? You think they don't look at the disclosure lists to make out their personal enemies list?" Michael heard the first strains of bitterness in his own voice, and it was not a pretty tune.

Chestnut agreed to proceed, but he left with his head down, as if his parents had just told him that Santa Claus was not real. Michael felt bad that he had shattered the man's image of a neat and tidy world.

Michael had crossed a line. He no longer cared about the law, only what Susie Jones, the reporter at the *Oxford Eagle*, had written about him when he was at the Bureau: "He is reminiscent of the code of the Old West where right was right, and wrong was wrong, and no shade of gray in between." The difference was that Michael was now defining right and wrong outside the paradigm of yesterday, and he was not nearly so certain and comfortable as he pretended—just angry. Very, very angry.

* * *

In the end, Shirley whipped Garcia going away. It was a rout. The Hallelujah Community of Faith had supported the incumbent because he told them, as he had Chestnut, that he was their friend and a man of God. The day before the election, they took down their yard signs supporting him and voted *en masse* for Shirley. After Michael called them and recited Garcia's midnight pledge to break up her family and run her out of Georgia, they decided that perhaps he *wasn't* a man of God.

People showed up with money and votes. There were those who were scared of Ricky and abused by him, like the rent collector he had belittled on the phone. Even the gay community showed up for a Republican primary bearing money—and casseroles for office workers; Ricky was using them in the pink leaflets. It was a strange alliance of citizens who didn't let rules rule them.

Bill Cook was in mourning. He had failed to deliver for his bosses, and reports of his threats against the new legislator had become public knowledge. He lost his job and accused Michael of "smearing him." The ophthalmologists were already calling Dr. Randy Patra to ask him to put in a word for them with the new representative. Ricky's drinking partner, Rep. Joey Tomlin, was stunned, angry. He vowed to get Michael.

The phones were ablaze with, "Have you heard?" The pundits were calling it the biggest political upset in Georgia in fifty years.

At the end of the day, Michael and Susan sat quietly on their deck watching as the world was slowly suffused with an eerie, orange tint. The clouds turned an end-of-the-rainbow gold as the sun moved behind them. Reflections of the golden rays tinted the rooftops around them, and the earth's color changed to a cleansing, liquid yellow. The rustling pampas grass seemed to whisper "hush, hush" as a sudden quietness enveloped their hillside.

Michael told her, "I'm not sure it's over. Maybe just beginning, honey. The attacks are already coming. It's not Governor Davidson and his allies this time, but it's the same old game. As the parrot said about Congress: 'Different places…same people.'"

Susan reached over and took Michael's hand as a brown thrasher ran in the flower beds beneath them. Like Thoreau's thrasher in *Walden*, the bird sang what sounded like "Get ready, get ready! Armor up, armor up! Put it on, put it on!"

CHAPTER EIGHTEEN

"Broken windows and empty hallways...Scarecrows
dressed in the latest styles, with frozen faces to keep
love away...I think it's going to rain today."
—Randy Newman

"If ye love wealth better than liberty...Crouch down
and lick the hands that feed you. May your chains
sit lightly upon you and may posterity forget ye
were our countrymen."—Samuel Adams

Michael arrived at the headquarters for BellSouth in Atlanta under a pewter sky. It was a nondescript day, no sun, and a stillness that seemed ominous. As he stepped from his car to meet with BellSouth executives, he saw a sign that said, "Atlanta—No boundaries, just possibilities."

A bright-blue and orange bluebird flew up to him from the shelter of trees and ornamentals that framed the corporate headquarters near Ashford-Dunwoody. There seemed to be sadness in the bird's eyes that mirrored his own. Its song, so painfully sweet and plaintive, seemed just for him, and pinched his aching heart. He walked toward the building like a condemned man on his way to execution and hummed, "Somewhere over the rainbow, bluebirds fly...why oh why can't I?"

Michael remembered what John Edward Collins, his father figure and MBN founder and director, told him in a moment of candor when Governor Davidson was about to force him to choose—give in or get out. With sad, weary eyes, he asked Michael, "Are we but enforcers for a corrupt system, enablers of it all?"

Michael thought, *The more things change, the more they remain the same* and wished for a moment where he was someone else, anyone else. He wished that he was in some other place, any place but here where minds were so open to everything to justify their compromise with the world, yet so full of nothing.

The elevator doors, emblazoned with the logo of Bell, opened onto a floor of opulence. Massive and ornate wood doors awaited him like the mickle gates to a forbidden city. Everyone in the outer room looked at Michael with hooded eyes, recognition of what was to come in the office of the new state president, a ruthless man appointed to replace the former president, who was too accommodating of what corporate gatekeepers called "rogues in the ranks."

Any last requests, their eyes seemed to beg of the condemned. Michael thought of the day he came here for a meeting when the company announced that he and other managers would have to be temporarily designated as lobbyists for legal reasons. They asked the quiet assembly of yes-men if there were any questions or concerns. Only Michael raised his hand and said, "I just hope my mama doesn't find out." It was greeted with nervous glances from his peers and a grinding of teeth by his vice-president, a lifelong lobbyist.

The door opened, and Shawn Warren, the prematurely gray corporate staffer and lobbyist who partied with and schmoozed the legislature, invited Michael into the inner sanctum. Somber-toned and primped in the raiment of dead men who walk but do not live, he was there as the witness for the kangaroo court in case Michael sued later.

Seated in a large black leather chair at the other end of a long and expensive maple wood conference table was Bill Benjamin, the state president, a man with unruly, bushy-black eyebrows which always had the need of a comb.

"Thank you for coming, Michael," he said gravely and dryly, as if Michael had a choice. Then he unloaded with both barrels.

"Michael, did you think that you were going to be immune forever? Did you think your record was going to insulate you on this little island you live on, and you'd never be held accountable? We need these people you have irritated with your little meaningless crusades. You have upset a lot of hard work by many people—me and Shawn included. Representative Joey Tomlin is upset, and he upset the Speaker. Big Jim called in our lobbyists and put our bills on hold. Because of you, Michael—you!

"For what, Michael? For what? Do you think you're better than the rest of us, that you are some kind of Don Quixote free to run around jabbing at these little windmills in your mind?"

Michael took a deep breath as Shawn looked away momentarily from the brutality and ugliness of the moment. "Sometimes you encounter something so wrong that your silence is agreement, that looking the other way is just unbearable. That's the way it was this time. It wouldn't let me go," Michael answered.

"Wrong? Wrong? Says who? Who are you, mister? Grow up! These wrongs you whine about, they made it possible to pay you those nice bonuses you enjoyed for all these years you've been in Georgia! Now you suddenly want to complain when these legislators who once liked you do something you judge to be wrong? Who died and made you God?"

In his animation and anger, little globules of spit came across his desk like missiles with one projectile sticking to a picture of Benjamin and the governor. Michael thought that the ball of saliva now affixed to the top of the head of Governor Holcomb looked like a crown of sorts, homage to political royalty.

"Who're you kidding, Michael? Your voice is too faint to ever be heard, to ever change a thing. The world doesn't know who you are, what you're saying, and won't miss you when you're gone. You're nobody, just some do-gooder desecrating and spoiling important deals we have with powerful political people. You're going to have to agree—no more politics, no more crusades. You're going to have to learn your place in life and keep your mouth shut."

Beyond the jabbering spokesman for the corporate and political cognate was a large window covered in the faintest of sheers that blew and billowed like ghosts when the air-conditioning kicked on. Outside the window and this room of avarice and close-fistedness, Michael could see a storm that was moving closer. The sky grew increasingly black and gray, mirroring the moments in this room with air so charged with the emptiness of its orator.

The lightning flashes captured Benjamin in strobe-like moments of arrested movements like scenes from an old silent film. His eyes were angry and accusing, gums showing above the white of teeth in a twisted sneer of anger and contempt. Michael would only remember this day and his accuser frozen in herky-jerky movements—an arm raised, a finger pointing, a yapping dog whose mouth only opened and closed. Elliptical words, like the speaker who spoke them, were vacant and barren. He was but a caricature of many Michael had known since the MBN, an illusion and projection of people in the incestuous coupling that was politics and corporatism, and already—fading from view.

Then, when the sheers blew open, exposing all of the innocence beyond this cavern of coldness, he saw the male bluebird, clinging to a branch outside the window. He was holding on with all of his might to a thin, precarious branch. Tiny claws had a vise-like grip on what seemed but a twig, incapable of withstanding this storm that raged and roared against him. The bluebird seemed to look directly at Michael with a message…"Hold on!"

Michael closed his eyes for a moment and said, *Little bird, fly up to the top of the tree of my mind, and sing your song of faith in me.*

Michael rose at that moment, and said, "I'll be filing for early retirement and the current downsizing buyout that is being offered to those managers who you once told me were subpar—the guys who 'couldn't cut it,' you said. You told me that I was in that cadre of managers who would never be listed among those who didn't seek, strive, and stretch for excellence and dream of something better. Yet, here I am.

"I'd like to say that it's been fun, but my grandmother always told me that if you can't say something good and true, then say nothing at all. Consider this my official thirty-day notice and add to that my annual and sick leave to which I'm entitled. My paperwork will be in the mail tomorrow."

Clay was right when he warned him about carnal and instinctual men who think truth is expendable—that if you believe there is truth, you're dangerous, and that they'll turn on you and peck you to death when you threaten the established order.

Michael suddenly heard Pearl's timeless words from an afternoon of goodbye talks as her health grew frail. "Remember, son, there are folks who would rather sell their souls to rule in Hell on earth, than to serve eternally in Heaven."

He turned at the door and looked back at the two inmates of this prison of their own making, and said, "This is Jonestown, but you can't see it. Everyone's had a long drink of the Kool-Aid. Just turn out the lights, this party's over."

So Michael walked out, and an era ended. No bands were playing, no toasts were raised to the man who would be missed, no gold watch, and no likeness of him would be struck for a plaque in the corporate hall of fame to inspire new, young managers.

Only Susan, the girl he had come to miss even when he was with her, the girl with tear-filled eyes and trembling lips, was waiting outside in the car to greet him. Rays of sunlight were breaking through the passing storm in a world that seemed to have been holding its breath and now breathed a long, deep sigh of relief.

CHAPTER NINETEEN

"I found myself in a dark wood. I had wandered from the
straight path…I can't offer any good explanation for
how…I strayed from the right path."—Dante's Inferno

"I don't know why I came here…Clowns to the left
of me, jokers to the right, here I am, stuck in the
middle with you."—Stealers Wheel

A golden sun lingered over Atlanta, its aureate reflection mirrored in the windows of the Twin Towers, home to the Georgia Department of Education. Across from the gold dome of the Capitol, the familiar towers were surrounded by the endless labyrinths of parking decks housing the day dwellers of agencies and businesses that fed off the workings of government.

The garages and bridges were home to the blue-gray pigeons that left presents on unlucky vehicles. The dove-like birds tried to hide in the concrete recesses of the garages, seeking refuge from the peregrine falcons nesting atop the high-rise buildings of Atlanta. The falcons loved to dine on the pigeons in another of the symbiotic—and symbolic—relationships in Georgia's economic hub.

Just down the street from the education headquarters was a historic old cemetery that visitors to the legislature passed on the way to see government in action…or inaction. The story circulated for years that a veteran of many battles with Atlanta officials, while walking with a friend on the grounds of the graveyard, paused to read the words on an old headstone. It read, "Here lies a statesman and a politician." The man turned to his friend and said, "I didn't know they buried two people in the same grave!"

Michael was in Atlanta to talk with Mary Ruth Robinson about her offer to become one of her four deputy superintendents. Congressman Deaton tried to rescue him with an appointment as U.S. Marshal for the Southern District, but all his attempts had failed. Michael's friend and mentor, Senator Dale, would have been the sole arbiter determining federal position appointments in the new Bush administration, had he not died of an aneurysm. Therefore, those jobs fell to the infighting of several congressmen, each of whom wanted their own people appointed.

Congressman Brown from Savannah, who wanted to be senator one day, felt that Michael shouldn't be rewarded for the unforgiveable sin of defeating Ricky Garcia. Granted, none of them liked him personally, but as Brown observed, "If Parker would do that to him, how can we count on him not to do it to us?" So Deaton and Michael finally agreed that it was time to give it up. No amount of meetings with empty suits in Washington would ever turn the tide.

The superintendent rose from behind her desk as Michael entered her office. She shook his hand and sat in a chair opposite him after retrieving a Coke for him from her fridge. He saw that she had been reading a novel—something with "Camelot" in the title. She was tidy and trim and resplendent in a royal-blue dress, accessorized with matching necklace and earrings. Her false eyelashes were matted with mascara. Lining the shelves and the window sills in her office were angels of all kinds. She was an avid collector.

There was no talking round and round with her. She got right to it.

"I'm sorry you didn't get your appointment, Michael, but the administration's loss is my gain. Come help me fight Governor Holcomb and all of his corporate and congressional cronies. I need help. Everything's changing, and there are few here I can trust."

The familiar role Michael had played was now reversed. She was offering him this position to help herself, but it would also act as an instrument of revenge against the corporate-government monolith which had stepped on him—much like his offer to Sonny in Memphis and to Jim Chestnut in Augusta.

"I don't know, Mary Ruth. What would I be doing?" he asked.

"What do you want to do?" she countered quickly. "Name the areas you'd like to supervise."

So they talked for a long while and structured a new division that included the responsibilities of the previous deputy, who had vacated the position she offered him. She also included areas that Michael requested—

legal, public relations, buildings, transportation, the constituent call center, the field directors, and the new department for federal programs. More than that, he was given an unofficial role as a sort of political consigliere. Mary Ruth might not be with the Mafia, but the type of role she needed Michael to fulfill was straight from their playbook. She wanted a close, trusted friend and confidante without personal ambition, one who would dish out the good news, the bad news, and disinterested advice—at least that was the plan.

"When would I start?" he asked with an uncertain grin.

"How about right now?" she asked, with the satisfied smile of a dog leaning out the car window, its face in the wind. He could almost see her ears flopping in the breeze.

"Welcome aboard, Mr. Deputy Superintendent!" she said as she took his hand. Her hand looked older than her face, and she withdrew it quickly.

Michael had just crossed the threshold of two moments in life that change everything—those moments when you say "Yes" too quickly and those you say "No" too late.

Michael stopped to call Susan and said, "It looks like we're going to Atlanta, honey."

He walked through the department. The curious covertly watched him, stealing glances at this new fodder for water-cooler chatter, fresh grist for the rumor mill. Heads turned, automatic smiles were employed, and offers of help were forthcoming.

Some weren't the idle curious. A few were informants for Hank Holcomb and his newly appointed State Board of Education of partisan hatchet-bearers. Some viewed him as just another transient traveler in the passing parade of political appointees. They knew they would outlast him as they had those who'd come before him. Some were hard of heart, while others were porcelain-hearted appointees glad to have a job and determined to not offend anyone lest they lose it.

Department of Ed employees constantly assessed all new entrants for the calculation that framed their world. There was a determination to be made about how to react, who to back in the great game of winners and losers, and who to betray at the first opportunity. A few, who should have been grateful that Mary Ruth had not fired them for their lack of loyalty and merit, were very quietly and carefully undermining her. She seemed blind to it, either by choice or necessity.

These were the ones who sensed closeness between Michael and Mary Ruth and bore suspicions that he was different, a hard case loyal to the superintendent. How could they erode that confidence she had in him and keep him from threatening what was, what always had been, and what always should be? Thus began a steady *drip, drip, drip*…poisoning of the well of trust between Michael and his new boss; small lies—and the occasional whopper—were already being devised in preparation to be whispered to Mary Ruth at an opportune moment. These reprobate minds sniffed the air and stalked their new victim.

Ed Thomas, a field director in Michael's group and an Elvis tribute artist in his spare time, walked him through the department, saying, "The veterans here have seen all the reformers and political appointees come and go. They wait them out. They know the grunts go on forever. Most are only worker bees who worry about making the next pay grade. They take out hospital and medical coverage plans they couldn't afford elsewhere, and they secure the department's burial plot installment plan for their gray years.

"It is all they know, Michael, and you'd do well to realize that it's just cradle-to-grave for most. It's not personal. The department heads view your rumored fights for 'just causes' as foreign concepts—not with the contempt of your former BellSouth bosses, but something remote to their universe, like the man in the moon."

As he traversed his new environment, Michael noticed a strange sense of sameness and irony about the workers, as well as a great deal of intrigue which churned just beneath the surface of the daily grind. *This is the belly of the beast*, he thought. *I've gone down the rabbit hole. What better place to plant the flag and make a stand?*

He walked through the Constituent Call Center and into his new office; it was suitably impressive. Sandy, his cheerful assistant, had a mouthful of Jimmy Carter teeth and skin tones that reminded him of Agent Merlene Johnson. She was already mysteriously finding furniture and accessories for him as only a veteran government operative or an Army first sergeant could.

Department heads stuck their faces in his door and introduced themselves. The computer gurus rushed in with access codes and "keys to the kingdom." Earnest-looking accountants placed piles of documents on his desk and requested his immediate signature of approval, quickly adding, "If you approve, of course."

A solemn-faced Human Resources rep came with cards and forms for tax withholding, charitable designations, the flower fund check-offs, and insurance and retirement designations. Retirement—he smiled at that unlikely option. He was given a schedule of deputy-superintendent and department-head meetings and a list of phone numbers for everyone in the DOE.

His phone rang often, as other deputies welcomed him to the madness and assured him of undying friendship. Finally, he turned around to find a cup of hot, steaming coffee on his desk, courtesy of Sandy. He told her that he didn't drink coffee. That fact mystified the veterans of the Twin Towers, who thought that based on this evidence alone, he might be a troublemaker.

The workers began to leave in a rush, scurrying to the parking garages so they could enter the outward bound streams of traffic and fight their way home. Michael found himself almost alone as the sun began to set.

Sandy walked in as Michael stood before his wrap-around windows which overlooked the city and the gold dome of the Capitol building. He marveled at the ever-changing hues of the city.

"May I get you anything else before I leave?" she asked.

"Look at this sight," he said as he motioned Sandy over. "Pollution sometimes subdues color, sometimes enhances. If the pollution particles are small, they can scatter the light and redden it to our eyes. This must be a clean sunset because the oranges and reds seem vibrant as the sun drops below the thin haze under those stratus clouds by the river. I don't see any of the pale yellows and pinks when dust and haze fill the air. Isn't it beautiful?"

"Hmm," Sandy said, as if her brown eyes had never seen what Michael saw.

"It's 'Red sky at night, traveler's delight,'" he told her as she left. He saw two mature peregrine falcons with a juvenile riding the currents, floating, it seemed, just outside the plate glass windows.

If they can make it here in this concrete jungle and thrive, maybe I can, too, he thought.

CHAPTER TWENTY

"The budget should be balanced, the Treasury
should be refilled, public debt should be reduced,
the arrogance of officialdom should be tempered
and controlled."—Cicero to Rome, 55 B.C.

"It was the best of times, it was the worst of times…spring
of hope…winter of despair, we had everything before us,
we had nothing before us…"—Charles Dickens

The visitor in Michael's new office was cast in the dappled morning sunlight. The sunbeams gave him a patchy look as he rattled on, saying much but revealing little: an acquired talent of mass media minions. James Peterson, reporter for the *Atlanta Journal-Constitution*, was a wiry journalist with piercing eyes. He dropped by to meet the new curiosity in Atlanta.

"How do you like it? Is it different than Bell? Do you have any hard feelings toward them?" The questions came like the bursts of a Gatling gun, and the reporter watched Michael intently with eyes that matched his inky-black, pomade-enhanced hair.

Michael nodded and smiled, and revealed little of himself. *Two can play at this game*, he thought. *En garde.*

"Why won't Mary Ruth see me this morning? What's up with that? I heard she was seen leaving the governor's office," Peterson noted. Pick, pick, pick…

"Just give me an exclusive. Something—anything! I will cite you as an anonymous source, and I'll always protect you. You can trust me," he said with a straight face.

Yeah, right, Michael thought. *I'm from the media, and I'm your friend.*

The superintendent had, in fact, visited Governor Holcomb. She went alone in a bit of testosterone gamesmanship, much like Reagan did when he walked out to greet Gorbachev in Iceland. It was freezing, and the stakes were high; yet here was the old man striding out confidently in only his blue suit to greet the younger Communist in his overcoat, gloves, hat, and scarf. The imagery was powerful and intentional.

Mary Ruth was playing a bit of this game herself. She arrived at the governor's office, her blonde hair poufed to record heights, glistening as brightly as the fresh gilding of gold leaf on the Capitol dome.

She wore what she called her "Nancy Reagan attire"—a brilliant-red power dress with matching red earrings, necklace, and pumps. The governor was a stark contrast in the smoky gray of a rumpled lawyer suit. It matched his personality and his wavy, gray-black hair.

But he was not alone. There were six men with him—aides, legislative figures, and a man named Billy Joe, a gofer for the Speaker of the Georgia House, who told friends that he was as happy as a "Mississippi pig in mud" to be invited to such a meeting. When Mary Ruth entered the room, all of them stood up and offered her a chair—all except the governor.

He remained seated, smoking a foul cigar and eyeing the state's only elected female officer. With a mocking disdain, he blew cigar smoke directly at her. It seemed that two could play at this game of one-upmanship.

After a long period of silence, Holcomb said, "How're you, Madam Superintendent?"

"Fine, Governor, and you?" she asked very softly, just above a whisper.

"Oh, can't complain. Wouldn't do any good now, would it? I appreciate you coming to see me." This was a reminder that she had come to him, not the other way round. He leaned forward and watched her intently for a moment before he spoke.

"Your second term can be easy, or it can be hard. I want to make it easy on you," said the cat to the mouse.

"Your new Board of Education is not like the lapdogs my predecessor gave you. These friends of mine are pit bulls and hard to control. They're going to nip at your heels, tie your people up in endless demands, and make life miserable for you in board meetings," he said.

The meetings had already turned into brutal inquisitions and interrogations. One employee broke out in hives and had a miscarriage after her relentless grilling by Holcomb's appointees, who did nothing without his approval. As a long-time state employee once told Michael, "I know that there must be something redemptive in the board members— something good—but by golly, you'd have to get a shovel and dig to China to find it!"

The governor continued, "I might be able to put them on a short leash and make your life a bit easier for you. There could be less tension, no leaks to the press every time you make an honest mistake, and maybe—just maybe—no more of those nasty editorials by the AJC on how unfit you are for office, your manner of dress, your, uh— idiosyncrasies, and so on."

Nervous and admiring glances ricocheted around the smoke-filled room like errant darts.

"Here's what I want. I want to whip Georgia teachers into line. So when I give my State of the State address, you will stand up next to me as I announce my intentions. You don't have to say anything; just be my window dressing. It's what you do best." Slight "aha" smiles creased the faces of his admirers.

"It's like I told Governor Jeb Bush in Florida—the first thing you got to do is break the backs of the teachers. That picture of you next to me will be worth a thousand words anyway," he smirked, sucking on the stogie until it burned a bright red-orange; then exhaling in a long and loud demonstration of just who was the ruling rooster in the Georgia barnyard. Billy Joe Estes positively blushed with admiration.

"Oh, another thing," Holcomb continued. "You get a boat-load of money each year in federal education funds. I need you to be kind to me regarding my requests for some of that largesse. Be generous in signing off on some of my board's requests for funding of some of our more ambitious projects. We'll paper over it with some cover for you so you can tell the Feds that it was approved for education-related test beds and such—that flex-ed stuff the Bush White House likes to talk about. Your bureaucrats will know how to word it. Some of them are in my camp already and just waiting for you to join the Holcomb parade."

In perhaps her finest hour, Mary Ruth Robinson squared the shoulders of her red power dress, calmed the tremble of her lower lip, and quietly cleared the frog from her throat before she said, "I'm the Superintendent of Education, elected by the people of Georgia—not you. I *will not* violate that trust. I won't throw teachers under their own school buses. I won't give you federal funds in violation of federal law. You want it? Come and take it if you can—King Henry!"

Eyebrows shot up in the room, and men leaned back in their chairs, eyeing each other in disbelief. The old political warriors didn't think she had it in her, but Holcomb wasn't surprised.

He smiled and said, "So be it, Madam Superintendent. Just remember that I warned you." Billy Joe's hands were clenched so tightly that they had turned a red-white. They quivered in a reflexive manifestation of his indolent brutality as they hung by the belt where he was known to carry his snub-nosed .38 special.

No one cared at the legislature. No one cared in the superintendent's own party. Mary Ruth was a woman and had never been popular with the "good ole boys" of either party; some were the ostrich with head in the sand variety, some had made a treaty with what they called *reality* to avoid things they didn't wish to see; others were absorbed by life, work, and family; and then some were just garden-variety chauvinists.

The superintendent had recently spoken at a gathering for members of the legislature, which was attended by a silver-haired legislator-pharmacist named Steve Palmer from outstate Georgia. He'd had a snoot full, and with all the charm of a greasy weasel in a henhouse and the subtlety of a ten-dollar prostitute, he had followed Robinson down a corridor to her room and demanded admittance. It was getting out of hand until the Speaker's policeman, Billy Joe Estes, showed up to drag him back to his room.

Palmer protested to Billy Joe, "I've had them all, all these heifers that come up here thinking they're this or that. We all know who they are and what they want. Who is she to pretend she's any different? She's nothing…less than nothing! Who's she to say no to me?!"

* * *

Michael knew all of this and more but shrugged his shoulders at the reporter. The fullness of the sun suddenly flooded the room, causing Peterson to squint. "Beats me. I'm just the new guy here, kinda out of the loop, you know?" Michael said.

Peterson looked at him with a long and skeptical appraisal through narrowed peepers and finally said, "Okay, just tell her to call me when she's in the mood to talk."

Michael said, "Oh, you probably need to talk to her scheduler or her chief of staff to get word to her."

"No," Peterson said as he paused at the door to leave. "I think that this is the office to get word to her now."

After the reporter left, Michael looked at the cards now piling up on his desk from this sudden rush of visitors—the AJC, legislative aides, the new board's hired gun, and some internal players—all the usual suspects. He looked out his window at Miss Freedom atop the gilded dome of the Capitol, gleaming golden in the harshness of midday.

Sandy, always ready for a juicy tale, rushed in with her high heels clomping, and asked, "What'd that snake want, boss?"

"Oh, not much. He just wants to be our friend," he said with a grin. "Look down there, Sandy. Not *all* the bordellos in Atlanta are confined to Piedmont and Ponce de Leon. Those are just the underbelly of the political materialism so prevalent in a government that reflects official Atlanta. It trickles down permission to the street urchins with a wink and a nod in a strange blend of political chicanery and moral relativism. Their mantra today and all days: 'We are all prostitutes.'"

Sandy looked at him with wide eyes and a slight shake of her head. As she scurried out to move more paper from her inbox to his, she turned to him and said, "Boss, you sure are a deep thinker. How'd you ever wind up here?"

Michael laughed and walked out of his office on the thirtieth floor. He wandered through the sections, nodding at the occupants of the cubicles who seemed remote and withdrawn. All seemed manacled to barren cells of fear and ego, longing for the coveted window desk where they could peer out and dream. What they really sought, Michael suspected, was not a window, but an escape hatch from this world that promised so much but delivered so little.

They seemed strangers on a distant shore, across an abyss so wide it seemed beyond the reach of all bridges. He thought, *How different are they from me? Here I am, juggling all these balls, trying desperately not to drop any with the help of my doctor's meds—trying to keep up the mask and the masquerade and not quite making it.*

He looked at these gray, anonymous faces—mere pawns in Machiavellian games they could not conceive of, used by remorseless people. They were drenched, blinded, and stupefied by the noise of the collective, and some quietly longed for an end to it all. They were becoming near and dear to Michael, these fellow captives.

He saw a man with a long, white beard who was leaned back at his desk at the cherished window cubicle with his hands behind his head and thought that he looked like a prophet of old. Maybe that was what they needed—a prophet. The man opened his eyes and smiled. Then he tapped on his office window and made bird wings with his hands and arms, making flapping motions like he was soaring.

And Michael understood then why there were no windows that opened on the thirtieth floor.

CHAPTER TWENTY-ONE

"'When I use a word,' Humpty Dumpty said... 'it means just what I choose it to mean—neither more nor less.' 'The question is,' said Alice, 'whether you can make words mean so many different things.' 'The question is,' said Humpty, 'which is to be master—that's all.'"
—*Lewis Carroll*, Through the Looking Glass

"One does not simply walk into Mordor. Its black gates are guarded by more than just Orcs. There is evil there that does not sleep."—Boromir at the Council of Elrond, The Fellowship of the Ring

After a long day at work, Michael walked to the upper levels of the mammoth parking deck attached to the Department of Education. A whispering rain was softly brushing the city, and a stubborn wind blew the mist under the eaves. Shadows falling over the empty concrete garage cast bent images in the corners, where crooked crosses and ominous headstones seemed to materialize. Every creaking sound and sway of the structure was magnified by the acoustics of emptiness. The moans and groans of steel and concrete echoed again and again down each level of the tomb-like skeleton, and the wind made a *woo-woo* banshee wail.

Settled over the city was a haze that he imagined would taste like soot. He was startled by a flush of birds roosting atop the pillars supporting the deck. He turned twice to look back—that cop feeling that he was not alone. He rounded one turn of the garage. Then, like a scene from the classic film *The Third Man*, a figure stepped suddenly from the recesses of an elevator bank and blurted out in the husky voice of a long-time smoker, "Michael Parker!"

Michael stopped cold, and his heart rate elevated. "Who's asking?" Michael answered.

The ghost-like apparition said, "I've been reading about you! Are you for real?"

Michael adjusted his eyes to the cast of light and said, "Wait, let me check."

The man laughed nervously and walked closer. He was just under six feet and had squinty eyes that matched the creases in his face. "You need to be more careful here in Atlanta," he said. "You never know who may be waiting in these dark shadows."

"Well, next I suppose you're going to tell me that you are Barnabas Collins," Michael quipped, with a reference to the old vampire-themed soap opera.

The man laughed again. "If I was, that silver Jesus fish on your car would have melted me like butter."

"A gift from my secretary, who agrees with you," Michael said.

The man introduced himself and gave his "bonafides," as he called them. A friendship was born that night between the long-time employee of the Georgia Department of Transportation and the former MBN agent. He offered to feed Michael insider information on Governor Holcomb's controlled burn of state government.

Michael, who had met many would-be informants in the MBN, eventually decided he was genuine and not a plant by the other side, sent to gain information. He laughed out loud when the informant issued a heartfelt warning: "Trust no one in Atlanta, Agent Parker."

Michael said, "You've watched too many *X-Files* episodes. And you can drop the agent title."

A relationship based on trust began to grow after Sam (his real name) furnished information Clay would have labeled "1-A" for the best intelligence. He told Michael what was going to happen in state government before it occurred. The meetings and cryptic messages took Michael back to countless musty, dusty rooms where the clandestine currency of information was all there was for nameless and faceless players who scurried about, ready to topple the powerful or avenge some perceived wrong.

Sam told him, "You and I are kindred spirits who won't settle for the answer that there *are* no answers—never have been and never will be. We know there are answers. They might not be pretty. They might be deadly and dangerous. But there are answers for those crazy enough to seek them out. We want to know, and we're the kind who can look death right in the eye and kiss evil right on the mouth because—we gotta know."

Sam began to call with increasing frequency. One day, he was agitated more than usual.

"Michael," he said with an almost squeak to his voice, "you won't believe it!"

"What?" Michael asked.

"The governor has taken over roads and bridges!" he gasped.

"Uh, he's the governor. Isn't he already over roads and bridges?" Michael asked.

"You don't get it, Michael," he exclaimed breathlessly. "This isn't business as usual. This is terraforming. They're changing the whole landscape, the whole environment, making all agencies hospitable to takeover, and remaking it all in the image of Hank Holcomb. He has bypassed the legislature and put in a super-director at DOT loyal only to him, making *way* more money than what the director makes. They're planning to take over projects large and small—to control everything that moves. This isn't the usual graft and political trade-offs and get-rich schemes of politicians. This is the stuff of dictators. This is apocalyptic!"

Sam paused and launched into it again. "He has also taken over the Port Authority, put in his people there. He's using that tiny agency for things it was never intended to do and that it has no statutory power to accomplish. The governor is morphing it into some kind of stealth agency in their master plan and seeding money there for extra-statutory activities.

"He plans to install super-directors over every agency in Georgia; no legislative approval, no oversight. It's coming, and it's coming fast. There're some things that he can't do due to money and budget restrictions and the debt limit, but they've got a judge who is set to rule that they can unilaterally raise the debt limit.

"I mean they're so bold as to say that the Constitution doesn't really say what it says on debt! If they can do this, they can do anything! The fix is in. A secret quickie hearing is set for tomorrow at the court-house at 3 p.m. That's when the lawyers are coming to present the request and get the ruling so they can move forward." Sam stopped, like a tire suddenly gone flat.

"You know, if anyone in the ruling elite of government or the media was listening to you now, they would call you a nut. They would be about having you committed—or at least tarred and feathered," Michael noted.

"I know," he said, "but it's true. This ain't Kansas no more, Toto."

Michael asked for the name of the compliant judge and told him not to worry.

"One more thing," Sam said with even more urgency in his voice. "He's going to come after you guys, big time. He'll set up a well-paid education czar to bypass Superintendent Robinson and pay him well. He has to have money to do all of this. They want those billions in federal money you have. They want it bad and are willing to do anything to get it. They're not going to stop at education. They want to create new agency heads loyal only to Holcomb who'll bypass all the constitutional officers elected by the people."

"They can't divert federal money," Michael said. "That would be supplanting. You can't take an existing state agency or a new monster, as in this case, and decide to save state money by using federal money. It's illegal, irrespective of other federal laws."

"When're you going to learn, Michael? They don't give a rip about legal and illegal," Sam said. "You guys had better batten down the hatches. The hurricane is coming."

With that, the whirlwind of government whispers was gone again. Michael had grown more careful about how he communicated with Sam on department phones and computers. After some things were leaked to the governor's office, Michael requested that some old friends at Bell run a physical scan on all department lines and on the mainframes of the switching center in downtown Atlanta. It was time to see if there were unfriendly bugs crawling around.

* * *

A meeting was called at the legislature by friends of the governor. Paul Robbins, a former DOE department head and budget expert, had been tapped to convince Robinson's management team that diversion of federal money was not supplanting, and that it would be okey-dokey to open up the treasury to the whims of Hank Holcomb.

Beneath the pink blush of the Georgia marble in the legislature, the meeting went back and forth. Robbins was a hunch-backed, older man with thick, gray brows and a wild mane of gray-black hair. He was girded for battle and went right at the members of the DOE management team, many of whom he knew from the old days.

"Now, Harry. You know this isn't supplanting. Why, back in our time, we'd siphon off some here and there, pretty it up for the feds, and everything was fine. Later, the auditors would rule "Ok" and give us a wink and the thumbs-up. Words in budget documents only mean what we interpret them to mean, that's all. C'mon, boys. We can just label our deal as part of this 'flex-spending power' that the new Republican President seems so fond of."

"That was different, Paul, and you know it. Look at this request and cite me the statute that makes it legal," countered the cagey Harry Jenkins, DOE budget director.

Robbins dug and dug through reams of Georgia statutes, but each one that he tried to produce to provide cover for the governor, Harry shot down. Finally, exasperated, Robbins leaned back and pasted on a Cheshire-cat grin. "You got me, Harry. I trained you well all those years ago. I tried my best, and now whatever happens is on you guys and your boss."

There was lots of back-slapping, and Robbins acknowledged in a whisper of confidentiality that he knew it was a losing battle, that any diversion was, in fact, illegal.

As everyone was about to leave, Robbins turned to Michael and said, "Who are you over there in the corner, so quiet and making all those notes?"

"I'm nobody important," Michael said with a shrug.

Robbins smiled and said, "Well, *they* know who you are. That's all that matters."

* * *

Judge Thomas Hendricks was a tall, hollow-chested Superior Court judge with a Wyatt Earp mustache. He was never that good as a lawyer in private practice, so he went into politics. He typified the general rule in Georgia—the most incompetent and/or ethically challenged attorneys wound up as judges.

He certainly hadn't made the money he needed for retirement, but that nice young man they called Hoss explained to him that he deserved to be rewarded for loyal service to the state. A favorable ruling on the debt limit could be his ticket to a vacation in Tahiti as well as some stock in a company that was about to skyrocket and split shares due to favorable action on some large government contracts.

"Wouldn't that be insider trading and illegal?" the judge asked Billy Joe.

"No, not at all," Billy Joe assured him, "just a favor for a friend. What's the use in having insider information if it can't be shared with people who love Georgia? Buy low and sell high, Your Honor."

The judge smiled, took another swig of bourbon from the small bottle he kept in his desk, and rose to don his black robe for the hearing on that very matter.

* * *

Michael's cell phone buzzed like an angry Georgia Tech Yellow Jacket. It was Sam.

"How'd the court hearing go?" Michael asked.

"Oh, the crowd you arranged showed up with placards denouncing corruption in government, and one reporter from a small weekly paper was there, too. When the lawyers saw all of that, they didn't even slow their luxury car down. They hightailed it out of Dodge. Friends in the court clerk's office said that the judge abruptly cancelled an extended vacation to paradise after all the commotion," Sam said.

Michael laughed. "Well, it's good to know that there's a few honest people left in this dirty old city…and at least one reporter who's either unafraid or so bored that he decided to show up for a scoop."

Walter Pettigrew, a lanky man with a wisp of gray hair, an infectious laugh, and an endless supply of bad ties, ambled into Michael's office as he hung up with Sam.

"Nipped that in the bud, huh?" he asked in his Walter Brennan voice.

"Yep," Michael said. "The weekly newspaper guy followed the bread crumbs we dropped. In the required filings for the judge, who was prepared to sanction a new debt limit, campaign disclosures showed a sudden influx of donations, delivered in cash. Contributions came with ready-made names of donors to attribute them to, good party loyalists in state agencies...but it just didn't work out like they planned."

Walter smiled a grasshopper smile. He had been appointed by Mary Ruth as her personal money cruncher and bird dog over the budget and federal programs. She already had deputies over those programs, but she wasn't so sure of them. So she brought Walter in, and he reported to Michael. Between the two of them, she figured she had it all covered. She had watchful, loyal eyes over the political and financial fronts. It wasn't long before everyone began to view Michael and Walter as mercenaries in the superintendent's private army.

Walter said, "I found all kinds of things in reports and budget directives lately. I found some money, small stuff mostly, that was hidden away in a request originating with the board. I called up the manager involved and told him that he was in violation of this and that statute, and the superintendent would not sign it. He told me that he didn't work for me or you. I reminded him to check the new organizational chart and see that the superintendent gave me the authority to supersede all budgetary decisions involving federal programs."

"What happened then?" Michael asked.

"Oh, the deputy over the budget called and huffed and puffed, and tried to order me to stand down." Walter cackled a now-familiar laugh that was unmistakably his own. "I told him that we could go meet with Superintendent Robinson right then. He got real quiet and asked me if I could just come through him and not embarrass him in front of his people. 'Why sure,' I told him."

Walter laughed deeply again, as he did whenever he talked about the two things that made life worth living—old bird dogs and George Jones's honky-tonk homilies.

"Anything else I can do for you and our boss?" he asked.

"No, Walter, we're doing all that we can, but it's going to get much worse. They're going to come after all of us with every big gun they have," Michael said.

After Walter left, Michael looked out at the twinkling of the city and resumed his relentless self-examination. *Yes, the hurricane's coming. Why are we fighting so desperately to defend something that is broken? Public education: Is this the Holy Grail? Can we say education as we know it is a panacea for the moral bankruptcy that we find ourselves in? Do we risk all to defend the free thinkers, agnostics, and old hippies who populate the administrations of many public schools? It seems the absurdity of all absurdities to pick this fight here and now, but the system is all we have. As Benjamin Franklin said about religion: If man is wicked with it, what would he be without it?*

Michael's head hurt thinking about it all, and he felt like an orphan—the most frangible orphan in all of Atlanta, just waiting to shatter into a million pieces.

CHAPTER TWENTY-TWO

"Evil is bad sold as good, wrong sold as right,
injustice sold as justice…a thin veil of right can
disguise enormous wrong…"—John Hartung

"Your god, sir, is the World…"—Charlotte Bronte

Michael walked to the superintendent's office after the board meeting. The State Board of Education meetings had become little more than surreal spectacles where sacrificial gladiators were trotted into the coliseum for the amusement and sport of the minions of Caesar.

Clutched in Michael's hand was a crumpled email from one of his section chiefs.

> *DOE employees scheduled to speak today on routine budget and program matters were running to the restroom to throw up before and after the ordeal. We know boards attract crackpots, eccentrics, and oddities, but not these cruel, chest-out, clenched-fist sadists who have no qualms about attacking low-level career employees. To get to and embarrass Mary Ruth, the enemy of their patron, Hank Holcomb, these bearers of coarseness are willing to make young women cry and old men tremble and sweat.*

> *It's open season. It's sport. It's insuperable. It's a vessel run aground on the isle of moribund. They speak of altruism, usually the things Holcomb wants to do with federal funds he wants them to divert. And in the next breath, they skewer hapless program managers who have no skin in their political games. The fear in the room today was palpable in employees who are beaten down by abuse and some who have been broken by it.*

> *Their inner light has gone out, Michael, and they'll never fit together again exactly right. Years from now, they'll claim to be mended, but the small cracks will still*

show around the edges, because they smelled fear in themselves in those meetings. They know their peers saw it in them, and it has forever soiled their self-image.

The board members amuse and fatten themselves in the Holcomb pecking order by instilling fear and confusion in witnesses they summon before them, often turning decent men and women against their fellow employees and neighbors. The objects of their cruelty just want to return to their cubicles, to be anonymous again. They only want it all to—stop. Can't the superintendent help us?

Michael was angrier than he'd been since Governor Davidson's people tampered with his witnesses in Mississippi and agents were abused by the system for his failure to play along and exonerate the guilty in his internal affairs investigation.

He tried in vain to interest the Atlanta media, but no one cared at the *AJC*. They yawned at the TV stations. When Michael asked them why they didn't cover all that was developing with the governmental in-fighting and Holcomb's bullying, there were no combative words, no real hostility—just indifference and incomprehension that he could possibly think any of it had anything to do with them.

Michael laid the email before Mary Ruth, who looked up underneath glasses she never wore in public. She read the email, looked up at Michael, and shook her head, asking, "Have you ever seen anything like it?"

"No," he said. "It's much worse than those who tried to kill me at the MBN. They never pretended to be anything other than what they were. These people in their fine attire are political assassins of the first order. They are merciless, and they like it. Time seems to stand still in the board sessions. There are none of the better aspects of man's nature, just the law of the jungle, this brutality."

It is a hard bed to lie on, Michael thought as he walked out of the superintendent's office. *It can't be allowed to be the end, but a point of beginning.*

* * *

While Michael yearned for new beginnings in Atlanta, U.S. Assistant Secretary of Education Gayle Powers sifted through the agenda of another meeting with her subordinates on Maryland Avenue in Washington, D.C.

She was one of those temporary occupants of federal agencies, political appointees who came to earn the title, pad the resume, and think long-term about the political and social networking possibilities that could feather a nest for a lifetime. Some came with idealism and hopes of changing the world, but any such utopian thoughts were soon crushed by the weight of the Washington bureaucracy.

Gayle, an attractive woman in her early forties, had brown-blonde hair and walked the halls of U.S. Ed with a free-swinging stride that bespoke her confidence in the rightness of things. She had the honor of being the one who assisted U.S. Secretary Rod Paige in matters large and small. In-between the drudgery of staff meetings, she traveled with the secretary and took care of logistics, speeches, and the list of people who would show up for photo ops and handshakes.

She surveyed the room full of managers who were responsible for programs and expenditures—most of which the average American had never heard of. "Good morning," she said. "Before we get into the set agenda, does anyone have any pressing issues to discuss?"

David Billings, a veteran educator from Tennessee who had come to Washington in search of adventure, spoke up. "Yes, Gayle, we have some potential problems in Georgia. These requests keep coming in from the State Board of Education there about the use of federal grant allocations for special board projects."

"Board projects?" the assistant secretary asked. "We deal with the Georgia Department of Education, don't we? Since when do we have queries from board members? They're not the agency, and from what I recall, they're only part-time appointees."

"Exactly," he said. "The Georgia Department is the only legal and constitutional recipient of federal funds. They're who we hold accountable and the only statutory agency with the power to receive and disburse funds."

"What are these board people asking for exactly?" she asked.

"The letters have been increasingly bold and speculative about their powers to direct money where they wish. We've responded with quotes straight from the Title programs and explained it all in a very professional way, but they won't let it go. Our sources say there is some kind of power struggle underway between them and the state superintendent," Billings said.

"Well, what's so urgent then?" the harried assistant secretary asked.

"We had a training session last week and many of the Title coordinators from Georgia attended. For the first time that any of us can remember, Marcie Henry, a board member from Atlanta, invited herself. She kept interrupting the speakers during the training."

"Really? A state board member was here at our sessions? What did she say?" Powers asked.

He frowned and replied, "She said, 'Rules, rules, rules! Can't we use the money for whatever we want?'" Eyes rolled around the conference table.

"She did what?" Powers asked incredulously.

"Yes, we were horrified and told her, 'No, you can't!' But she wouldn't let it go, and actually began threatening our instructors! Now we're getting feelers from the governor's office down there asking for *carte blanche* to spend federal money for whatever they choose, or they'll 'go over our heads,'" he said.

"Go over our heads? How much could be in question in Georgia?" Powers asked.

"Potentially, one billion dollars," the budget guru at the end of the table piped in.

"Who's our contact in the Georgia Department of Education?" Powers asked.

"Mary Ruth Robinson is the superintendent, but we show that our prime contact for such matters is her deputy, Michael Parker," Billings answered.

"We're adjourned! We'll continue this meeting later," she said, an angry woman on a mission. "Get this Parker on the phone."

* * *

After Michael left the superintendent's office, he walked through the department and cataloged the merciful end of another board meeting. Employees with large stains of sweat visible under their arms were making their way back to their offices. Drained and exhausted, they consoled one another with the fact that it would be thirty days until it all started again. One noted that after a week or two, the dread would begin and hang over their cubicles like evil spirits of gloom and fear. Board members had also begun to show up unannounced to demand private audiences with managers. Those meetings didn't carry the intensity of the pack attacks, but they invoked the bad memories and served as a reminder and conditioner of—"You'd better cooperate, or we'll summon you to the next inquisition."

Michael caught an elevator to find Grover Gault, chairman of the board, as a fellow traveler. He had the worst halitosis of anyone Michael had ever met, almost the smell of…sulfur. He was a wealthy businessman who, by all accounts, was ruthless to his employees. Some reportedly prayed his marriage would produce no children, because "the evil seed must stop."

The chairman said, "We must have lunch, Michael. Some of your friends back in Augusta speak fondly of you. You and I are on different sides here, but Fred Davidson, the former chancellor at the University of Georgia, told me about your wife's health problems and how you care for her, move mountains to find the best healthcare for her, and raise money to find a cure for her disease. That speaks well of you as a man."

"That's very kind of Fred," Michael said stoically.

Just as the elevator doors opened and Michael turned to step out, a face from yesterday stepped in to join the chairman and his aide. Michael looked, then looked again to confirm that it really was Billy Joe Estes, a furball coughed up from his nightmares. As the doors closed, the two refugees from Mississippi exchanged looks that spoke volumes and needed no words.

* * *

When Michael arrived at his office, he closed his door for a bit of solitude and to think about finding Ace Connelly's gofer in Atlanta. He finally picked up a book he'd been reading and grabbed his usual brown-bag lunch. Then the phone rang, and Michael almost didn't answer.

"Hello," Michael said.

"Is this Michael Parker?" a female voice asked.

"It is—or what's left of him," he joked.

"This is U.S. Assistant Secretary of Education Gayle Powers, liaison with state education agencies for U.S. Secretary Rod Paige." Michael sat up a little straighter and was at full attention at that mouthful of titles and authority.

"Yes, ma'am. How may I help you?" he asked.

"Mr. Parker, we're hearing some troubling things out of Georgia," she said bluntly.

"Well, you should be here at ground zero," he said.

The conversation began very formally with stiff and carefully worded inquiries. As the long discussion wore on, it became pointed and got down to the real nitty-gritty. All the pleasantries and legalism fell to the wayside.

"Some of your board members and other politicos are trying to strong-arm us on federal funds coming to the Georgia Department of Education. We've never seen anything like this! States are usually just so happy to get federal money to help fund their schools that we get few complaints. Lately, it sounds like disputed delegates at a 1960s political convention. Who'll be seated, who won't…Forgive me, but it sounds a bit like a banana republic!" she said.

Michael laughed. "Madam Secretary, you don't know the half of it."

"Call me Gayle," she said, an intuitive warming to a voice so far away. "A bit off-topic, but do you know that you can spend up to five percent of all money we send you for administrative costs? That's legal, and it's something you might consider if push comes to shove. Your department has cut overhead from what we see, but the superintendent isn't claiming that five off the top as she legally can. It's probably an admirable thing to push every dollar you can out to your districts. I'm just informing you of your rights and authority. If you ever need to move some of that money around, there's nothing anyone can do about that."

"Thanks, Gayle. I'll pass that along. We're under siege here, and they're trying to raid federal funds to do what the governor wants. They are relentless. Anything you can do to protect us as our rear guard in Washington would be most appreciated," he said.

"Well, I'm not supposed to be political in this job," she said, "but this is a Republican administration. Your governor is a Democrat, and these board members are Democrats. So I don't think you have anything to worry about on this end. The party people are nothing if not partisan. This nosing around, trying to get us to give away money, is the craziest thing we've seen lately, and believe me, that covers a lot of ground," she said with a hearty chuckle.

"I hope you're right, but I'm not so sure about your bosses at the White House," Michael said.

"Well, in any event, you hold the line down there. We'll slam the door here. We'll prosecute anyone who attempts to divert federal funds to uses not sanctioned in federal law. We won't tolerate theft of federal money meant for education. We're behind you. Don't give in to them and divert funds to places they shouldn't be," she warned.

"You don't have to worry about that," he said.

"Secretary Paige and I will be in Atlanta soon. I'll see you then, and we can talk more. Call me if you need help on this end. The secretary's a good man—the President, too—so don't you worry," she assured him. With that, his new best friend in Washington was gone.

Michael thought about the call, Billy Joe Estes, what it all meant, and the coming storm Sam predicted. He hoped she was right about Washington, but he'd seen too much.

She came through Atlanta shortly thereafter as promised, and Secretary Paige was with her. He stood in a silent but stoic profile as Powers told Mary Ruth and Michael unequivocally that they would prosecute anyone who stole federal money. Her parting words were, "Stand firm. We are with you."

As he watched the representatives of official Washington leave for Hartsfield that day, Michael understood journalist Lewis Grizzard's longing for home and whispered to himself: "If I ever get back to Mississippi, I'm going to nail my feet to the ground."

CHAPTER TWENTY-THREE

"No one can serve two masters, for either he will
hate the one and love the other, or he will be
devoted to the one and despise the other…"
—Matthew 6:24.

"The illegal we do immediately. The unconstitutional
takes a little longer."—Henry Kissinger

Pennsylvania Avenue Northwest.

The windswept Ellipse was the field south of the White House where Michael, as a fingerprint tech, had played baseball on the FBI team in 1966. Just across from there, a young journeyman government employee was now struggling with greater issues than strike-outs and fly balls.

Deep within the endless labyrinths of the Eisenhower Executive Office Building west of the White House, Jamie Sebren was in the thickets of what seemed an insurmountable dilemma.

The young man, with a shock of blonde hair and a baby fat jelly-belly, occupied a small corner office in the EOP, the Executive Office of the President. He was a young patriot with big and deeply embedded ideas about liberty and doing the right thing. He sometimes thought that writer Henry Adams might have been correct to call the old building the "architectural infant asylum"—at least the parts about infantile behavior and the inmates who ran the asylum. He had seen so much since he came to the White House, things that had shattered his tenuous faith in public officials and shook his naiveté about great crusades.

He was the son of a wealthy contributor to the current party in power. His father had asked for and received a low-level appointment for his boy. He had moved from the Office of Management and Budget, where he had courier status for routine NSA documents, to his current position as an assistant in the chief of staff's office.

He was always told to forget everything he saw and to repeat nothing, but he had seen and heard some things brewing in Georgia that didn't compute for him. He believed political parties actually stood for great and grand ideas and ideals, and he believed you never, ever got in bed with the other side—especially at the expense of your own.

One letter he delivered, a communiqué from the governor of Georgia, caught his attention. It was from home, so it was interesting to a homesick kid from the Peach State. He saw that it was one of a series of letters trying to strike some bargain with the White House, a tit-for-tat deal of some kind.

He began to sift through documents he had been told to forget, and he was horrified at what began to come together. Georgia Governor Holcomb, whom everyone he knew opposed and who was persecuting Jamie's friends back home, was trying to cut a deal with the White House. The signatures he saw were of some very powerful people in the administration; people he admired, principled people—or so he had believed. *There must be some mistake*, he thought.

Jamie went to his boss, the deputy to the deputy in a place that was long on impressive titles that often meant very little.

"Uh, excuse me, Richard. You got a moment?" he asked of his boss, a Virginia native who wore red bow ties and was fresh from the fraternity life at UVA. He was not much older than Jamie.

"Sure, what's on your mind?" Richard asked.

"I kinda got wind of some things, heard some things from people in the chief's office, and I'm confused," he sputtered nervously.

"What kind of things?" Richard asked, suddenly all ears.

"Well, I think the Georgia governor is asking the President to make a deal to support our education bill, No Child Left Behind, and…"

"Where're you getting that? You know this isn't our business," Richard snapped.

"Yeah, I know. But Dick, it sounds as if he wants us to throw Superintendent Robinson under the bus down there, and get us to say he can just steal federal money and help him destroy *everything* the party's trying to do in Georgia. I know that can't be right, Dick, and don't believe the president would go along with it if he knew what was really going on and how wrong this is…" Jamie finally stopped to breathe. His heart was running away, practically halfway home to Georgia already.

"You done now?" a visibly furious Richard hissed. "I'll tell you what you're going to do. You're going to forget all of this. You're nobody, and what you don't like means nothing. These people above us have a vision. They can see far above the treetops. We can't begin to see those things down here in the forest. They know what's best for America. There are tradeoffs in life—the greater good, you know. You're messing where you don't belong with some very powerful people close to the president."

Richard, the sun freak whose forearm hairs were bleached white from weekend beach trips, was piqued. "Karl knows what he's doing and doesn't need your advice. So what if Holcomb gets some federal money? The bloated education budget will never miss it! The Treasury will just print more. Let him tinker down there in his Georgia playpen. If he becomes the only Democrat to endorse our bill, he gives us cover, and all this other is just a cheap price to pay. It's in the best interests of the party. That's all that matters. It's the way of the world. Grow up!" he fumed.

Jamie was reeling and sick at his stomach. He wanted to run, but he had no place to go. He was in the throes of an awakening that all idealists must eventually suffer, when the way things *should* be collide with the way things *are*. The mask is torn off the Lone Ranger, bullets no longer bounce off Superman, and it suddenly seems that "God didn't make the little green apples, and it don't rain in Indianapolis in the summer time. And there's no such thing as Dr. Seuss or Disneyland and Mother Goose, and no nursery rhymes."

He stumbled out of Richard's office and ignored a fellow neophyte who ran up with a new poll and said, "Hey, Jamie, the president is up four in the latest polls. Ain't that great? We'll get a second term for sure!"

He almost walked over a baby-faced female staffer, who said, "Hey, Jamie, I got passes for us to be in the gallery when the president speaks to Congress about the State of the Union."

Jamie stopped then and turned to her. "I guess he'll tell them that everything is just hunky-dory, huh? Cause he's up there above the treetops, high on the mountain—some kind of visionary, breathing that rarified air that only polls and political contributions can impart—not God. Man, he's the blind leading the blind. He can't see nothing!"

As Jamie stormed off, the staffers gawked at him and looked at each other in disbelief. This was the most gung-ho guy they knew! "What happened to him?" one muttered. What, indeed?

Jamie once saw clearly in black and white. Now he saw only opaque colors in his new opaque world. He thought they were the good guys, only to find out there were no good guys in Washington, D.C.—only those who were with you in the thick, not the thin. If you wanted a friend in the Capitol, you'd best find a dog.

Jamie was up all night thinking and praying, and finally it came to him. To right his world that had been knocked from its axis, Jamie called his dad. He told him everything, including what he wanted to do. His father, a contributor to Robinson's campaigns, gave his son her cell number. Jamie dialed the number with trembling fingers. Somewhere in the background at an official function, the band played "Hail to the Chief."

"Superintendent Robinson, I'm sorry to bother you at this hour, but this is Jamie in the White House, and I think there are some things you need to know."

He went on to tell her all that he had pieced together. The President's people had signed off on the deal with the devil. The command had already gone out to U.S. Education to make nice with Holcomb.

"Ma'am, friends told me the White House encountered some protests from the purists at U.S. Ed who still believe in federalism and the rule of law, but..." The words choked in his throat as the young man struggled. "Our staffer's response was, 'Let them the governor take what he wants from education. We've got bigger fish to fry. We'll attribute it to giving the states more discretion over spending, and tell the Conservatives that we are freeing them from the regulation of the central government. That's all those dimwits want to hear.'"

A long silence ensued as he struggled to maintain some semblance of composure. "Ma'am," he said, "they've thrown you guys under the bus. I'm so sorry."

Mary Ruth thought she heard him softly crying. "Son, don't worry about this. It's not your fault. Thank you for calling me."

She dialed Michael at his apartment, informed him of the call, and said, "Those card-carrying red-white-and-blue patriots have thrown us to the wolves."

Michael hung up, and Susan asked him what was wrong. He thought of Gayle and her faith in her political bosses—how the Georgia group was safe because of partisanship when dealing with the other party. *The rules have all changed*, he thought.

He looked at Susan, and said, "Nothing, honey. The hurricane just arrived."

CHAPTER TWENTY-FOUR

"Yeah, my blood's so mad feels like coagulatin'...
I can't twist the truth, it knows no
regulation...We're on the eve of destruction."
—Barry McGuire

"We're sailing on a strange sea, blown by a strange
wind...turning flesh and body into soul."
—Waterboys

As Michael pulled into the state parking garage, his Bonneville made a sick *tink, tink* sound in the Georgia heat. A large crow flew by to mock his car with a boisterous "caw, caw, caw" which sounded a lot like "car, car, car." It was par for the course as the days of conflict turned into weeks of siege in Atlanta.

Objects around him seemed to be framed by blue-white halos. Stress was off the chart. He wasn't getting enough sleep, and his eyes were sagging and swollen. As he plopped in his office chair, he had a two-day stubble of beard and his gray hair was tangled. The Xanax his doctor prescribed wasn't working so the dose was increased again.

Michael began to think about wins and losses, regrets, and the day that the breath would go out of him. Now and then he could hear the slamming of the big door that night with Freddie. He didn't know what would happen if he woke up on the wrong side of the door and out of options. He still wasn't sure.

A card of Irish blessings was on his desk. Mary Ruth was of Irish descent and obsessed with all things Ireland. Michael believed there were times when she used Irish fables and romantic songs to escape from memories too difficult to bear. He sensed she was like one of the porcelain angels in her office, one dropped in the past. He'd heard whispers about a night in the woods where the angel may have splintered and cracked. There'd been a cosmetic reconstruction, but the tiny fracture lines showed when you looked closely.

Mary Ruth stuck her head in his office and gave him a crinkly smile. "Hold down the fort. I'm off to do an interview on the federal funds."

"Good luck," he said.

She turned once more and said, "You know, if we had met when we were young, we could've conquered the world." Then all of her bounced out of the room, except for her perfect hair lacquered with Final Net, extra hold.

Michael was surprised by her statement, but chalked it up to her mood. She was, after all, dressed in Irish shamrock green. While fielding questions in a recent education forum, someone asked her if she had lost her way as an educator and was hanging out with the wrong crowd.

She replied bluntly, "I *am* the wrong crowd!"

* * *

Phil Kincaid, the immaculately coiffed, silver-haired anchor at WSB-TV, peered into his teleprompter with all the gravitas of Walter Cronkite to read his script to Metro Atlanta.

"State School Chief Mary Ruth Robinson is going head-to-head in a battle with Governor Henry Holcomb and his State Board of Education over who decides how Georgia uses eight hundred million dollars it will be receiving each year in federal education funds. At stake is the money Georgia is due under the No Child Left Behind Act signed into law by George W. Bush and written in conjunction with Senator Ted Kennedy in the new bipartisan spirit in Washington.

"Here at home, Governor Holcomb has requested that the U.S. Department of Education give Georgia 'state-flex designation' to give the state flexibility to meet our unique needs. This would enable Georgia to align its education reform initiative with Bush's education act, but Superintendent Robinson wrote a letter to U.S. Secretary of Education Rod Paige asking him to deny the request for state-flex designation. We have Superintendent Robinson with us. Good evening, Madam Superintendent," he said.

"Good evening, Phil. You're correct. We don't seek flex status for Georgia. We have a political situation with a power-hungry governor who wishes to remove all safeguards from federal funds so he can divert them to further an agenda that has little to do with students. The programs Governor Holcomb pushes for education are layered with bureaucrats and whole language, not phonics. The governor's trying to raid the federal piggy bank to build the personal kingdom that he longs for. Why would Republicans want to partner with him and Ted Kennedy to expand the U.S. Department of Education and give us more one-size-fits-all dictates from Washington?"

"Well, even your own party is against you, Ms. Robinson. State Republican Chair Wayne Zeigler said, and I quote, 'Even as we oppose much of this governor's agenda, it seems this is one of those moments where our President is trying to overcome partisanship to give locals control over federal funds in keeping with our great party's belief in the Tenth Amendment.' The state board issued a statement today which reads, 'We've tried so hard to work with this superintendent and are surprised to find her opposed to allowing those closest to the children to decide where funds are allocated. After all, it's about the children. She's lost her way.'"

"Phil, if I could just respond," Mary Ruth interjected.

Phil droned on. "The governor issued this statement: 'We support No Child Left Behind, a model for what President Bush did in Texas as governor. We are supported by our good friend, Florida Governor Jeb Bush. I was proud to overcome the partisan divide, do the right thing for our children, and become the first Democratic governor to endorse No Child Left Behind.'"

"Phil, if you'd allow me to respond," an exasperated Mary Ruth tried again.

"I'm sorry," the anchor said. "We're out of time, but we appreciate you coming on." He hadn't even wrinkled his conservative Rotary Club blue suit, and he could still see himself in the buffed gloss of his dress shoes as he reached in his anchor-desk drawer for a breath mint.

The segment faded out with a smiling picture of the king of Georgia. The fix was in.

* * *

Washington had suddenly gone silent for Michael Parker. Their new strategy seemed to mirror the mission of the old submarine movie — *Run Silent, Run Deep.*

He tried repeatedly to reach Gayle Powers at U.S. Education, only to be told time and again that she was not in. He tried to reach the secretary, but he was out of the office. When would he be back? No one knew. No one knew—anything.

Michael pressed the emotionless voice, "When do you expect Gayle to return?"

"We don't know, sir," the autonomic Washington voice said.

"This week, this month—this year, maybe?" Michael pressed.

"We don't know, sir," was the flat reply.

"Do you know anything?" he asked sharply.

Betraying all of her intense training that sought to sanitize all emotion and empathy from her interaction with the public, the civil servant blurted out unvarnished honesty: "I know that she'll never be in for you—sir!"

Michael chuckled. "Well, I think I heard the *ding, ding, ding* of the pinball machine. We must've hit the bumper button just right. Could you take a message for her?" he asked.

"Sir, that would be admitting I have contact with her," she said in Washington speak.

"I'm not going away," Michael replied.

A long sigh of exasperation, "All right then," she conceded.

"Gayle, wherever you are, I hope you're—holding firm. That promise you made is about as useless now as a screen door on a submarine."

There was a slight, suppressed giggle on the phone, and then, "Will that be all, sir?"

As Michael hung up, a sense of despair and anger engulfed him. He walked out onto 20th Street to clear his head, and he heard the strains of the best blues he'd heard since Mississippi. A weathered, old black man in dark glasses was sitting on the sidewalk playing his guitar, hoping for donations for his version of "The Thrill is Gone." Michael dropped a bill in the blind singer's pan, and the man said, "Thank you, sir."

"Great music," Michael said. "Makes me think of home."

"You're carrying a burden, aren't you, son?" the old man asked.

"Seems so," Michael answered.

"You got to stop fighting the devil by yourself. The battle belongs to God. That ole devil's sneaky, too. He doesn't come around with a pitchfork and a pointy tail. He walks up on you dressed up like everything he knows you want," he said.

"Thanks. I'll remember that," Michael said.

"Son, keep on speaking the truth even if your voice shakes. But remember, if you want to sing the blues, you got to pay your dues."

CHAPTER TWENTY-FIVE

"They do not learn…A small sacrifice to save many.
It is necessary."—Oliver Bowden, Assassin's
Creed: The Secret Crusade

"Let God speak within you. Every path leads
homeward, every step is birth, every step is death,
every grave is mother."—Hermann Hesse, Bäume,
Betrachtungen und Gedichte

Politicians develop instincts which stand guard like sentinels against bad decisions. In their apparent slumber after the disaster on WSB—surrounded, hopelessly outnumbered, and politically penniless—Mary Ruth Robinson decided to go for broke and attack.

She announced she would run for governor.

When Michael asked her why she did it, her glassy eyes clouded and she said, "Time is short and risk-taking is the only thing that gives you that rush to slow the clock."

Immediately, the scorched-earth campaign began. The usual suspects came out to rake her over the coals. They regurgitated their old columns, criticized her for the things that they deemed to truly matter in governance—her hairstyle, clothes, soft demeanor, intransigence, support of parents who chose to home-school their children, disdain for unions, and an unwillingness to compromise. And from those champions of women everywhere, the subtle implication that somehow her gender rendered her—even as governor—incapable of matching the old bulls in the legislature.

It was another mugging by the political class and all of their allies.

When Mary Ruth returned to the department after the news conference, she asked Michael to come to her office. She was sitting in her chair reading a romance novel when he entered. The fine weather-lines around her eyes showed as she licked her index finger to turn each page of the book. He thought sometimes that she was trapped within some kind of Peter Pan syndrome, buzzing like a fly on very old flypaper.

She looked up, saw him, and said, "James Johnston, a retired Georgia state trooper, wants to meet me tonight for dinner. Given your expertise, I'd like you to go with me."

As the quiet of the night fell and a milk-white pocked moon spotlighted their drive along I-20, they traveled to the eight o'clock meeting in Carrolton, not far from the Speaker's home. Turning onto Highway 61, Michael noticed a neon sign in front of a small, wood-frame church just outside Carrolton. Two or three black letters hung askew, but the message was readable—"This is the highway to hell. Do you believe in hell?"

As they entered the quiet Carrolton eatery, a very tall black man rose and motioned them over to a small table in the rear of the café. Michael wondered how the big man had ever managed to fit into a standard police cruiser.

Former trooper Johnston stepped around the table, hand extended and smiling. He took Mary Ruth's hand and did a brief bow of respect. Michael noticed that the knuckles of his hand were sunk in, the tell-tale sign of officers who hit too many people over the years when their slapjack failed. He also noticed that Johnston noticed him noticing.

Over a meat-and-potatoes dinner, Johnston eased past the small talk to his main menu. "Mrs. Robinson, I've come here to warn you that troopers were in meetings at state patrol stations all over Georgia today after your announcement. They were told that if they catch you out on the road, for whatever reason they can manufacture, they're to stop you, ticket you, arrest you, and even—hurt you."

That wounded butterfly fluttered around the table as his eyes never left Robinson's. Michael cocked his left brow and broke the trance by asking him, "Hurt her? How good is this information? Even with these guys, this seems—to put it mildly—a bit far-fetched."

The likely veteran of many clandestine government projects himself in days of yesteryear, Johnston bestowed a benevolent smile, shook his head ever so slightly as a father would to a child, and said with a voice like Pavarotti, "You don't know these people like I do. They think they can get away with anything. It doesn't matter if it was said in jest or if it was even said at all. That story is traveling the grapevine in trooper circles all over this state tonight. Some told me. I tell you."

He leaned back in his chair and spread his palms up. "While most officers will be appalled, there'll be a few who got their jobs through political patronage and have no hope of advancing by merit. They'll hear the orders and view it as their ticket to favor and power. They will do anything to honor these instructions, idle gossip, or wishful thinking by those boys downtown who hate y'all. And make no mistake—they do hate you."

Mary Ruth was uncharacteristically quiet, perhaps stunned. Michael's eyes bored into Johnston's as he asked him, "What do you want out of this?"

He nodded back and smiled. "You're a suspicious man, but that's good. Former MBN captain, weren't you? I just want to help out now and then. I'm available if you ever need—security, a little muscle, you know."

Michael wasn't satisfied. "There had to be a genesis of this story if it's real. Who put out the word to the trooper stations?" Michael asked as Mary Ruth looked intently at Johnston, engaged for the first time.

Johnston had a look on his face that reminded Michael of a great blue heron he had once seen at Hilton Head. The giant bird snatched a snake from the water, and as it was positioning to swallow its prey, the snake was striking wildly at the giant bird, trying to stay alive. The heron kept its own neck just out of reach, bobbing and weaving, until suddenly—gulp, the snake was dinner.

Finally, Johnston decided that answering Michael wouldn't come back to bite him. He leaned forward and said, "It came from on high, but my friends tell me that the delivery boy was an old friend of yours, Captain Parker. The one they call Hoss—Billy Joe Estes."

Johnston smiled. "You of all people should know that there are real enemies who lurk at old service stations, on railroad trestles, and even in the dark of friends' homes. Yeah, I heard those stories."

On that sobering note, the dinner ended. Not much was said on the drive back to the office, but Michael could tell that Mary Ruth was scared.

She was very quiet and kept licking her dry lips, trying to work up some spit or some—grit.

Peter Pan didn't look much like a candidate for governor at that moment—more like a little girl from rural Georgia, in way over her head.

* * *

Early the next morning, a coral sun rose to illuminate rush hour traffic and jammed commuter lanes. Mockingbirds heralded a new day with painfully innocent melodies for a guilty world, and the commuter traffic subsided as worker bees landed at their desks. Train brakes squealed at the local yards as the brakemen switched tracks. Then a quiet stillness fell over the state parking garages.

Billy Joe Estes' hands were wet with sweat as he drove an old Chevrolet Impala onto the lower ramps of the garage attached to the Twin Towers. The car, best described as greenish-blue or sea green, trailed black smoke and smelled like thirty-weight Quaker oil. It seemed to measure efficiency not by miles per gallon but by miles per quart of oil. It was as nondescript as its occupants. The car had no visible markings and an untraceable tag that had never been issued by the state.

Riding shotgun with him was Slim Maloney, so painfully thin and emaciated that he was given the moniker "Boney Maloney."

Slim had honed his considerable mechanical skills while a guest of the Georgia Diagnostic and Classification Prison in Butts County. To hear him tell it, he had single-handedly maintained the state's fleet of cars in his ten years there until Governor Holcomb pardoned him. Holcomb had once represented Slim and was successful in getting some charges dropped. Slim was forever recommending Holcomb to everyone inside who needed a good lawyer.

Famous for mixing his metaphors, Slim told everyone that Holcomb got him a "decease and desist order," and that he was the kind of man who knew how to "grab the bull by the tail and look him in the eye."

Now here he was, assistant to Billy Joe, for whatever talents he might lend to the regime via these unsanctioned operations. Today, it was pretty basic stuff—"Operation Boll Weevil," as Billy Joe called it. He would drop off Slim in the state parking garage where Mary Ruth Robinson parked in a marked space, and some adjustments would be made to the wheels of her car. The security cameras would suddenly go blank for a few minutes; no registry of cars entering and leaving would be captured.

Tires squealed as Billy Joe hit the ramp up to the fifth-floor deck, dropping Slim near Robinson's car without coming to a complete stop. He slid out the crack of the car door as only a thin man could and moved to her car with his fully-charged power tools in hand.

Ninety-six seconds later, Hoss came back around and picked up his accomplice.

"Everything done, Slim?" Billy Joe asked as he gunned it down the ramps *clankety-clank*, scattering pigeons left and right.

"Sure, boss. You coulda knocked me over with a fender. Thing's gonna wobble now for that little boll weevil," Slim said through a toothless grin.

As they drove away, Billy Joe smiled and recited his latest poem. "Mary Ruth was a little lamb, she could've been our sheep. She wouldn't cooperate*, so now she must fall asleep."*

* * *

At 5:30 that day, Mary Ruth was driving her car out of the state garage to head home. She noticed a loud bumping and thumping as she accelerated to merge onto the I-20 ramp to Augusta. A man behind her began to blow his horn and flash his lights.

She finally pulled over to a side street, and the man, who recognized her, ran up to the car and said, "Oh, Superintendent Robinson, thank goodness you stopped before you got on I-20! Your left front wheel looked as if it was about to fall off!"

"What?" Mary Ruth asked. "What did you say?"

They walked to the front of the car as rush-hour gawkers rubbernecked. The wheel, like Mary Ruth, was barely hanging on. The lug nuts had been loosened almost to the end.

The man said, "Isn't that strange? I wonder how that could've happened."

Just as Mary Ruth grabbed her cell phone to call Michael, Billy Joe and Slim were having a burger on the other side of town.

Billy Joe told Slim, "Here's some cash for a job well done. Sign here on this voucher to cover me for the walking-around money I paid you today."

Slim hesitated and finally said, "Dang it, I can't write, Hoss."

"Well, just make your mark," Billy Joe said.

Slim made one big X and another small x beside it.

Billy Joe looked at it and asked, "What's the little x for?"

Slim said, "I'm a junior."

Slim saw the look of amusement in Billy Joe's eyes and said, "Finding me, not Daddy, was like looking for a needle in a hayride. I wanted to use that little x so I would stick out like a sore throat until I can get my curve ball straightened out."

You just can't make these things up, Billy Joe thought.

CHAPTER TWENTY-SIX

"Politics and crime—they're the same thing.
Politics is knowing when to pull the trigger."
—The Godfather III

"Only dead fish swim with the stream."
—Malcolm Muggeridge

Once upon a time in what was left of America, Michael received "the call" from Washington—one of those moments Gandhi warned of, when men with dirty feet try to walk through your mind…a moment when events might turn a man toward the shadows.

"Mr. Parker, this is Megan, conference operator at the U.S. Department of Education. I have you on the list to add to a conference call about to begin. Are you able to join now?"

"I'm sorry, but I wasn't expecting a call from Washington. Who arranged this conference?" Michael asked.

"I don't have that information, sir. Are you able to join the conference now?" the dryly efficient and almost mechanical Washington voice repeated.

"Sure, why not?" Michael said.

The call came up with a *beep* when he was added. Within the hollow echo of the link, he heard lots of empty chatter about Senator So-and-So, as well as the happy voices of Washington insider collegiality describing the party last night on K Street. It was reminiscent of the corporate conference calls at Bell that he so despised.

No good can come from this, he thought.

"Ah, so it seems everyone is here now," the voice of the moderator called. "Let's get started now that we have Mr. Parker on the line. Everyone go around the table and introduce yourselves so he will know who we represent."

Michael saw the "us versus you" agenda shaping up, and he had the uneasy feeling that he was the main course on this buffet for hatchet men.

So round the conference table they went. He could almost see them: Title 1 expert for this-and-that division, under-secretary for such-and-such, aide to Congressman Hill Billy, teacher union lobbyist, political consultant to the party, and several special counsels—one to the White House Chief of Staff's office. Michael was the only one not in the room.

He steeled himself.

"Mr. Parker, we've called to tell you that some decisions have been reached in the Department of Education and at the White House."

"Excuse me," Michael said. "I don't believe I heard the names of the people I've been dealing with—Secretary Paige and Assistant Secretary Gayle Powers."

There was a pause and the sounds of shuffling of paper and chairs squeaking.

"No," the moderator said flatly, "they won't be attending."

"What we have decided, Mr. Parker, is that the requests from Governor Holcomb and the State Board of Education will be honored, and they'll be allowed to designate federal funds for, uh, extraordinary projects in Georgia. We'll apply it under what the White House calls 'flex spending' to allow locals increased flexibility for use of federal funds. I know that's something a conservative Republican will support. You were in Reagan's campaign, weren't you?"

So it begins, Michael thought as his heart began to race. "Is that not illegal? Supplanting laws, the troublesome Constitution? Gayle certainly thought it was when she promised to prosecute anyone who diverted federal funds; she told me to stand firm," Michael interjected.

"Well, we don't know about all that, but we have decided to allow the use of the money for these projects and to defer decisions of legality and prosecution until after the fact, to some point in the future," an anonymous voice squeaked.

Yes, at some point when you are no longer in office and you have done your dirty deeds, Michael thought. He wanted to bridge the world onto this call and say, *Come, listen to who these people really are, these people you think you know.* It was brazen. It was the Constitution for lunch. He was but the minor belch in the meal. These were the "same people" the parrot described in Congress. Then the other shoe fell, one that even Michael couldn't anticipate.

"We also have decided that money will no longer come from Washington to the Georgia Department of Education. We will henceforth deliver funds directly to the Georgia State Board of Education," the moderator announced.

Michael reeled. He felt as if he had been punched in the face and then the gut. The rats that gnawed at his innards in the ICU returned with a vengeance, and the walls of the hospital ward began to close in again. He was, for once in his life, almost speechless.

"The Georgia DOE is the only legal recipient of federal funds!" he fired back in a defense that he knew was futile. "The board's not an agency; it's only a pustule of political operatives with no staff and no framework to receive or disburse money. The leopard is on the prowl and hungry, so *your* response is to cut off the horns of the gazelle?! This is not flex spending. This is criminal!"

All the façade of decorum evaporated, and the murmurs in the background indicated that the term "criminal" was just way out of bounds, objectionable in polite company.

"Our decision has been made and is final," moderator man said. "We feel that it will hold down trouble, conflict, and political bloodletting. If you have no other comment, this call is terminated."

"All of this—millions in federal funds—for an endorsement of No Child Left Behind! We're talking about a bill from a *Republican* administration that expands the top-down management of local education! There is no 'Texas Miracle,' as the White House is calling it. You can't do a one-size-fits-all bill that makes no distinction in school districts. This is going to be a disaster and result in massive cheating when you make it 'low score—out the door' for teachers and administrators," Michael declared.

In the true nature of central government, the moderator decreed, "The purpose of this call was not about determining who's right and who's wrong, and we are certainly not here to be lectured by you, Mr. Parker. It was merely a courtesy call to inform—not debate. You blundered into our world seeking answers. Sometimes there are no satisfactory answers—never have been, never will be."

It was just another soulless call by soulless bureaucrats who had been called upon to do the dirty deed for the White House. They would all go to lunch now at one of Washington's fashionable restaurants and talk of legislation or a pretty new staffer, and then have that extra drink or two or three to drown any pangs of conscience that might nag at their coreless existence, Michael thought.

Michael said, "Oh, pardon me. I understand now. You guys are kinda like a reverse Wells Fargo when they hear that there are bank robbers in town. Like good central bankers, you call the local banks and say, 'There are bandits in town. To hold down conflict and bloodshed, we've decided to have our armored cars deliver our shipments of money directly to the robbers.' After all, that's what good central bankers do, right?"

Before they could comment, Michael slammed the receiver against its cradle. He thought, *Some cultures love their neighbors. In that one, they eat them.* He deeply and soberly realized for the first time that he and Mary Ruth were alone in the fight. No cavalry would be coming.

He looked at another devotional left on his desk by the ever-vigilant Sandy. "And your ears shall hear a word behind you, saying, 'This is the way, walk in it,' when you turn to the right or when you turn to the left." (Isaiah 30:21)

But Michael wasn't listening. The Boy Scout and knight of lost causes had departed Bell when he should have stayed and dared them to try to muzzle him. He came to Atlanta to make his last stand, to slay the dragon, but this time the dragons were bigger and nastier than he could've imagined. The son of sons of Puritans had gone over the edge and was now in uncharted waters. He fished from his pocket another of the peach Xanax pills that always made the world stop moving under his feet and began to hum…*We're on the eve of destruction.*

CHAPTER TWENTY-SEVEN

"Some of them want to use you...some of them want
to abuse you... Everybody's looking for
something."—The Eurythmics

"Three can keep a secret if two are dead."
—Carlos Marcello

When Billy Joe Estes sauntered into the Capitol Club high over old Atlanta, he was so far up that the blue seemed to be kissing the vast black curtain of night.

He was awed, for he had always dreamed of this kind of opulence and privilege—from the rich wood paneling and crystal chandeliers to mauve-colored carpet so deep and plush that a Mississippi boy might just sink past his Buster Brown loafers, all the way up to his fake alligator belt. He had finally arrived at the gates of the gilded Nirvana he so richly deserved.

This is a far cry from the Dixie Mafia retreat near Memphis, he thought. *Those old boys worked hard to recover after Ace Connelly went down. They bought an old club on Shelby Drive and converted it to a ranch, where they invited unsuspecting sheriffs up to wine and dine them. I brought in working girls, and after we got a few drinks in those good ole boys, the girls would love on and make pictures with 'em. Then we'd set the deal we needed to move into their counties. We had to start over when we were rousted out of De Soto County after Michael Parker's raid. We wanted to move into Lafayette County and had the sheriff up under false pretense. Things were going well, but who shows up with him that night to queer the deal? Parker! He was like a bad penny.*

As Billy Joe extricated himself from memory, the attendant checked his name against the approved guest list and motioned him to the fourth room on the left down the hall. As he walked a tunnel of tribute to icons of business and politics, ornate oil paintings of Atlanta's power brokers peered down at him.

He passed one room and heard Sinatra singing the ode to the players of a certain generation—"flying high in April, shot down in May…when I'm back on top in June." The next room, filled with social and business climbers who had obtained a provisional membership in the club, dined to the modern beat of the Eurhythmics, "Sweet dreams are made of this. Who am I to disagree?"

When he reached the final room, he heard no music playing behind the massive door; there was only a tomb-like feel at the end of the hall of fame. He knocked, and an elderly black porter dressed in a smart white coat, black pants, and a shiny, black bowtie opened the door and bade him to enter.

"Come in, Mr. Estes. We've been expecting you," said a graying, distinguished man with a beak-like nose. He sat in an ornate chair that Ricardo Montalban might have described as "rich Corinthian leather."

You can feel it. Lots of cojones in this room, Billy Joe thought. *Probably one of them "cultural imperatives" I heard about in these places of opulence*, he reckoned. *Heck, these old boys are no different than Ace Connelly or the Mafia boys behind ole Hal Davidson back in the day. They can dress up in their pretty suits, but they're no better than the rest of us trying to scratch out a place in this world.*

Despite his silent observations, he noticed that his hands were sweaty and he suddenly had a nervous tic of the right eye. His skin seemed to crawl behind his left ear. Billy Joe was intimidated. These men gazed at him with a look of contempt that went right through him—a look of condescension that made him want to check and see if his barn door was open.

"Sit down, Mr. Estes. These gentlemen seated here with me are…well, we'll just say, Mr. Smith and Mr. Jones," he said quietly. They nodded at Billy Joe.

"We have an interest in what's best for Atlanta. We invest in her future and attempt to be a positive force for the common man and common good," he said.

"There've been delays in receiving some federal monies that the city and state need for our progressive plans. That's unfortunate. There have been some victories and people should be rewarded and encouraged to get on with it now—no more delays."

"Yes sir, I know. The White House helped us. Well, not helped us, you know, but fixed it so we could all scratch each other's backs. We tried to take care of that local problem with the patrol boys and us fixing that car, and…"

"Mr. Estes!" They cut him short.

"You weren't invited here to speak but to listen. You're not to involve us in any of your pedestrian activities. You're a tool to us, like the people on the board are tools. You're no different than all the other lazy and venal fools we deal with, who endure *National Enquirer* lives, where every week is just a perpetual cheat-your-best-friend week. You're only here because our friends say you are useful to do things they can't do themselves. As far as you and the rest of the world is concerned—we don't exist!

"Don't look so shocked. Political parties mean nothing to us," he continued. "They're all one and the same—nothing like the peasants think. The occupants of the governor's office and the White House are only temporary occupants. We go on forever. We're building the new Athens of Pericles here, the Rome of Hadrian, and the China of the Tang and Ming dynasties. There's only the aristocracy, Mr. Estes.

"Now, for the reason you were called here. In this valise are envelopes of appreciation that you're to take to the political people on this list. Many people from all walks of life are ready to help us dispense with the impediments to tomorrow." Billy Joe nodded, took the case, and turned to leave.

"One last thing, Mr. Estes. We understand you know this Parker man from your past. Is he approachable and—reasonable?"

Billy Joe laughed long and hard, forgetting himself for the first time.

"What's so amusing, Mr. Estes?" the man asked.

"Pardon me, sir. Parker thinks he's Lancelot, Elliot Ness, or maybe the Lone Ranger. Most people pretend to be whatever it is others want them to be. Not Parker. He wouldn't be too impressed with you guys—no insult intended. I think he's a fool, but fool or not, he's going to die the way he is."

"Why so fatalistic, Mr. Estes? Every man has his price," Beak Nose said.

"I don't think Parker *can* change! It's only a matter of time until someone ends it all with a convenient *accident* or another tragic Atlanta *mugging*. Maybe you folks will sic the cheap government hustlers you own on him—those who preach about the rule of law but don't practice it. He makes too many of the genteel folks on your payroll—those with their crinkly smiles, polite dialogue, and chittering women—very uneasy. Parker reminds them of the time when they still cared about the world and thought they could make a difference. They don't like being reminded."

"You sound sympathetic, Mr. Estes," the patrician said, arching his left eyebrow.

Billy Joe smiled and felt that at that moment he might have more in common with Parker than with these men, who he knew would step on him like a bug if it suited them. "No, not at all," he said, "but I understand him. We were born out of the same stew.

"Well," he sighed deeply and shrugged, "gotta go and deliver these thirty pieces of silver shekels you've given me. That was the price of a slave and the cost of betrayal, wasn't it? It didn't work out so well with the judge, though. Reminds me of the days when we were buying votes for sheriffs in Mississippi with pints of whiskey. Just a bigger pond to swim in here in Atlanta.

"Well, I'd better get going on my errands for you folks. No rest for the wicked—huh, gentlemen?"

He paused. "Oh, I forgot—you boys convinced people that you don't exist. Kinda like the devil convinced people he ain't real while he robs them of their souls, huh?"

Billy Joe opened the door and turned back again. Shrugging his shoulders, he made one final statement: "I may be wrong about him, but an associate of mine learned one night in Tupelo that Michael Parker is a hard man to kill."

CHAPTER TWENTY-EIGHT

*"The mask makes vice seem beautiful, turns squalor
and nastiness into glamorous thrill, seduces the
onlooker into the game—and leaves him…with the
corpse on his hands."—Jennifer Birkett*

*"Money can buy…police order. Justice is sold to
the highest bidder."—Rohinton Mistry*

As night fell like a gentle comforter from heaven, peregrine falcons scrunched together on the narrow ledges of pea gravel beneath the eaves of buildings across from Michael's office. He stared out his window at the purple-brown tones in the Atlanta troposphere and considered the world in which he found himself.

After the conference call from Washington, Mary Ruth's insurgents moved quickly to claim the five percent of funds that were available to her, as Gayle Powers had suggested before she was whisked away. The board thought they had crushed the opposition and were furious when they discovered that millions had been allocated to local school systems, just one step ahead of Holcomb's Herd. Threats were made. Their patron wasn't happy.

Michael also planted a trap for the Judas within. A false information item was shared in the deputies' meeting, and within hours, Sam the informant called Michael to say the word had been leaked to the governor's office.

The department's computer guru quickly found the origin of the email: Deputy Superintendent Roger Curry, who had long been suspected of divided loyalties. Mary Ruth sent Michael to Curry's office with the "vacate the premises" order.

Roger Curry had smoky-gray eyes hidden under thick gray-black brows that framed his eyes like hedgerows. He also had the same coarse hair growing out of his ears in a silver bush. Curry was a lifelong educator/administrator who had held too many sedentary jobs, and

Robinson—against all good counsel—had appointed him as one of her deputies. He had a history of betraying everyone who had ever shown him kindness. One of the superintendent's many weaknesses was poor judgment in those she chose to surround herself with. Michael realized some would include him in that crowd.

The email Curry sent to the governor's chief of staff read, "I haven't been able to ascertain how the money you wanted was sent to the school districts, but the superintendent is clearly in over her head. She has no vision, no gravitas. She isn't worthy of her position or of a man for his time, Governor Henry Holcomb. I'm flattered to be considered for the czar post and honored to be useful to the cause from inside the gates of this poorly run agency. Be assured of my loyalty and willingness to put the funds from Washington to good use in our new education department."

When Michael arrived in Curry's office, Curry was indignant and snorting.

"I don't know who's feeding you these false accusations. I've always been loyal to Mary Ruth. My leadership is vital to the department. Who's to guide her if I leave—you and her other mercenary poodle? She's nothing without me. This is outrageous. I've never been treated this way in my life. I'm a professional educator," he sputtered.

"Well, Roger, justice is a train seldom on time, but it's just pulled into the station," Michael offered. "Your secretary will gather your personal items. All the department files and computers stay—no more data leakage."

Heads turned in the department as Curry was marched unceremoniously to the front door. It was an embarrassing spectacle that would feed the gossip mill for weeks.

No sooner was he out the door than the governor's office received their spy with open arms, gave him his blood money, and announced to the world that he'd been appointed education czar in the new kingdom of Hank Holcomb.

Alone with his thoughts that night, Michael looked high above the arc of Atlanta where a billion white, yellow, and red stars twinkled and blinked. Some had burned out eons ago. Michael's own light had dimmed and then burned out in it all—the betrayals, death threats, sabotage, theft of funds for a political payoff, and politicians trampling the Constitution.

So many blind men walking in this world, he wrote in his new journal. *The self-lovers aren't actually blind, but they find no worth in people or in the beauty that falls upon their deaf ears. All the flesh-and-blood people are merely props on the stage where the self-anointed preen. In patronizing indifference, people become only things to be used or abused, the easier to do unspeakable things to with no remorse and no acknowledged consequences. These players mimic the polite, social relationships at kissy-face society events, but in their "evolution" they're little more than suit-wearing, cigar-smoking, knuckle-dragging troglodytes who are carnal and instinctual. "Me want, me take. Me want, me must have. Me—entitled."*

They'll eventually come full-circle to stand alongside their ancestors. The only difference is that they use man's law—not clubs—to lurch through life, killing and maiming in pursuit of their DNA. They may be judged less human than the progenitors of their gene pool when future archaeologists find their remains and begin to measure and compare their skulls. They speak in polysyllabic utterances of the pseudo-intellectual but are incapable of feeling the beauty of words. If they see at all in their vacuity, it's only to classify by outward appearance: Can someone be useful or mere doormats to wipe their feet on? Travelers to camp with for convenience, or prey to be bludgeoned and dragged back to their lairs?

As their arteries harden and their frail vessels weaken with age, they discover they are utterly and awfully alone. When temporal power fades away and doors close around them, they suddenly realize that the journey from womb to tomb is a very short one after all. They become Biblical in defense of the corrupt governments they created and plead, "Render unto Caesar what is Caesar's," without ever understanding that God owns everything. Finally, when the shadows lengthen, they face forever with their whimpering protest: "But I really wasn't such a bad man—was I?" The only real purpose they serve is to be an example so others will see their ugliness and be moved to take a long look at their own.

* * *

In the aftermath of Roger Curry's forced departure, intrigue lingered in every nook and cranny of the department. The superintendent was looking for a safe and dependable caretaker replacement for Curry. Michael and Walter recommended Nita Crickenberger as the new deputy. The governor's office zeroed in on her, thinking they could muscle the new kid on the block and replace the loss of their mole inside the department.

Michael's phone rang, and anxiety oozed out of Nita's squeaky voice.

"Michael, the governor's chief of staff called and wants to come over to meet me. What should I do? I don't want to meet alone with him. Will you come to the meeting so I won't be flying solo? I'm not up to facing these people," she pleaded.

"Sure," Michael said. "Let's see what they're up to."

Kip Berry, a Georgia Tech graduate who wanted to play in the big leagues, signed on to manage Governor Hank Holcomb's affairs. Not the kind to normally dirty his hands with the unseemly, Berry would handle the political while others who had no such qualms did the things that Kip and his staff put a pretty face on.

He walked into Nita's private conference room all smiles and boyish charm, hand extended. He was attired in a trendy suit that Atlanta clothiers described as tumbleweed pink-brown. His new, pearly white caps were gleaming until he saw Michael, who stood and extended his hand, saying, "I'm Michael Parker."

"Yes, I know who you are," he said in a tone a bit too revealing, but then he corrected with a quick smile and eyes like shoe-buttons that never left the target at hand.

"Well, I wanted to come over, meet you, wish you well, and tell you that we want to help you in any way we can," he told Nita. "Roger Curry speaks highly of you."

Berry had the look of an indifferent player, one never fazed by anything. Glibness masking flintiness, he was the ultimate charmer at cocktail parties—the bright young man who all agreed would go far. It was easy to imagine the same fatuous smile affixed to his face no matter what news was delivered to him—your stock fell today; protests are expected at the Capitol; or the world just ended. "No matter," the look would imply, "it can be fixed."

He had the degrees, the tool and tech of a new generation. He had the breeding, the pedigree, and the ability to frame anything—however disgusting and wrong—into a politically and commercially viable, glib acceptability. He was the kind of compulsive liar who bent the truth about everything that the Hank Holcombs of the world could use.

It was an awkward game of cat-and-mouse, and the cat didn't feel comfortable playing with the mouse while Michael was present. Berry saw it was the wrong time and the wrong place, and after some perfunctory mewling chatter, he decided to retreat to his litter box in the governor's office.

"Well, it's certainly been a pleasure," he said as he rose. "Let's stay in touch."

"That'll be fine," Michael said, "as long as your friends stay out of the piggy bank and out of state parking garages."

Berry showed a flicker of anger or amusement. He turned at the door and, in a rare moment of candor, said, "You know, Mr. Parker, you act as if we are lepers, gangsters...or Communists. We're just living the American dream like you. You need to learn to loosen up. You're wound so tight, you're going to break one day, and it won't be a pretty sight."

"Communists?" Michael asked. "No, you're not Communists. They actually believe in something, however wrong it may be."

Berry studied him with a stony gaze, as passively as a man about to squash a bug, and said, "There are no absolutes, Mr. Parker, but we have values, too."

"Do you really believe that?" Michael asked.

"Absolutely," Berry said, before he realized he had been suckered. He turned a shade of appropriate imperial red, and almost swallowed his Adam's apple.

Michael smiled. "The Dixie Mafia had values. Governor Hal Davidson had values. You have values. But virtue? Now *that's* another question. Do you bring the king his scepter each day? Everything's just situational, isn't it?"

Berry only nodded and walked out the door. Nita sighed.

Her hands were trembling. She fumbled for a cigarette, forgetting that it was a no-smoking area. "Whew! Glad that's over. What do you think they'll do now?" she asked.

Michael was far away on the island of memory, after the raid on Ace Connelly's club, his hunt for Fredrick, and his challenge to Governor Davidson.

He finally said—"Come after us."

CHAPTER TWENTY-NINE

"...there are people who have never been defeated.
They...never fought."—Paulo Coelho,
manuscript found in Accra

"I...felt the torrent come; to rise I had no will,
to flee I had no strength."—Charlotte Bronte, Jane Eyre

Michael felt vulnerable and exposed—the butterfly from its cocoon, the hermit crab that lost its shell. His world had become fractionated and sanded down by the sharp edges of life. He remembered the talks with Pearl and wished he could speak with her once more. He longed to find that unconditional love again in those private moments where the beacon of truth always seemed to find and warm his heart.

"Do the right thing. Always do the right thing, son," she told him.

"How do I know what the right thing is, Grandma?" he asked her.

"You'll know, Michael," she said. "The hard thing to do is the right thing."

The memory of Pearl pinched his heart and made him yearn for simpler times. Back then, there were none of these gray traps that now seemed to lie in wait for him around every corner of this artificial world. Lines in the sand seemed blown away by the wind. The differences between friend and foe narrowed and then vanished, as portable fences separating good and evil shifted to counter opponents.

The board reacted to the millions they lost with all the volume and venom of an unruly child in full tantrum. U.S. Education informed the board that there was nothing they could do. The superintendent had the authority to claim five percent previously issued for overhead and management. The White House praised Governor Holcomb for his endorsement of No Child Left Behind and his spirit of bipartisanship.

Mary Ruth, the highest ranking Republican in Georgia, wasn't invited to a presidential appearance in Atlanta. Only by crashing the party did she get a picture at the event. It was a sad, almost tragically comic image of her standing beneath the President's table to capture a picture for her campaign. All on the mount of power pointedly ignored her, amused at this beggar seeking crumbs from the nobles.

Georgia DOE employees were called to testify on who sent money where, and why this hadn't come before the board. It was a display of bloodletting not seen since the days when doctors used leeches to bleed patients. Board members began to turn on each other, and the chairman was unceremoniously dismissed by the governor. No one mourned him, even as he gave political cover to the governor, claiming he needed more time with family. No one honored him in his hour of despair. No kind words were spoken except those offered by his adversary, Michael, in a private gesture.

It may have been only a Pyrrhic victory scored by the department, spending the funds before the board could divert them to Holcomb, but it was an unforgivable sin. The chairman's successor scrambled to assume his position. While she was awash with crocodile tears before the cameras, she was all giggles and high-fives in the back rooms with her supporters, who had helped backstab the former chairman. They were as gleeful as Roman senators wielding daggers for Julius Caesar.

Threats and ultimatums were issued, and Holcomb allies in the press began to attack Michael for the first time. Former BellSouth executives, who were fond of Michael but didn't share his politics, asked him to dinner, ostensibly to catch up on old times. Michael waited patiently over dinner for the other shoe to drop—usually over dessert.

The earnest corporate citizens leaned over the key lime pie and asked, "Michael, what're you doing in that mess down there? You've had your adventure. You've got a good reputation. People like you. You need to get out before something unfortunate happens—before your name is irreparably harmed, or you're ruined. You're a smart guy, but you aren't acting smart. We can recommend you for a job if that's what this is all about."

Deep down, he knew that they were right, but the more they jawboned and counselled, the harder he dug in. The obsessive-compulsiveness his doctor had diagnosed had begun to cloud his judgment. *They must not win*, he thought. *They mustn't, no matter what.*

* * *

Michael and Walter celebrated the routing of the federal funds to local schools and bamboozling the board. They enjoyed some laughs with the superintendent, but they knew it would be short-lived. The day was bearing down when the Alamo would be out of bullets, out of any good options, and as far as the eye could see, only Santa Anna and his army.

As the days of melancholy wore on and the superintendent hit the campaign trail, Michael filled in for her at foreign embassy parties and university dinners. Late one evening, Mary Ruth called him to her office.

"Michael, I need you at the campaign. We have no money, and no one knows what to do," she said with resignation and a bit of feigned helplessness. Many already thought she was too dependent on Michael and couldn't find her way to the ladies' room without consulting him. Some who'd waited since day one for him to fall called him the "Guard Dog," and that was one of their nicer names for him.

"I don't know, Mary Ruth. How would that work?" he asked.

"We have a campaign manager, but you would be chairman and run the show. You can return to your post after the campaign. If we win, you can go to the governor's office as chief of staff. If we lose, we all go home. You get to work longer hours, be gone more from home, and not get paid a dime for it," she laughed.

Michael knew that he was no miracle worker and doubted that anyone could make her bankrupt campaign take off, any more than a plane could fly without fuel. Nevertheless, he agreed and knew almost immediately that it was the wrong decision, one that Pearl would have cautioned him against. As he walked away, he took a long look at his reflection in the mirrored framing above the elevator doors.

He was emotionally overextended. The pills prescribed for panic attacks were now a crutch. Susan's health had taken a serious turn for the worse. Life had gone on without him at BellSouth, as it had at the Mississippi Bureau of Narcotics. Corruption was still a problem—here, there, and everywhere. The woman he'd risked everything to elect in Augusta was now cozying up to the very people who had threatened him and all the others who had staked their lives and careers for her. She had become a sophisticated player. Her seducers, those who had attacked Dr.

Randy Patra, told her to keep her distance from Michael's old-fashioned intransigence and hard-headedness. "You're a player now," they told her. She believed them.

What's it all about then, Alfie? he thought. *Is it just for the moment we live?*

Sam the informant called on a bad connection, his voice like sandpaper on a dry board. "Michael, it looks hopeless. What're you doing? Get out while you can."

Michael said, "I know with every fiber in my body this is a fight that I should walk away from, but it's like a scene of horror that transfixes people—car wrecks that gawkers must slow to see, or voyeurs mesmerized at the scene of a suicide even while bemoaning the tragedy. I can hear the train coming, growing louder and picking up speed, rushing toward the moment when I realize I can no longer control my destiny. In that instant, the questions of why decisions were made will be beyond my control. That will lie in the province of others who'll be merciless in reducing life to the basest and crassest of motivations. Still, I can't seem to look away."

"So you're going to wait and let the gravediggers and vultures pick your bones, clean the carrion, and relegate all of the right and wrongs of life to mere footnotes—if they mention them at all! There'll be no one left to mourn you as they tamp down the fresh earth around you. The very scoundrels who plant you in the field will be the emotional paupers who ran with the pack, and they will write your history. If you know that and don't walk away, then that is part of the bargain you make. No amount of what-ifs and pitiful postmortems will change one iota of the consequences for you," Sam said.

* * *

Michael rode the elevators up to the top floor of the department to a service elevator that took him to the roof. A melancholy slice of cheese hung over Atlanta's night air—a strange mix of pollutants, auto exhausts, the rancid odor of broken dreams, and whispers of a million complaints from the masses. The giant night bugs seemed to be mutants birthed by city pollution, like the legendary sewer gators of New York City.

He could hear snippets from a hundred banal and repetitive songs—seven-eleven tunes, seven words repeated eleven times. The punchlines of television jingles, the *ding-ding-ding* of *Pac Man* and *Space War* commandos at the arcade, and the blare of discos near Underground Atlanta bombarded his ears.

He stared down at what seemed an orchard full of decaying trees and apples rotten to the core—presided over by the Holcomb interregnum government, which seemed poised to await the final collapse. He felt he was only a hiccup in a bad dream and had the impulse to wash his hands of the bad news this world seemed to deliver every day.

Mary Ruth had been coming to see him in his office with some regularity. He sensed that she had been slowly and carefully diminishing his personal space, the private emotional and physical separation that seeks to avoid uncomfortable closeness—the breath on the nose or the crowding of the cushion guarding secret thoughts.

The distance had narrowed between them as she deftly advanced via the bridge of his hero complex, his need to rescue. It was becoming an uneasy intimacy. It was not physical but it *was* an unhealthy co-dependency between two people isolated by the players in the land of Oz. They were looking for solace, for affirmation that they were still on the right side—the good and green valley side of the walls—before they were forced to leave the citadel waving the white flag of surrender.

As the knight errant walked toward the roof door to leave, he heard the refrains of CCR drift up to the roof from below. "I hear hurricanes a-blowing. I know the end is coming soon. I fear rivers overflowing. I hear the voice of rage and ruin. Don't go round tonight, it's bound to take your life. There's a bad moon on the rise."

* * *

Senator Horace Kent, the leader of the Republican Party in the state senate, responded to a poll that showed Mary Ruth within striking distance of Governor Holcomb. "That's not *her* strength," he said with venom in his voice, "but *his* weakness."

The party recruited a lifelong Democrat to run against the only Republican woman in the state. The Democrats protested publically, while privately calling to see how to expedite the ongoing raid on the U.S.

Treasury and exhorting a media on the make for fresh scoops and free meals to attack her for campaigning and missing board meetings.

Then came a call from Jasper Hart, the nasal-voiced chief of staff for a Georgia congressman. Jasper had small, skeptical eyes in a big face of perpetual, slow-burning anger framed by a short, second-lieutenant military haircut.

"Hello, Michael. How're things in the big city?" he asked with a false buoyancy that he was adept at turning on and off at will.

"Interesting, Jasper, but it could be better if you and your boss would help—actually help—raise some money for Mary Ruth and stop telling her long-time donors to close their checkbooks to her," Michael replied.

"Now, you know that's pitiful rumor and idle political gossip. We're prepared to give her all the money she needs if she'll give up this run for governor and run for re-election. Why, we love her! Please tell her that. We want her to be a school teacher as long as she wants to be…for life if that suits her. It's really the best thing. You know, and I know—she can't win," he said.

"Why are y'all so worried then?" Michael asked.

Jasper lost his cool, dropped all niceties, and barked, "She's an embarrassment, that's why! She says things that hurt the party and hurt the cause. You never know what's going to come out of her ignorant trap when she opens it. She has no respect for the accepted way. She doesn't pay homage to our elders. She hasn't paid her dues. She needs to peel off those false eyelashes, read something deeper than *Vogue*, and get in line. Then *maybe* she could be anointed one day."

He paused, sighed deeply, and recovered.

"You know, Michael, some of us were talking about you. You've got a lot of power. You're the number two guy there, all that power—and you didn't even have to run. You've got the business acumen she doesn't. Everyone knows she has a drug problem, and there are rumors of… indiscretions. You should be superintendent."

"What?!" Michael exclaimed.

"Hear me out. You've got influence. She trusts you. We arrange an intervention of her friends, people in the party, and some long-time donors we've been working on. We ease her out with an early retirement. There'd have to be a special election, but we could reach across the aisle on this one and ask Holcomb to slow the call for the election with you as interim superintendent and no serious Democratic opposition to you.

"Just agree to help us, and we'll see that no Republican files to run. Bingo! You are superintendent over all that money with no real campaigning. Think about all those people who did you wrong at BellSouth, that weasel Ricky Garcia, and those low-rent journalists who came against you. They'd all have to come crawling to you then. Archie Bunker was right, Michael: Revenge is the best way to get even. We'll help you," he said.

He paused again in what writers would have painted as a dusky, back-of-the-cave silence—one hiding the burning red eyes of something that wants to devour your soul.

"All you have to do is give Holcomb the money he wants. He'll be happy. The White House will be happy, and you'll be in the catbird seat to do all those things you used to write about in your corporate op-ed pieces...for as long as you want. You don't have to hang out with the trailer-park Republicans anymore. Come in from the cold, Michael. For once in your life, warm your feet by our fires," he said with all the affection of his House mentors, the ones who had sired him and a thousand others.

Michael didn't think he could despise them any more than he did, but suddenly there it was: anger growing into rage by the moment. He wanted to hurt this weasel, but even more so the system and his handlers, who cheapened everything in life.

"Jasper, that's a mouthful there. By the way, I thought about you when we flew into D.C. recently," Michael said.

"Oh yeah? Why?" Jasper asked.

"Some of your friends were alarmed. They thought they saw vultures mating with snakes, but I told them not to worry, that's just how chiefs of staff are birthed."

Michael smiled and hung up as the obscenities began to fly.

CHAPTER THIRTY

"I pushed my soul in a deep, dark hole, then I
followed it in. I watched myself crawling out as I
was crawling in. I saw so much, I broke my mind. I
just dropped in to see what condition my
condition was in…"—Mickey Newbury

"Never simplify what is complicated or complicate what is
simple…respect strength, never power…never look away.
And never, never to forget."—Arundhadti Roy

Susan greeted Michael at the door to their condo in Atlanta, her eyes like wet chocolate floating on pools of salty sadness. Her lower lip quivered, and deep worry lines creased the bridge of her delicate nose. It had only been a week since she had suddenly fallen ill when they were shopping for groceries in Atlanta.

After years of dealing with her illness, Michael knew what to do in such moments: the sudden insulin reactions; cooling her fevered body as she teetered at the edge of a coma; finding her unconscious from unexplainable maladies; midnight awakenings to grab receptacles as nausea overwhelmed her; and long recoveries from surgeries in Augusta's University Hospital. Again and again, she left the temporal world only to return from the long tunnel and white light of peace—of no more pain.

At the grocery, Michael told them that an ambulance wouldn't be necessary. At Susan's insistence, he secured a cart to get her out to the parking lot and their car, where she whispered, "I'll be all right. Just get me home, Michael."

Susan's health was erratic, and recovery from each episode grew more sluggish. The once tried-and-true remedies were no longer reliable. She longed to leave the oblique world of Atlanta and return to the quiet gardens Michael had tended for her when the plastic arteries in her legs made it impossible to bend her knees. But Michael was caught up in the grips of obsession and a worldly battle that had come to mean too much—

a conflict consuming and blinding him. So he told her, "Soon. We'll go home soon."

Today her eyes were red and swollen, and her mascara was streaked down her cheeks, but she wasn't physically ill. She was heartsick and bearing some burden she wanted to spare him but knew she couldn't.

"It's Mr. Collins. He's gone," she said. Her lower lip trembled, and she seemed to want to recapture each word she had spoken and withdraw it.

This news would have been devastating on any day, but in this season of sorrow, it was almost unbearable. They hugged, cried, and rocked back and forth in their grief. The dam of emotion Michael had been holding together by sheer force of will began to visibly crumble in the small condominium.

He knew that John Edward Collins, the founder and first director of the Mississippi Bureau of Narcotics, had been sick for a while. They had talked several times. Some of the talks with him had been reminiscent of the conversations and cautions from Marlon Brando to Al Pacino as the old Don was nearing the end in *The Godfather*. Much like Brando's character, Collins warned him to watch for this betrayer and that black-hearted enemy behind quick-and-easy smiles. Mr. Collins would have objected to the analogy. He had refused to see *The Godfather,* a movie he felt had romanticized the Mafia.

"Michael," Susan said, "they tried to reach us with the arrangements for the funeral but they didn't have our number here in Atlanta. In the note with this package, they say that the funeral procession was like a long train of blue, all flashing lights and people pulling over in respect, up and down Interstate 55 in Jackson. There's a letter inside this envelope. The note says Mr. Collins wanted you to have it."

Michael took the brown mailer and walked out on the lanai overlooking Atlanta. He carefully opened the package, and there was the unmistakable handwriting of the man who had sent him many cryptic communiqués—the man he respected, feared, and loved like a father. As he read the letter, he could hear the graveled voice of authority.

Dear Michael,

If you're reading this letter, it can only mean that I have left this ole temporary world. I've been hearing the conductor calling "All aboard" for some time now. Don't weep for me, boy. I was tired, real tired of it all. I had some things that I wanted to say to you and a few others. Clay's gone, but we had a talk before he left us. I can't wait to see him on the other side.

All those years ago when you walked into Bureau headquarters to apply to be an agent, I thought you were impudent, naïve, impatient, a world-shaker in the making—everything I was looking for. I told you and Clay once that you boys had true grit. I knew you would go to the gates of Hell to do the right thing. We had some good boys, but they were weak. They said the right things, what they thought I wanted to hear, but they were "deader than a beaver hat," as the Duke said. Some of them wound up doing some bad things in the end, the same ones I hired, trained, and gave a chance and then a second chance. They sold out to those who wanted us to be just as corrupt as everyone else. That's why I made sure you and Clay were made captains before I left. It wasn't much maybe, but I knew you boys would do your best to hold the line if I gave you a little help.

I was in law enforcement through some turbulent times in Mississippi. I was asked to do some bad things for political leaders, and tried as best as I could to avoid doing them, or at least to mitigate the consequences. I so wanted to build the agency to be something better and unique, to protect you from what I had to deal with. In the end I guess some would say they won, but they don't know the whole story, do they? Once, when Davidson and his goons were all around and about to force me out, I told you that I wondered if we were merely enforcers for the status quo, used for evil purposes we couldn't see. I know that hurt you and you didn't understand then, but from all I've heard and all you've told me, I think maybe you understand now.

I have never been one for this sentimental stuff, and that's not to my credit, but I wanted to set some of it right in these letters. I hope this note found its way to you, and that it found you holding firm. Be careful, Michael. Protect yourself. You stumbled into so many situations at the MBN where you could've been killed. Someone was watching out for you. If I get to meet Him, I'll ask Him to keep on watching over you.

I appreciate the sequel to Lonesome Dove *that you sent me to watch when I was so sick. I appreciate so many things—son.*

John Edward Collins

Michael sat there alone for what seemed like forever amidst the sounds of the city. Music wafted up from the lobby far below, where residents employed by the Atlanta Symphony practiced on pianos and wind instruments. Beneath their apartment, he heard the summons of an elderly man for the giant, male companion who cared for him. Flying in the breeze across the way were unmentionable dance outfits drying on the balcony of exotic dancers who performed at the club with the green door. All were residents in this eclectic mix of wayfarers.

He looked up and pondered the miracle and mystery of it all—this blue sphere that hung precariously in the far corner of a universe that scientists said was ever-expanding.

Why did this island in the galaxy survive and not spin off into oblivion in the constant expansions of the murky Milky Way? Why did it not move closer to the sun and burn to a crisp or move in the opposite direction and turn into a ball of ice, ending this divine experiment that began in the Garden? Scientists say we only have four billion years left before we collide with Andromeda, he thought. *Maybe we'll get it right by then. There must be something redeemable in it all. Else the day would be upon us when the Great Doorkeeper arrives with his big ring full of keys a-jangling to announce—"The party's over! It's closing time!"*

He stared at nothing and everything. He waited for the revelation that never came. Then he heard a soft and sweet humming from the next-door neighbor's balcony. It jarred him from his grief and introspection. A small girl with brown, braided hair, maybe five or six years old, sat on the edge of her wicker chair in a cotton print dress, swinging her legs and singing in a quiet whisper. He leaned forward. "Hi, honey. That sure sounds pretty. What's that you're singing?"

She looked at him, the full embodiment of the innocence he longed for, and said through massive eyes as blue as the firmaments—"He's got the whole world in His hands."

Michael dropped his head into his hands and began to sob.

CHAPTER THIRTY-ONE

*"The slightest carelessness can rot a man's
integrity....What we call character is held together
by all sorts of tacks and strings and glue."*
—*Willa Cather,* Consequences

*"There's no medicine that can manage the pain of
keeping lies."—R.M. Ford*

Michael walked to the Twin Towers from the Capitol. A hard rain had water-logged the city. A low-lying side street was temporarily lake-like. On impulse, he bent over and picked up a flat piece of slag, grasped the edges with his thumb and forefinger, and skipped the stone across the new pond, just like old times.

One...two...three skips, and concentric circles wrinkled the water! It would have once garnered bragging rights with friends in Parker Grove, but a car splashed through the puddles, spoiling the imagery and reminding him that there were still gauntlets to run in the land of perfidy. Deceit and betrayal seemed to be the only absolutes in this disjointed world.

Michael hurried to his office and caught the ringing phone on the fourth ring.

"Hello, Michael," said the familiar baritone voice of Dr. Todd Hartin in Augusta, friend and dispenser of advice and medication to help Michael with his panic attacks. There wasn't much Michael had kept from the man with the Freudian gray-brown beard in their talks.

"Hey, Doc, it's great to hear from you. Is this a social call or professional?" Michael asked.

"You're never home anymore. I guess telephone sessions are all we have left," he said.

"It would seem so," Michael answered.

"How are you?" he asked. "Are your prescriptions holding out?"

"It won't be long before I need new scripts, taking more as the stress ratchets up. It's been intense lately," Michael admitted.

"You're not taking too many, are you? That can be a problem," the doctor said.

"I don't know. How much is too much in a world where you feel like the proverbial duck in the barrel in a shooting gallery?" Michael asked.

"I've been hearing some things, Michael. Things that I felt I needed to talk to you about," Hartin said.

"Oh? Like what?" Michael asked.

"Risks you're taking, things that don't sound like you," Hartin ventured.

Michael hesitated and said, "Things are far worse here than I ever imagined, Doc. Enemies are all around and they don't fight by Marquess of Queensbury rules."

"Michael, I want you to listen to me for a moment, pretend we're just talking in my office in Augusta. You're a fixer. You've been one since you were a kid trying to protect your mother and grandmother from unpleasant things in your family. You come by it naturally. I've watched you when you encounter an obstacle. You bang your head against it until you're bloody, trying to break through. If that doesn't work, you tunnel under, go around or crawl over it, but you won't be denied, particularly if you think you are pursuing a just cause. I'm afraid your obsessive compulsiveness is driving you to fix things that can't be fixed," he said.

"But, I don't—" Michael tried to say.

"No, let me talk. You're what we call a 'white knight.' They're drawn to troubled women who need a champion. The women may be genuinely in distress, emotionally handicapped, or victims of abuse or addiction. The knights see them and want to rescue them from themselves, but wind up lost in their sickness. They're usually very smart guys who, because of their romanticized view of women and the rightness of the cause, cast caution to the wind.

"The knight is an easy mark for the false drama of the tortured woman who can be very manipulative. She may play him for money, extraordinary requests, ask him to take great risks, and then convince him that it was all his idea in the end.

"The more he does, the more she demands while telling him that she is helpless and fearful and couldn't make it without him. He is pulled in until there's nothing left of him. Her demands increase until she wants him on call day and night. He'll make excuses for her and tell his friends that she was abused, doesn't deserve her fate, and it's his duty to help her. He surrenders his personal life eventually and though he'll deny it, he has nothing left for the ones who really need him. Finally, he wants out, but it's too late. He doesn't know how to get out and feels if he stays a bit longer, she might make it.

"That kind of woman is an emotional vampire, a user and abuser who learned it the hard way and is passing it on. She may actually hate her chivalrous and gallant rescuer but tells him evil will consume her if he goes away. She counts on his sense of responsibility and uses guilt to keep him her emotional slave."

The doctor sighed and paused to catch his breath.

"Don't become one of those poor slobs who try to fix the unfixable. Pack up and bring Susan home now."

Michael was stunned. It was a body blow by someone he respected, but all he said was, "Thanks, Doc. I miss our talks. See you the next time I come home."

* * *

The city that Michael had come to conquer refused to yield. Modern Atlanta was as far removed from the Atlanta of *Gone With the Wind* as the frozen moons of Saturn were from the warming and life-giving rays of the sun.

Some said that the current incarnation was just a natural extension of Scarlett's vow to never go hungry again—at any cost. If the chivalry Michael longed for in his idealism ever existed, it wasn't to be found in the new South. Dueling and pugilism had been replaced by the blood sport of socially and politically annihilating adversaries or using the institutions of government to terrorize or criminalize those who got in the way.

The inhabitants celebrated their maturation from physical violence to a civilized society, but they were ruthless and relentless in a savagery that held no modicum of respect for opponents. Their lack of honor would have startled Southerners of old. They sacrificed their pawns in gambits to further their "chess game" and confuse adversaries, evidenced by the "man overboard" status of the former Board of Education chairman.

If Michael was the knight come to capture the king, what would be his next move? "He can move two squares at once and even two directions at once. But he can't move twice," said Faulkner's Gavin Stevens. So the commander of absolutes found himself in a bifurcated world with one move left and no acceptable retreat.

To complicate it all, Mary Ruth developed a serious problem with narcolepsy. Her condition seemed to grow worse by the day. Some whisperers saw her nodding at public events and attributed it to drugs. In the middle of speeches and school visits, she began to fall asleep. During a visit to a local school, she was supposed to read to children. Instead, she became incoherent in front of them. The hall was filled with teachers who had admired her, but they now wore a look of disbelief and disenchantment as she staggered to the car, supported by her faithful but conflicted deputy.

The narcolepsy, as well as a growing dependence on OxyContin for back problems and a propensity for doctor shopping when prescriptions ran short—such was the stuff her political enemies used to further undermine her. All concerned parties should have known it was time to flash the house lights and announce, "Everyone go home to Augusta." Instead, Michael dug in to rescue the damsel in distress, who now appeared anemic and bore a ghostly pale countenance. He took leave and became chairman to try to steer the *Titanic* to shore.

Kevin Carney, Mary Ruth's campaign manager, was paid on commission for donors recruited. Carney, whose fricative voice was as pleasant as fingernails on a chalkboard, had a simple approach to fundraising: "You can't have a skyscraper destiny on a chicken-coop foundation," he was fond of saying.

Carney was finding doors closed to him, like they were to Robinson in general. It wasn't the cup of tea that he envisioned. He always wanted money to tide him over, knowing full well there was none. The campaign coffers were empty.

He met with Mary Ruth and Michael at the end of a long day, when gold and red colored the earth's ever-changing palette. He came to tell them that a businessman wanted to support Mary Ruth, but he wanted an audience with her to pitch his business products for official blessing.

Carney leaned back in his chair, locked his fingers behind his head, and crossed his ankles. "I think he'll make donations. He has been shut out for not paying off the good ole boys," Carney said through flinty eyes under heavy brows.

"It could be big—really big," he said, flicking the ashes from one of the cigarettes that seemed to dangle perpetually from the chain-smoker's lower lip.

"Well, I think we'll meet and see what the vendor offers," Mary Ruth said. "I don't think it could hurt. What do you think, Michael?"

She looked at him, hushed and waiting, as if time had halted between her breaths and the world had called "time out" to hear his reply. Her hazel eyes were suffused with a wet glow of anticipation, and the fluorescence of the room caught the golden flecks in them. There were no sounds anywhere in the room, the building, or the busy city that Michael could hear. All paused to await his response.

"Is there any *quid pro quo* expected?" Michael asked.

"What's that?" Carney asked a bit too innocently.

"A tit-for-tat arrangement, where he does something for us, expecting us to do something for him. It's Latin, meaning 'something for something.' It's key to the Hobbs Act, which makes it illegal to extort property under color of office. We can't trade campaign contributions for promises of official actions or inactions by Mary Ruth," Michael said.

"Hey, we're the good guys here!" Carney said.

"You don't have to tell me that, but convincing a prosecutor of the relevance of that statement in the world they live in is quite another matter. I'm just saying that's the test: the moment it crosses over into something that's illegal under Hobbs," Michael said.

Mary Ruth jumped in. "We're looking for more avenues to keep federal money away from the governor. We won't do any of that *quid pro quo* stuff. If they have good products, we'll look at them. If they earn contracts with the department, that's just more friends to help us keep money from the governor," she interjected in a wide-eyed imitation of little-girl innocence, as if she believed it with all her heart.

"I guess it won't hurt to see what product they have. But no matter how much we want to fight the board and Holcomb and divert money from them, there must be *no* promises that we will do anything that is not merited by the vendor's products. The ends *cannot* justify the means," Michael said weakly, as Mary Ruth watched him intently. He realized for the first time that she seemed to be aware of him in a way that was unsettling.

The cracks in Michael's armor were widening. He knew this kind of trade-off was done all the time in government contracts, but they were amateurs who didn't know how to navigate treacherous waters. It was that first step out on the thin ice of a winter pond, the tentative one foot after the next, even as you feel the sickening crack-crack and watch transfixed as the spider-like seams appear, running here and there beneath you.

A voice had begun to whisper to him that those moral absolutes had outlived their usefulness. All that was left, it said, was to rise above these impediments that put him—that put right and the armies of good—at a disadvantage. He was ceasing to say "I shouldn't" and beginning to embrace "I want." By conquering the enemy, he was, at the moment of his own consummation, conquering himself. The whole bank of ideas that were sacred, firmly in the "no" category, had been moved to the "maybe" column.

He had taken the first step on the path of the temporal world, where the floodgates of the fatalistic here-and-now proclaim, "Let us eat and drink, for tomorrow we die."

CHAPTER THIRTY-TWO

*"Hear that whistle...don't go ridin'...That devil's
drivin' that long, black train."—Josh Turner*

"...you will never conquer her fear of the devil."
—Pierre Choderlos de Laclos, Les Liaisons Dangereuses

Ring, ring, ring...

On a Saturday afternoon, Michael was napping and dream-walking in the woods near Louisville, Mississippi. As the phone rang in his condo, Captain Parker was once again searching for an MBN agent who had gone missing. Benny Jones had missed his required check-in at headquarters, and his parents called to say that they feared the worst.

Some suspected foul play, and others worried because Benny had been depressed of late. He'd finished an assignment on the Gulf Coast and decided to take some time off. A motorist reported seeing his car in a remote area of pines and thickets near his mother's Winston County home, but he never showed up.

Michael walked the dusty gravel roads in the rural area where Jones was last seen. He found tire tracks in the soft, red sand. They seemed to go across a shallow ditch and into a wooded area shielded by a dense growth of cane. Some of it was broken, and Michael walked deeper into the forest as the sun began to set. Following the broken undergrowth, he eventually came into an opening, and there sat the agent's car.

Michael proceeded cautiously toward the car and found it empty but stocked with all of Jones's personal items. He surveyed the thickets around him and saw what appeared to be a recent disturbance of cane and briars near an old cottonwood tree. As he moved through the undergrowth, he smelled Benny before he found him in the clearing.

Benny was lying on his back, eyes fixed in the forever death stare, and the dried, black blood staining his white Polo shirt. The flies swarmed around him, and his service revolver lay nearby. The cylinder contained one spent round, probably the one that had blown the gaping hole in

Benny's chest. It seemed a wound that might have caused a lingering death.

The director appeared, urging Michael to "come with us to the autopsy in Houston tonight." Michael told him he just couldn't bear it, as he shooed the buzzing flies away. Some animals had been at Benny, and it was not a pretty sight. Michael felt nauseous from the smell; it sickened him to see this vital young man whose days had run out long before they should have.

He bent over the body of the young agent and whispered—"Why?" In his dream, Benny's eyes popped open, worms crawled out of hollow eye sockets in a skull of death, and snakes slithered from rotted lips that whispered, "You're next, Michael Parker!"

Michael recoiled from the dream horror as a distant irritant tried to extricate him from his prolific vending machine of nightmares.

Ring, ring, ring...

"Hello," Michael said, awake, sweating and heart pounding.

"Michael, can you meet me in my office? I need to talk with you before we meet with the vendor," Mary Ruth Robinson asked. She sounded out of breath and on the edge of disaster when Michael answered his cell phone.

"Sure, I'm on my way," he said, shaking the cobwebs of the dreams from his mind.

As Michael drove downtown, a strange churning began to sweep across Atlanta. The world looked strange and out of focus, as if a curtain had been drawn. Ominous shadings caressed the skyscrapers, and he felt a tug from something beyond the moment—something lost but familiar. Within the swirling images that formed and dissipated in the rolling thunderheads, there seemed an awareness of mortality, danger, and the fragility of life—encrypted messages rated "E" for eternal.

When Michael arrived at Mary Ruth's office in the Department of Education, her door was closed and locked. He knocked, and the door creaked as it slowly opened. There was no one visible. The shaded room smelled of incense, and the flicker of candles around Mary Ruth's desk seemed to scream at him—"Run!"

Mary Ruth was plastered against the back of the door, foggy-eyed, pale and haunted. Her speech seemed slurred, and he thought she must be hitting the OxyContin again. She glanced quickly around the edge of the door and slammed it shut behind him.

He thought she suddenly seemed older than her years. Her meticulous grooming was nowhere evident at this bizarre moment and place. She had been crying, and just for an instant—before she masked it—he saw ugliness behind her tears. Years of an acquired hardness from pain and abuse revealed a fleeting glimpse of the abrasion on her soul. She was drooling, and her lower lip was reddened and swollen, as if she had been gnawing on it.

"What's wrong, Mary Ruth?!" he asked, alarmed at her countenance.

The staleness in the room seemed to rob his lungs of air, and the drapes were tightly drawn across her picture-window view of the city, creating a tomb-like sepulcher where nothing existed but the here and now. Her legs appeared wobbly, and her hair was tangled. She began to recite a rambling and unfocused tale from the crypts of her heart. It was a tale of a life spoiled and stolen—the night in the woods so long ago, the incantations, playing poker with the devil for the highest stakes possible, and horrid tales of abuse by those closest to her.

Listening to her, he remembered picking her up for speaking engagements and seeing the telltale signs—extra heavy-duty makeup to cover what appeared to be black eyes, and long sleeves to cover the bruises—imprints of fingers on arms that had been violently seized. She embodied the libertine dream gone terribly wrong for restless, anonymous people—perpetual adolescents who had bartered away innocence to assuage their boredom.

Transfixed by this almost-unrecognizable imitation of the woman he had come to admire, she suddenly seemed a sad and shocking figure. The more she recited from her catalogue of remorse, the more her presence repelled him—even as it attracted the rescuing knight within him. She seemed pathetically vulnerable…and incredibly dangerous.

She waxed from virgin to vulgarian in a breathless quatrain, detailing nightly vigils with candles around her bed to protect her from the approach of demonic assaults. It seemed as real as anything in the physical world to her.

All the signs of her unraveling were there in the most fastidious person he had ever known…the bitten nails, the stains on her blouse, the smeared makeup, and her soiled neck. He was inside her perimeter of illusion. What he was witnessing was rapidly erasing all previous images, yielding to schizophrenia or true demonic possession.

"I've reached my end. I know this is too much to ask, but I don't know what else to do. The voices have grown so intense. The deeper we get into these battles at the department and the campaign, the louder they become. Will you read from this book for me? I got it from the fortune teller I've been seeing. Let's see if we can purge these voices. Will you try this exorcism for me?"

Exorcism?! he thought. *This is the stuff of Linda Blair in Hollywood movies. What am I doing here? Who do I think I am, some kind of rent-a-hero?* He knew that he was in over his head, but he could not bring himself to leave this tortured soul in her misery.

He nodded and whispered, "Okay, Mary Ruth. We'll try."

She pointed him to the giant, gold-leaf book bound in red sitting alongside an old, silver cross. Then she reclined on the couch like a sacrificial offering in a pagan ceremony or a princess who had consumed the poisoned apple and awaited her prince.

Michael opened the ancient *Rituale Romanum*, containing the rite of exorcism, and began a dangerous journey to confront evil or madness or both. He bore no armor of God to shield his descent into a realm for which he was unprepared. Nevertheless, he began to recite The Lord's Prayer as the text instructed, attempting to undo the backwards recitation that Mary Ruth's group had chanted years ago.

Then he began to read from the text. "God, accept our prayer that this servant of yours, bound by the fetters of sin, may be pardoned by your loving kindness. Everlasting God and Father of our Lord Jesus Christ, your only-begotten Son was sent into the world to crush that roaring lion. Hasten to our call for help, snatch from the clutches of the devil this woman made in your image, and strike terror in the beast attacking your vineyard. Let your mighty hand cast him out of your servant, Mary Ruth

Robinson, so he may no longer hold captive this woman it pleased you to redeem through your Son who lives and reigns with you in the unity of the Holy Spirit."

Michael struggled to believe that he was in this room and a part of this ritual, but he began to speak directly to the demon or demons. "I command you, unclean spirit, along with all your minions now attacking this servant of God, by the mysteries of the ascension of our Lord Jesus Christ, that you tell me by some sign your name. Obey me, and do not harm in any way this creature of God or this bystander."

Michael laid his hand on the head of Mary Ruth as instructed in the text. He prayed a prayer from the book as his hands shook and his heart pounded like a captive trying to escape its prison. "God, I appeal to your holy name, humbly begging your kindness, that you graciously grant me help against this unclean spirit now tormenting this creature of yours. Amen."

The exorcism had only begun. Mary Ruth appeared comatose but began to shudder and shake. She was sweating profusely and murmuring in what appeared to be a foreign language, but one that he did not recognize. She sat straight up from the couch and opened her eyes, but they were not her own. A voice came from her lips—but it too was not her own. It was the rasping, choking voice of something evil, eternally perilous, and somehow familiar.

"Go away...go-o-o...away...now! Lilith is ours."

Terror and disbelief grabbed Michael by the throat, but he heard himself say, "Leave her, unclean spirit!" A sizzling, hissing, shushing sound filled the room.

"Who are you?" Michael asked, not believing he was here at this intersection between heaven and hell.

"Go away...you're too good. We don't want you here!" the voice more spat than spoke.

"Unclean spirit, leave this poor woman...in the name of Jesus," Michael said.

"You are not bearing the armor, Michael Parker. You're not the one to battle us."

Then the whispered utterance..."I know you. You know me."

"Know you? No, who are you?" Michael said.

The voice growled, echoing a million voices in eternal torment, the warning cry of a thousand feral cats, and answered:

"Fredrick."

Michael recoiled in disbelief and horror. Images swirled in his mind—the night he almost died on Church Street, and the murder scene from Dixie's condo. In abject fear, he grasped the cross with trembling hands and began stage three of the exorcism as he teetered at the abyss.

"I cast you out, unclean spirit, along with every Satanic power of the enemy and every specter from hell in the name of our Lord Jesus Christ. You are robber of life, corrupter of justice, root of all evil and vice; seducer of men, instigator of envy, fomenter of discord, author of pain and sorrow. Why do you stand and resist? Leave in the name of the Father, the Son, and the Holy Spirit. Amen."

Mary Ruth's lips ceased to murmur or to channel whatever it was that had her in its grip. The thunder rumbled outside, rattling the pictures on her walls and interrupting his words in a symphony for the macabre.

Michael took a deep breath and returned once more to the text. "God, look down in pity on this your servant, Mary Ruth, now in the toils of the unclean spirit, now caught up in the fearsome threats of man's ancient enemy, who stupefies the human mind, and overwhelms it with fear and panic. Repel, O Lord, the devil's power…"

He marked three crosses on Mary Ruth, just as the text commanded, and resumed the archaic recitation. "Keep watch over the innermost recesses of her heart; rule over her emotions; strengthen her will that the evil spirit terrorizing this woman may retreat in terror and defeat. Let this servant of yours render you service through Christ our Lord. Amen."

Michael then addressed the spirit as exorcists had done through the ages. "By the judge of the living and the dead, by the Creator of the whole universe, depart forthwith in fear, with your minions, from this woman who seeks refuge in Christ. The mystery of the cross and the saving mysteries of our Christian faith command you."

He paused, out of breath, and watched Mary Ruth, who had gone limp and lifeless. Her eyes were open and rolled up into her head. The sweat poured from Michael's forehead, dripped from his nose, and his hands were on fire as the lamps flickered. The intermittent lightning illuminated the room in strobe-like flashes. He felt a tightening pressure, like fingers around his throat, but he pressed on.

"Depart, transgressor, seducer, persecutor of the innocent. Give place to Christ, who has laid waste to your kingdom, bound you prisoner, and plundered your weapons. He has cast you forth. Depart from this woman in the name of the spotless Lamb," he said as he touched her cold and clammy brow. She felt like a corpse.

"Tremble and flee from the Lord, before whom the denizens of hell cower. The Word made flesh commands you. Jesus is driving you into the everlasting fire, prince of murderers. God has willed this woman should be His temple. Why do you remain? Give honor to God. Your place is the nest of serpents. Give way to Christ before whom every knee must bend."

And so it went for hours. Day turned to night. The fading sun yielded to the moon, and the storm outside and the storm within raged on. Mary Ruth appeared drained of energy—if not evil. Michael feared to stop, and he feared not to stop—wanting to free her of things that the world says do not exist.

Swaying over the unconscious woman, Michael prayed the prayer repeated in ceremonies down through the ages. "Almighty God, we beg you to keep the evil spirit from further molesting this servant of yours, never to return. O Lord, may the goodness and peace of Jesus Christ, our Redeemer, take possession of this woman. May she no longer fear evil since You are with us."

Michael leaned over the woman he had chosen to befriend. Her breathing seemed regular, and the sweat had subsided except for a thin sheen of moisture above her upper lip. Her eyes opened and were clear—the deepest, unveiled look he'd seen in a long time. They didn't seem tortured and troubled, nor the eyes of the damned. She watched him for a moment, grasped his hand, and squeezed it until he thought it would break. Her eyes seemed to blur again and she whispered, "Thank you, Michael. No one else would've done this. Thank you for trying."

She was changed—no longer tortured, but indolent and speculative, with a challenging physical confidence and a sultry spark in the hazel eyes.

He began to draw back from her, hoping to look at her in a better light. Her reference to "trying" gave him cause to wonder if he had succeeded in his unlikely rescue attempt. She held him and began to sob into the crook of his neck. Her tears crashed around him like a million glittering diamonds suffusing the air. Pheromones dusted the night, and he fell into her world, exposed, unguarded, and compromised—a late arrival at the ceremony of his own dissolution.

As morning iridescence diffused color in the room, he watched her sleeping, surely as David had watched Bathsheba. He knew he should run as far away as possible, but abandoning her would be aiding and abetting the suicidal path she seemed to be on. She could be pristine and innocent or common as any harlot of the streets—the milk of kindness or the bitter vinegar of cruelty.

Where is the real Michael and what have you done with him? he thought. As a child, he had watched Samson and Delilah and remembered Cecil B. DeMille's words: *You cannot break God's law. You can only break yourself against His law.*

As he drove away, an FM station played Leonard Cohen's dirge-like song—melancholic, fragile, prophetic, and sorrowful. It was almost liturgical in its commentary on fallen man and the hint of redemption—a distant drumbeat to a funeral march, drawing nearer by the moment.

"She broke your throne, and she cut your hair, and from your lips she drew the Hallelujah."

CHAPTER THIRTY-THREE

"Four absolutes we all have in our minds: love, justice, evil, and forgiveness."—Ravi Zacharias

"The heart has its reasons which reason knows not."—Blaise Pascal

The day of the meeting with the vendor, Michael woke shivering and trembling from a nightmare. He had fallen asleep reading from the small King James Bible Susan had placed on his nightstand. It was open to Genesis 3:9—"And the Lord God called unto Adam, and said unto him, Where art Thou?"

He was Adam and Mary Ruth was Eve. He was hiding from God in the Garden. God was calling and calling him, "Where art thou, Adam? Where art thou?" In the dream he had stepped away from God, left the garden, and found that the world was cold, cruel, and unforgiving— beyond his comprehension. Michael ran from tree to tree, trying to cover himself as Adam did in Genesis. He felt the enormity of the pain he had caused, that he had broken God's heart.

He heard God whisper, "Who told you that you are naked? I created you without shame. How did you lose your innocence?"

Michael felt the full rush of all the pain that God never wanted him to experience. The guilt was overwhelming, merciless, and consuming. From a hillside overlooking the garden, he heard Cain ask the question that echoes in man's conscience—"Am I my brother's keeper?"

Michael fell back into the dream. Men in monk-like, long, gray robes, hooded and faceless figures with glowing orbs for eyes, were peering in his windows, and then knocking, and finally pounding on his door. They were chanting in a Gregorian rhythm—"Point of no return, point of no return—perfect storm, perfect storm."

He had come to Atlanta to right wrongs and to bring fire to the people, a modern-day Prometheus—but he had partnered with Pandora, and her jar had unleashed all the evil of the world into his life. The would-be drainer of the swamp was now waist-deep in alligators.

On the drive to the meeting, the superintendent was quiet, only occasionally sneaking smug and inquiring looks at him from behind a veil of schoolgirl coyness, a surreal mocking imitation of innocence.

A turkey vulture circled slowly in a mesmerizing arc overhead, riding the currents…the silver under its black wings shining, and the red of its head surveying the earth. Michael watched the rows of residential homes go by, homes under siege by the relentless advance of the ever-growing megalopolis that was Atlanta. Many would soon be displaced; the insatiable hunger of business interests sought land to occupy in pursuit of the very suburbanites they drove further and further from the heart of the dying old city. Michael imagined the stories hidden behind the walls of these stucco dwellings with gray stone chimneys. All kept secrets that could consume the inhabitants as surely as his own threatened to consume him now.

Do they know the Orcs and Trolls of Atlanta are on the march? he wondered. *These creatures consume one another, only ceasing if an outsider threatens their common cause. The modern variety preaches love of the kingdom—a perversion of the real thing—mimicking good behind bloody smiles. Their metrics are measurements of evil where up is down and down is up, and falling short is measuring up. But I don't measure up either, do I? Yet collaboration with the citizens of Mordor seems unthinkable. What would Tolkien think?*

As he neared their destination, he was jolted from his musings by the song on the radio as Mary Ruth sang along…"They say the best things in life are free, but you can give them to the birds and bees. I want money, that's what I want…I need money, I need money…"

He turned up the manicured drive that led to the headquarters of Russian Action Communications Incorporated, sheltered in an island of woods in the midst of the larger urban sprawl and deforestation. The massive glass doors were tinted to thwart prying eyes. When they entered, Mary Ruth seemed to be drifting into another wave of the narcolepsy that had become more prevalent. She appeared to stumble and her speech was halting.

A curly-haired man in wire-rimmed glasses approached them with boldness in his step and said, "Welcome to our corner of the world." Vitaly Antipova was the CEO of RAC, Inc. Besides having a heavy Russian accent, he also projected an intense physical presence with small, pinpoint umber eyes that peered from behind his Dr. Zhivago glasses.

Mary Ruth took his hand and almost curtsied. Antipova turned her hand and kissed it near her wrist. Michael felt that he no longer existed in real life but in Theater of the Absurd. Even there, he was but a bit player peeking through the keyhole. He waited for the curtain to go up on Act One in this place where actors recited their lines from a cavernous emptiness. They thought themselves invisible and free to do whatever they desired, free of repercussions or accountability—slaves to their appetites or needs.

What're we doing? he thought. *These needs of the moment sway our hearts and allure our souls. Aren't the parameters of right and wrong dictated by conscience? Is this all that's left us...fight the good fight, compromise and get away with it? Is this what all do—accept the ticket to ride in a corrupt world? Or is it the keeper of the furnace that whispers "Fight fire with fire"?*

The back-and-forth dragged on, and double-speak seemed to be the common language. Lots of nodding and parsing of words took place after the presentation of their wares and applicability to the department, and many reassurances flowed regarding their intended support for the superintendent. The phrasing was careful and tedious, but it surely bordered on *quid pro quo.*

"We'll deliver services to your schools for blind and deaf children, help them build communities of interest, and streamline their communications. Presto, we'll make it instantaneous and grow their family of common interests related to their special needs. We know they get the bottom of the barrel from your board. Maybe we can 'kill two birds with one stone,' as you say. Maybe the same stone you say you will hurl in your sling to bring down King Hank like Goliath," Antipova said as he slammed the desk and threw back another shot of Russian vodka.

"We watch your battles. You Americans know nothing about fighting the state. We'll help you defeat these evil men. They're like the

KGB. We know something about fighting evil and pledge to support you all the way—if we get your contracts to move ahead," Vitaly promised with a subtle wink.

Finally, as they rose to leave, he said, "Let's hope we never have to worry like your senators in Washington. When the roll is called, they don't know whether to answer present or not guilty! They have no Nativity scenes in Washington, because no one can find three wise men and a virgin!" He laughed uproariously, and one of his associates slapped Michael on the back so hard his teeth rattled.

The superintendent was suddenly subdued. Her mouth was pinched tight and thin, and she showed no interest, only a perfunctory smile at the new donor's jokes. They drove away in silence, not understanding that they had crossed the rickety bridge of no return; it was already burning behind them. They didn't speak of how vulnerable they were in this game of take-no-prisoners. A willful ignorance or a terminal naiveté had consumed them. They had bought the lie that there were no problems, only solutions—and everyone does it.

After the meeting, Mary Ruth had an appearance at a local church. As they entered the church, Michael felt a crushing weight on his chest. When Communion was offered, he refused. When "Amazing Grace" was sung by the congregation, he was mute.

"What's wrong with you? That didn't look good to church members!" protested a petulant Mary Ruth, a modern incarnation of Ado Annie, the character in *Oklahoma* who couldn't say no to the flirting and flattering of the world. She wanted to do better, but she just couldn't resist the manipulators around her. Why, none of it was her fault—was it?

He looked at her blankly and said, "I'm not worthy."

Michael, the caged bird, drilled down into his paralysis, trying to find a way out, to mine some vein of good in it all, and found none. He heard Pearl's admonition from long ago: "If you can't unscramble eggs, son—don't heat up the pan."

As they left the church, Mary Ruth called her husband, whom she wanted to do something he had no intention of doing. The argument went back and forth. Suddenly Mary Ruth shifted and morphed into someone else. "Oh, you big lug, you know I love you. I just need you to do this one tiny thing for me," she cooed, winking at Michael. He guessed this was a time-tested strategy.

The honey dripped from her tongue as the mileposts clicked by on Interstate 20. Transparent and breathtaking in her manipulation, she forgot herself after the victory and turned to Michael, her confidante inside the walls of her fortress of fantasy. To her, he was now no longer exactly male, but rather a neutered and privileged guest in her world of games.

"You see, that's how you handle men!" she bubbled giddily, in a high-five moment.

Michael stared at her for what seemed forever and asked, "Is that how you handle me?"

Caught, she shifted again, but not before failing to cover her deer-in-the-headlight gaze. "No-o-o, oh no-o-o," she stammered in full, blushing retreat. "I would never treat you that way."

It was at that moment when he finally realized she wasn't an innocent. She had become such a part of the dance of the abused and their abusers that manipulation was now natural and acceptable to her, just as it had been to all the abused women he encountered in the MBN. For the first time, he felt she could be dangerous.

He had a sudden flush of memories—warm Mississippi days, turning the old pole television antenna to capture flickering black-and-white images: "Grandma, can you see the Lone Ranger and Tonto now?" He longed for it with all of his heart—a place of butterfly kisses, chivalry, and herculean sacrifice—not this jaundiced corner of the world consumed by treachery and infidelity.

As they pulled out onto Peachtree Industrial Road, he saw a message on a church marquee that clawed at his heart and choked his throat:

"I shall have no excuse. I can't say I didn't know. You called me and I didn't go—empty words, empty passion." (Malcolm Muggeridge)

CHAPTER THIRTY-FOUR

*"We all live in a house on fire. No fire department
to call. No way out. Just the upstairs to look out
while the fire burns the house down...with us
trapped, locked in it."—Tennessee Williams*

*"When truth conquers with the help of 10,000
yelling men—supposing that which is...victorious is
truth; with the form and manner of the victory a far
greater untruth is victorious."—Kierkegaard*

Outnumbered and surrounded in Atlanta...that's how Michael felt. It reminded him of a time when he and five other Mississippi Bureau of Narcotics agents had stopped at a lounge in Baton Rouge after a training class. Two of the officers were black, and it was 1972 Louisiana... The patrons soon picked up bottles, knives, and guns and began to circle the MBN's finest. Michael saw what was coming and said, "We need to get out while we still can." Holding their guns and staring down their would-be assailants, the agents backed out of the club.

Michael had forgotten that lesson; otherwise, he wouldn't be so reluctant to leave the Department of Education now. It was dysfunctional. It was beyond hope. It was a place of stagnation and rot...but it was his last stand. Retreat was not as simple as it had been back in '72.

So he took Susan to their home in Augusta even as he continued to polish his rusty armor and dutifully rearrange the deck chairs on the sinking ship, which was listing badly at the bow.

The crisscrossing of the state went on unabated from Augusta. Mary Ruth kissed babies and shook her fist at the power structure in speeches and stops in mostly small, rural venues which were the center of her populist appeal. Churches, BBQs, grassroots meet-and-greets, and local grip-and-grins were beyond the control of the big money. They were her bread and butter.

She bounced up the steps to platforms to speak to crowds of six and sixty, embracing her image as the woman Atlanta hated most but could never defeat. Weekly papers took pictures and offered generous access to their pages, something the dailies would never do, because they were bought and paid for by the old political machine. The sizzle of catfish dropping in fryers competed with the *snap*, *crackle*, and *pop* of ribs on the grill. Music from bluegrass bands wafted in the air, accompanied by an odor Michael couldn't wash from his senses—the smell of defeat and self-loathing.

The vendor money flowed to the campaign under many names. The die was cast. Each posting poisoned the whole pursuit. Mary Ruth's image as a reformer worthy of trust dimmed in the reality of innocence lost. She awarded contracts to the vendor for new services at the state schools. Like Humpty Dumpty in the nursery rhyme, no one could repair the brokenness that had fractured Michael's world. He stood in front of the bathroom mirror before a campaign trip and stared at his image. He was bone weary, soul sick, and felt utterly and awfully alone.

"Who are you?" he asked. "I don't know you, and I don't like you."

Like Humpty's parable of the fall into sin, he felt beyond redemption as he wrote in his journal.

All the king's horses and all the king's men can't restore beauty. I heard a pastor on the radio today say that if man is to be beautiful, he must be created anew by the very source of beauty itself. That seems beyond me now. All the favor I had from God seems gone. The distant music no longer plays. The pursuing Presence seems to have left me. What do I do now?

To make it into the runoff, we need conservative teachers who vote Republican in the general election but in Democratic primaries for local races where Republicans have yet to offer candidates. They must vote for Mary Ruth in the Republican primary, else all is lost. It's hard to ask them to ignore local races that affect their daily lives to vote in one primary race. They said they'll show up en masse for the superintendent in the general election, but it'll be too late. If they're forced to choose between Mary Ruth and their cousins running for constable and school boards, we lose. It's too close with three candidates. If we can make the runoff, the number two candidate in primary runoffs often wins in Georgia.

The night of the election, a dour James Peterson called from the *Atlanta Constitution*. "Michael, your opponents say they'll make it to the general without a runoff against Mary Ruth."

"No, that's not possible," Michael answered, but he knew it was spot on. As the night wore on and the results began to trickle in, he knew the teachers hadn't heeded his plea.

The party got loud and cheered at Mary Ruth's momentary victories where she had support, but then the revelry died as it became obvious this long night wouldn't end well for the candidate or for those who had risked so much for victory. She missed the runoff by one percent.

Michael sat on the stairway of the old mansion, head hung low. A gutful of merciless guilt was eating away at him. All the stress, the compromise of the supposedly inviolable, the nights he should have been home with Susan, and the fights that weren't his—for what? People came by to console him, to tell that it would be okay. They said it was just a political race, and everyone would live to fight another day. But Michael knew better. He knew in his soul that the loss had left them vulnerable, exposed to the whims of the government and those who hated Mary Ruth.

In the days and weeks that followed, many chickens came home to roost. On the day of the general election, King Hank lost big—the beginning of the end of a hundred years of one-party control. Even Big Jim fell to defeat, after forty years of ruling the House with an iron fist. It was the biggest news to hit Atlanta since Rhett, Scarlett, and Coca-Cola.

Speaker Big Jim called Mary Ruth. "Little lady, I admire you. We threw everything we had at you, but you never wilted or backed down. I was Speaker and you were who you were. I couldn't treat you any other way than I did, but I sure like the way you hung in there. You deserved better," the crusty old politico said in a moment when there was nothing in it for him, no political edge to be gained.

Mary Ruth was living on that river in Egypt called "de-nial." She called Michael to tell him she was off on a taxpayer-funded trip to New Orleans. She invited him. He declined. She also used leftover campaign funds to get a facelift. After her trip and facelift, she returned for a night out on the town, courtesy of RAC. They went to the Cougar Club, the most notorious strip club in Atlanta. She said it was her duty to "chaperone" some impressionable young women the CEO was taking to "that dangerous club." As she indulged her fantasies, the Board of Education blocked RAC's services to the state schools, a precursor for one last act of revenge yet to come.

Billy Joe knew it was the end of the visions of grandeur he had brought with him from Mississippi, where he had left memories of Ace and Fredrick behind in hopes of finding something greater. There would be consequences for the party that feathered his nest, for his boss, the Speaker, and for his enemy—Michael Parker.

As he talked with Slim, he said, "I actually feel sympathy for Parker. We both came to Georgia as outsiders in this world, both from a home state that looks better and better all the time. I don't like him, but he's still better than all these pantywaist cowards who believe in nothing. They're born with that shiny, silver spoon stuck in their tonsils, everything handed to them in their designer cribs."

Slim watched him and asked, "What're we gonna do, Hoss?"

"We'll make do, Slim. A bunch of Democrats are just changing labels and joining the other party. No "R" by their names can change who they are. Those "Rs and Ds" don't mean nothing. They all hug the front pews and sing 'I'll Fly Away,' but that don't mean they will. As *you* might say, you can't change the spots on an old dog," Billy Joe said with a chuckle.

"Will our bosses mount a comeback?" Slim asked.

"No, they won't be coming back. They're blowing those dog whistles, reminding their mutts that they were paid well with that federal money Hank spread around. They'll ask them to lie low until King Hank rises again and then contribute big, but they're done. The pendulum has swung and swung hard, but don't worry. There's not a dime's worth of difference between old bosses and new ones. There'll always be places for men like us in government," he assured him.

Slim then asked his benefactor, "Hoss, what're we gonna do about the bad things we've done? We got to get all of our ducks on the same page. The fan's going to hit the roof."

"Are you afraid, Slim?" Billy Joe asked.

"I am, Hoss. God's been watching me like I was a hawk. Ain't you afraid?"

"Slim, did you ever read something called *The Iliad*?" Billy Joe asked.

"The what?!" Slim asked.

Billy Joe smiled. "An old, old book that Ace gave me. In it, this guy named Achilles sees the faces of all the men he's killed. They're all standing on the banks of the river Styx, waiting and saying, 'Welcome, brother.' Achilles said that we men are wretched things...and we are, Slim. We are."

"We done let the devil in our front door... Don't you believe in God, Hoss?" Slim asked.

"No, I don't," Billy Joe said. "But I fear Him. As you might say, I got lots of black sheep in my closet."

CHAPTER THIRTY-FIVE

"Everybody knows the good guys lost. Everybody knows the fight was fixed. Everybody knows that the captain lied..."—Leonard Cohen

"Whatever crime it may be to which they have confessed, their pertinacity and inflexible obstinacy should certainly be punished."—Pliny (the younger) (62-C. 113), Roman prosecutor

After the election, when more than a political race was lost, Susan's doctor told Michael that her diabetes had blocked her vascular system from head to toe, and that he should be watchful for possible heart attack, stroke, kidney failure, and dementia, which could result from plaque in the arteries of her brain. It was the straw that bent him to breaking, though Susan never complained. She assured him that it was expected, and she would be fine.

In the midst of that crushing news, Michael's mother called. Her cancer had returned, and it was stage four. Only hospice remained, and no one was there to care for her. Michael arranged for someone to stay with Susan, and then he went home to care for his mother in hospice during the last three months of her life. In a Parker Grove summer, where searing and suffocating Mississippi heat came in wave after wave, there was no talk of politics in this vigil for life—only things eternal. She spoke day and night of how fragile life was. She was overwhelmed by the world's subjective morality—the futility of its belief in endless, random possibilities compared to the sacrifice written in red on Golgotha so long ago.

Michael's heart thumped in a chest full of lead, and his feet were wooden as he walked to and fro, tending to his mama's final needs. She was a slim woman for her eighty-four years, with a curly cap of gray hair and a warm smile. This woman, who shared his dimples and nose knew he was carrying a heavy load, but she thought that it was her lingering death that weighed on him. She decided not to ask, instead choosing just talk to him of his tomorrows and the things of her faith—of the things she wished to impart before her voice was stilled and all of her words were muted for ten thousand years.

Finally, the talks ended. The spangling blue eyes closed, and there were no more tender words… "That back rub was good, son. That peach dish tasted fine, Michael." There were no more priceless gifts of "I love you, son." The day came when Michael carried her to the waiting hearse. Tears overflowed his eyes and washed down his face in rivulets that wouldn't stop. She was the last of family, and he loved her—would have done anything for her…but it was more than that which had driven him to stay and care for his mother in her final days. It was atonement.

* * *

While Michael was away, things were evolving in Georgia. A fresh crop of officials were swept into power with the new government. They paid a visit to Judge Hendricks, who had been prepared to rule in favor of ignoring the state's debt limit. The Cougar Club was padlocked by agents of the new district attorney, tipped by Billy Joe about the money laundering and the payments made to the old regime. Old Hoss knew how to deal with whoever was "in town and wearing the crown." He assured Dixie Mafia investors, "This is but a momentary rotation of the players. Nothing changes."

"The Midnight Special" was playing on the club jukebox when Carmen Rodriguez was again called to take the fall for new indictments, and he wasn't happy about being shipped off to federal prison at Edgefield, S.C. "You better not fight…the boys will bring you down. The next thing you know, boy, oh you're prison bound."

Not all was lost. The man called Romeo, that good ole boy whom Billy Joe had intercepted in his charge to defend the honor of Darlene the dancer, came back to take young Miss Honeysuckle away from the whole sordid mess. They were married, and she got a job in the garden section of Home Depot, where she swore to customers that honeysuckle vines were named after her.

* * *

The November elections may have settled questions of governance, but the U.S. Attorney's office still waited to dispense their own brand of justice—or a facsimile thereof.

The apparatchiks of central government scurried to and fro like pismires in the ant farm of the Russell Federal Building. Humorless and drone-like in their deficiencies, they saw people only as numbers or case files to be processed. They functioned as one convulsively pulsating lump that asked no questions and demanded no explanations of policy. Judgment was measured by their own collective scale of values, as interpreted in laws and regulations passed by Congress and selectively applied and distorted by agencies of the Executive Branch. They steered clear of value systems in discordance with their own, creating nothing—and sometimes destroying much—in the name of a nebulous public good, simply doing their jobs as honorable, tenured servants.

Alex Martin drummed a pencil on his gray, government desk, like the old second-chair snare drummer he was at the University of Georgia. As the up-and-coming Assistant U.S. Attorney for criminal prosecutions, he viewed himself as the vanguard of an occupying Union army in Atlanta. He didn't shun Sherman. He admired and emulated the man who "brought order to chaos or a necessary new chaos to an old order."

An effeminate blueblood by birth, he was born with a ready-made portfolio of blue-chip stocks and a disposition unsuited to the Justice Department—like a pyromaniac hiring on as a fireman. An ambitious prosecutor who hated his job, he viewed it as merely a stepping stone to his destiny—he planned to become the youngest Assistant U.S. Attorney ever appointed as a federal judge for life.

"For life"…he liked that part. No more worrying with his inferiors or trying to please his superiors by attending their boring Christmas parties and political events. He only visited those soirees to meet and cultivate the best connections to the White House, which dispensed such appointments to loyalists across the country.

Graylock Communications, along with one of Governor Holcomb's trusted disciples on the State Board of Education, had given him a tasty morsel that might facilitate his rise in the world.

Martin rang Agent Jim Barrows in the FBI office down the hall. "Jim, come to my office. I want you to meet Warren Booker, the agent from U.S. Education, just down from D.C. to discuss a new case." Booker, a tough-looking agent, was assigned to the U.S. Department of Education when he wasn't in Afghanistan, where he served as a sniper in the Army. He moved back and forth from the front so often that he forgot now and then where he was—on the battlefield where there was no Bill of Rights or in his role as a domestic police officer on U.S. soil. He spoke of "lighting people up" with the same cavalier attitude as someone squashing a roach.

As Booker and the prosecutor made small talk, Jim Barrows arrived. Barrows was not the sharpest blade in the drawer and had purposefully been assigned to the U.S. Attorney's office to do the grunt and gofer duties of case background research.

"Come in, Jim, and say hello to Warren," Martin said.

As perfunctory handshakes were exchanged, Martin said, "Warren just happened to show up on a matter that Grayson Communications brought to my attention. We didn't move on it before because we needed to see how the elections were going to sort out. Now that it's over, we need to take a look at this alleged diversion of money to Mary Ruth Robinson's campaign. Warren, why don't you fill Jim in?"

"As I understand it, there was a dispute over federal monies going to the governor or the Georgia Department of Education. The White House decided they should go to Governor Holcomb. Apparently some of the money was spent by Robinson before the governor could get it. That's not our concern. However, it appears some funds may have found their way from a vendor back to Robinson's campaign, and that would be of interest to us. Our liaisons in Justice want to see what's what," he said.

"In the new Grayson TV piece, the investigative journalists are doing a series called 'What happened to the money?' So I want you guys to take this on and see what the facts are. I understand the White House expressed interest to the AG," Alex said emphatically.

He could already see the possibilities—a nice, high-profile case for his career couldn't hurt. Alex had become expert at compartmentalizing and segmenting his life from his schemes—loving without love, warming himself by the fires of others but leaving as cold as ice, crying the dry tears of the wooden martinet.

"I thought the Georgia Department of Education was the one that was supposed to get federal education money," Jim offered to surprised looks and raised eyebrows.

"Hey, I'm just asking," he said, "trying to understand what the crime is here and what statute we feel is violated…the facts, you know."

"Don't worry about statutes, Jim," Martin snapped. "I'll find those. You and Warren interview folks and follow the money trail. Get everyone to talk about Robinson and this guy Michael Parker, who I understand is her right-hand man and confidante."

After the agents had departed his office, the prosecutor marveled at his good fortune. *This case has all the elements of a useful soap opera. The board member said it could be alleged the money was stolen from the state schools for the blind and deaf. That would rally public opinion against Robinson and her allies. No matter that the board had never allocated special funds to those schools before or that these contracts the board declared illegal DID provide new services from Robinson. No matter that the board blocked delivery of services to the state schools to divert it to Governor Holcomb. Who cares? It's a great story. I can get a lot of mileage in my press conference as "Defender of the Weak." The media will repeat our line as the gospel. Must call our friends at the* Atlanta Journal-Constitution *and get a new suit.*

* * *

The phone rang at Michael's home. It was Kevin Carney, the campaign manager who had concocted the plan to seek campaign donations.

"Michael, the FBI was here asking questions that I couldn't answer," he said. *That means they're still there*, Michael thought.

"Please tell me no money came to the campaign from the vendor they were talking about," he said with mock disbelief. Michael knew that meant that the call was being taped.

"I'm not sure what you're talking about," Michael said casually.

The give-and-take continued for several minutes, with the manager reading his script and Michael sticking to the noncommittal answer. He had a sick feeling in the pit of his stomach. The dreaded storm had arrived, worst nightmares come true. What would he do? What *could* he do?

Another call came from Walter just as the large bugs began to pop and buzz around the streetlamp outside. "Michael, they say they're going to indict us for money that came into the campaign. What'll we do?" Walter asked with a trembling voice.

"Don't worry, Walter. They aren't after you. They're after Mary Ruth and me, I suppose. Do what you have to, cut a deal…It's okay." There had to be some dignity left, Michael thought.

Late that night, a government-gray car slowed in front of Michael's house and then backed into his neighbor's driveway across the street. He watched the car through the blinds in the dimness of the street lamp. A match flame, a cigarette burn here and there, the white-green glow of electronic screens, and then it was pitch black. They sat there behind silent headlights, the eyes of some sleeping beast watching and waiting for the prey to emerge.

The neighbor's small, yellow mutt of a dog began to bark and growl at the bumper of the government car and then at the passenger door—a good watchdog defending his home. Then the window powered down, and an arm extended with a can of what appeared to be Mace. The dog began to yelp and whine and finally slinked back toward the garage— stumbling, falling, and rolling. The dog rubbed its eyes and snout on the grass, trying to stop the sudden, burning assault of the spraying.

Nice guys, Michael thought.

Finally, Michael had enough. He slipped from the side door and walked toward the car. His heart pounded as he mounted this last show of false bravado to confront the government agents—agents working cases as he once had.

As he neared the car, the driver lowered his window and a stern-looking agent peered out at him.

"Fee-bees, I would imagine," Michael said.

Badges came out and the moment had come.

"Agent Warren Booker," the driver said. "This is Agent Jim Barrows, FBI."

"Would you like to come in and talk or just sit out here and gas all the neighborhood pets?" Michael asked.

"We'll come in if you're ready to cooperate," Barrows shot back.

A mottled-brown night hawk in search of a meal screeched above as it followed Michael and the agents through the quiet subdivision. Michael's palms were sweaty, and he felt sick. This was one of those unthinkable moments, the impossible come true for the last of the Boy Scouts. This was the moment when the books were finally brought out for an accounting—risk worth the game, game worth the risk. He doubted they would be impressed by the right-versus-wrong, "somebody had to do something, or else the free world might crumble" defense.

He was correct.

"Mr. Parker, we know your past, your service, and we want to help you. If you just cooperate tonight—and it must be tonight—we're prepared to recommend certain points and reductions in the sentencing guidelines. We know your wife is ill and that you are her caregiver. Tell us what you know and don't hold anything back. This is your chance—your last and only chance," Booker dryly recited through a florid face and a Yosemite Sam red mustache.

"First, let's clear the air. You're not my friends," Michael said. "To quote Josey Wales, 'Don't pee down my leg and tell me it's raining.' Don't try to kid a kidder."

They're good, Michael thought. *For them, this is "Betray your friends week"—and THEIR friends too if necessary. We're having a special tonight, because we like you.*

He knew the drill. He'd recited it many times as a state agent, but not like these guys. He didn't like them in the Bureau days, and he didn't like them now.

A clock ticked loudly in the room. The central unit cut on with a *whoosh* of air.

"You know the Hobbs Act doesn't apply here," Michael said. "There was no tit-for-tat, hypothetically speaking of course. And where were you when they were stealing millions with the blessings of your bosses in Washington? We were holding the line just as the U.S. Education Secretary told us to. Where were you? Huh?" he asked, looking at one and then the other. He knew it was futile. They didn't give a fig about him—or right and wrong either, for that matter.

Barrows looked at Booker. They smiled smug and knowing grins. Michael wondered if this was his punishment come full circle for enjoying his own interrogations a little too much.

Barrows, a bulky, rubbery-looking man for his profession, finally laughed out loud. "We don't need the old Hobbs Act. You're behind the times! We have broad new laws to charge you under now, Mister Parker. Under the Honest Services Fraud Act, we can indict that streetlight out there if we wish. Intent means nothing. All those tools to fight crime, all the authority you and your friends wished for—pined for—in the old days? We got it *all* now, in the name of combating the bad guys. You may not be the classic image of the bad guy in the eyes of some, but as far as the government's concerned, you're Public Enemy Number One. Congress has given us power to combat terrorists and the Mafia, but they never told us that we couldn't use it just as well on you. Tonight, you're just another terrorist."

"Where can you show that I benefited one penny from all of this? It didn't happen. I'm not going to plead to theft," Michael said in a quiet, almost whisper of argument.

Booker smiled. "Forget that you didn't personally benefit. You cooperate with us, or let us explain what you are facing. Forget the fact that you are a first offender; that means nothing now. Forget all of your good works, the good-guy image you have in the community. That means nothing—less than nothing. The prosecutor could make Mother Teresa look like a harlot. And you won't just be charged with diverting federal funds to the campaign, either.

"Here's how it works. Under the sentencing guidelines passed about sixteen years ago, we have our big book to determine sentences. *We* do it, Michael—us and the prosecutor, not the judge. They're figureheads now. Under the guidelines, our good book of justice determines the sentence.

"We take the diversion, the theft, your theft, her theft—let's call it what is—and we see that you have a range to sentence of, say, forty-eight months to sixty-five months. But then we say the campaign received some money by mail; that's mail fraud. So we go to the guidelines and add another range of time on top of the first penalty. But wait—there's more! Some of the money came to the campaign by wire. That's wire fraud! So we go into the good book again, and we see the range for that is another few years, so we add that to boot!"

Booker chimed in, "We're not through yet, Michael. You and Mary Ruth talked about it with the vendor and the campaign manager. That's conspiracy! I think you get it now. Yeah, we go into the book again and add a few more years onto what the judge must sentence you to under law. You're looking at thirty years! Thir-ty years!!! The federal grand juries today never question the prosecutor's presentation of charges. The true bill rate of return is near one hundred percent, and we keep one sitting grand jury running at all times so we can indict who we want, when we want.

"This is power that you guys could only dream of back in your day. That's why our conviction rate is ninety-eight percent. Most plead. Only the stupid take it to court because they still believe in innocence and the Bill of Rights. That's justice today—former…Agent…Parker!" he added with dripping sarcasm.

"You speak so casually of this new world where first offenders are given sentences once reserved for those who scared us. Judges don't have the power to determine sentences, to consider mitigating circumstances or the entire life and record of people who make mistakes… We didn't dream of that kind of power," Michael said. "Those aren't dreams but nightmares, the kind of power that corrupts. We couldn't handle that, and you can't either."

"Don't look so glum," Barrows said. "We're just like you used to be. We're the same."

"The heck you are," Michael said.

The silence was deafening. *What now?* Michael thought. *What would Susan do if I had to go away?* A little late to worry about that, his conscience jabbed.

He knew they counted on him wanting to unload the bad news, the burden he was carrying. He was stressed to the breaking point. The thought of losing liberty, of losing Susan—of losing everything—overwhelmed him, but he knew terror would undo him.

Smug and ice cold, Barrows said, "It's obvious that you haven't made up your mind. You haven't accepted your fate. But unless you sign tonight, you lose points you would have gained, and points translate to years off of your sentence. It's going to be tough inside. You're not made for it. You've grown soft in your cushy corporate jobs, and if inmates were to find out you were a cop—if someone were to tell them…" He paused for effect.

He continued, "If they were to learn that you sent their cousin or uncle or daddy to the slammer for drug charges twenty years ago—well, time served would be the least of your worries. We couldn't help you then. No one could."

Booker nodded and said, "I know you know this, but whoever's first to plead is the one who gets to write what 'truth' is presented in court. So if you play ball now, you're the prosecutor's chief witness and your truth becomes his truth and our truth. However, if you allow Robinson or others to beat you to it, they write the truth, and you know how that'll go. It'll all be your fault. You'll be the fall guy."

Barrows jumped in with the one-two. "You know, Parker, the prosecutor is going to say these funds were taken from the schools for the deaf and blind. When he paints this as theft from those poor kids, well…let's just say it's sure not going to look good. Forget that no funds were really taken from them. Forget that Robinson got them new funds through the contracts she awarded the vendor. So what if the board wanted to give *none* of it to the kids and keep it all for the governor? It doesn't matter! That was sanctioned by the powers. What *you* people did wasn't."

Booker agreed. "The idea that they were getting *no* big increases before Robinson bypassed the board, or that they would've gotten *more* under your little Iran-Contra exchange is too esoteric, too obscure for a jury. It's a bridge too far for them. That's how it will be laid out by the government. You're going to look like Al Capone and Hannibal Lecter rolled into one."

Michael's chin was resting on his chest. Barrows leaned forward in his chair with his hands on his knees, drawing closer to him to say quietly,

"You didn't really think there would be no consequences for bucking the system, did you?"

"It is what it is," said Booker.

"John Ed Collins was right—just enforcers of the *status quo*," Michael said.

"What's that?" Booker asked.

"What's the penalty for stealing the truth?" Michael countered.

"What do you mean?" Barrows asked, frowning, creasing the wrinkles around his eyes.

"Your questions are autonomous. You already have your answers. This inquiry is perfunctory, a game to you. All those truths you ignore just sit there in your guts eating away at you like a festering poison. The truth will set you free, I hear," Michael said.

He stared at them and said nothing. They packed up their papers, leaving the house with a lingering stench or disturbance—an aura of violation. He opened the windows and sprayed a can of air freshener, trying in vain to cover the smell with a fresh, piney woods fragrance. Then he went in the downstairs bathroom, knelt down, hugged the commode, and puked his guts out until he spit blood and the water showed crimson.

After retching through a long round of the dry heaves, he rose, wiped his face with a cold wet cloth, and sat alone in the den before calling Mary Ruth.

"Mary Ruth, the Feds were just here," he said in a whisper, his throat hoarse from vomiting.

"What did they want?" she asked softly and absently, as if she was drugged.

"What do you think?" he snapped. "They're going to indict us."

"Why?" she asked in a little-girl voice. "We haven't done anything wrong."

"You may believe that, but they surely don't. I'm going to speak to my lawyer about options and about—any deal that can be made. I urge you to do the same," he said, recoiling at the actual verbalization of what seemed unthinkable.

"You're pleading to what, Michael? I'm not pleading guilty. We're not the bad people. We tried to stop the bad people. We'll just tell them," she protested.

"They have the laws, Mary Ruth, and they don't lose," he answered with resignation.

There was a long silence, and then she said, "Well, Michael, if it's really that bad, then you should fall on the sword for me."

"What? What did you say?" a stunned Michael asked.

"You're strong, and I'm weak," she pouted and purred in a coquettish tone. "You should say it was—all your fault. You should do the time for me. You can get me out of this. You would do it if you loved me. I'm not well," she said with a gallon of guile and not an ounce of shame.

"What? No! I must think of Susan," he replied.

"Oh, she'll outlive us all," she snapped.

He never saw it coming. He was numb—not so much at her request, but at her belief that she could talk him into it, and the cold manner in which she spoke of Susan.

"No," he said. "I must go."

Just as he hung up, the phone rang. It was Sam the informant.

"Hey, Michael, I wanted to call and see how you're doing," he said.

"If I was in Florida, I'd be Bush, barely holding on by a hanging chad," Michael said weakly.

"The Holcomb people are celebrating. They lost, but y'all are the consolation prizes. In your sense of fair play, you're like those big old jocks I used to torment in high school football. Every time I fouled them, they'd get mad and foul me back. I had already whispered to the refs, and they'd be the ones who got the penalty. Sometimes they'd jerk off their helmets and want to fight honorably. I'd keep mine on and beat the tar out of them," he said.

Sam sighed heavily and said, "They're pros. You're junior varsity."

He paused again and said, "You're going to lose this, you know?"

"I know. I know," Michael said as he hung up.

He cut off all the lights and felt his way up the narrow stairs to the master bedroom, where he could hear Susan softly crying. What would he say to her? How could he ever explain it to those who had believed in him? How—in a way they could understand?

It was like trying to capture a tornado in a bottle or a hurricane in a coffee cup. Saying this was hard and saying that he was sorry was like acknowledging that the sun is hot, ice is cold, nobody's right if everybody's wrong—or that politicians lie a lot.

CHAPTER THIRTY-SIX

*"Good morning, America…Don't you know me,
I'm your native son."*—Arlo Guthrie

"Angels and ministers of grace defend us."
—William Shakespeare, Hamlet, *Act 1, Scene 4*

The sharks smelled blood in the water, and they were always grateful for a free meal. They were circling outside Michael's front door, ringing the doorbell to surprise him.

When he didn't answer, a voice called out, "It's Robin Blanchard from Channel 6, Michael. We need a moment of your time!" They waited with a bank of cameras under a moonless night to catch the surprised victim in the glare of their lights—the prey-in-the-spotlight moment, where the home was no longer a refuge from those out to snatch *National Enquirer* moments from the misery of others.

The indictments had come down from Atlanta's grand jury, and the media was in a feeding frenzy with the news of Mary Ruth's fall and Michael's complicity. So many old debts were being settled by her enemies in Atlanta. Like seagulls flocking to a garbage dump, the media was eager to consume all they could. *Gulp, gulp.* It fit their script and was a "truth" they wanted to believe.

Franklin Dorsey, a television news director with a soothing, baritone voice, called to check on him. "I wanted to check to see if you're okay, Michael. How're you holding up, old friend?" he asked.

"I'm doing as well as can be expected," Michael answered, "but thanks for caring."

"Do you want to talk about it?" he asked with sympathetic tones

"No, I don't think so. Just a lot to digest," Michael answered. The news director's demeanor changed immediately. Gone were any residuals of concern or friendship.

"Well," he snapped angrily, "if you won't give me the exclusive, I'll have to ask you not to talk with anyone else if you change your mind. Remember, we called first!!"

So it began, the long process of separating the "wheat from the chaff," acquaintances from friends. Michael hung up after the call from his "friend" and called the sheriff's office to remove the riff-raff camping on his lawn. The police came, and the vultures moved on to less spectacular locations to frame their spots on the late news.

Michael sat in his den. He had the papers from the court announcing his indictment. He wadded each page to the size of a South Carolina peach and shot for the wastebasket across the room. As in games of old as a child, if he made the shots, his team would win. Tonight, if he made it, all of this would go away. He would be a free man once again, a free man who would never challenge the powers again.

He missed.

* * *

The day came when he accepted his fate, pled guilty, and received unspecified sentencing consideration on his sentence for cooperation—likely no time or a token sentence. He agreed to no further contact with Mary Ruth, who refused to give in. She began to bombard him with text messages of devotion, sorrow, and undying loyalty.

"How are you? Worried about you."

"We must hang together, or we'll hang separately."

"What do they say about me? Oh, never mind, I know you can't say."

"Have they turned you against me? I don't think they can, despite what others say."

"Let me tell you about my day. I'll just pretend we are talking."

"Tell your friends in the U.S. Attorney's office to…"

"I'm sorry for the earlier text. I know you don't like profanity."

"This will soon be over, and we can all go back to the way it was."

The texts came by the dozens; smeared and muddied words pelted him hour after hour, day after day, like a relentless storm eating away his resolve. It was a masterful campaign of subterfuge, guilt, and manipulation designed to wear him down; an unrelenting stream of one-way, digital dialogue from the half-light of dusk to the break of creeping dawn.

Just when things had quieted down, a package arrived. It had no return address but was postmarked Suitland, Maryland. It was a miniature of the Jefferson Memorial including the first few lines of the Declaration of Independence from panel one of the actual monument. "We hold these truths to be self-evident: that all men are created equal…"

Underneath it was a handwritten note: "Perhaps so, but wealth and power can buy immunity, render some invisible, and purchase acquittal. I underestimated my party. I'm sorry, Michael." It was signed by Michael's long-lost friend at the U.S. Department of Education, Gayle Powers.

As he read the note, the radio softly played Johnny Cash: *"I hurt myself today to see if I still feel. I focus on the pain, the only thing that's real…What have I become, my sweetest friend…I wear this crown of thorns upon my liar's chair. Full of broken thoughts I cannot repair…If I could start again, a million miles away, I would keep myself. I would find a way."*

CHAPTER THIRTY-SEVEN

"If beauty have a soul, this is not she."
—Shakespeare, Troilus and Cressida, *Act 5, Scene 2*

"I've seen the battle, and I've seen the war...
In prison I hear, there's time to be good, but the
first thing you see is the last thing you should...
We pray our lord's gonna meet us there."
—Black Rebel Motorcycle Club

Flame followed the explosion, and fire engulfed the house in the Holly Springs National Forest. In Michael's tortured dreams, the arsonist, who was seen casing his house near Oxford, had finally fulfilled his contract. The specialist for the Dixie Mafia had a preferred method, which was designed to blow the flame across the structure. Tossing jugs of gasoline and sticks of dynamite onto a roof created an instant inferno for the inhabitants and virtually guaranteed no survivors.

The symbolism was not hard to decipher. All of Michael's bridges were burning to the ground.

It had been a long night with the prosecutors in Atlanta. He didn't like them—Alex Martin in particular—and they didn't like him. Over several intense sessions, they alternately clubbed him and then smiled upon him. Instead of building him up and preparing him for testimony, the sessions were acrimonious and brutal.

Michael attended the last session without his lawyer—a big mistake.

"I don't think you're remembering all the pertinent facts, Mr. Parker," said Alex Martin, sneering over his reams of documents in the conference room of the Russell Federal Building, where the dusty venetian blinds rattled like so many bleached bones—all that remained of those who had traveled this road before him. Michael thought the Assistant U.S. Attorney wore his suit as a kind of uniform to mask his emptiness and hollow core. He was a bully who enjoyed tormenting and ridiculing those who came within his sphere of power.

"I think you might be protecting Robinson. Now, didn't she really say this here? Don't you remember it now that you've had a moment to think?" he coaxed, with nods from Agents Booker and Barrows. He was browbeating and toying with Michael in some kind of pointless, sadistic game.

"No," Michael said. "I'm telling you all I remember. The meds and the fatigue from that time may have obscured some minutia, but I'm giving you what I can swear to under oath. That's what we're supposed to be doing here, isn't it?"

"Don't get cute with me," Martin snapped. "You're not out of the woods yet. If you want our recommendation to the court for a favorable sentence, you'd better worry about pleasing us and have an epiphany tonight. We have a lot on the line here."

I've never seen such ruthless ambition and sadism, Michael thought. *Is he trying to provoke me?*

"I think you want details where there are no details and facts where there are no facts—support for the drama you're constructing," Michael shot back in anger.

"If I'm fishing, Mr. Parker, you aren't biting, are you?" Martin scoffed.

"No, I'm not. Your lies stick in my throat like old fish bones," Michael said.

The session melted down. More bitter words were exchanged, and Michael left Atlanta in a rage. He was tired, dog-tired of being under the thumb of people who had no respect for right and wrong. He was angry at himself most of all, because he was out of control. He took more pills, desperate to quell the helplessness that smothered him so intensely he couldn't breathe.

When he returned to Augusta, he did something that would come back to haunt him. In his anger, he violated his plea agreement and drove to Mary Ruth's house to assure her he would tell the truth on the stand if she went to trial.

She seemed surprised at first, but then acted as if he was an expected guest.

"Michael, I wondered when you might drop by. Come in," she said.

The den was as disheveled as she was. Her eye and face enhancements seemed to have faded under the stress. Books and magazines were strewn around the room—mostly romance novels and celebrity periodicals. The windows were propped open with sawed-off broomsticks. A sudden breeze parted the sheers and the white moon burst through and illuminated her den, as a whippoorwill called from the hollow below.

"How do you like my new jumpsuit?" she asked as she spun around like a model on a runway. "They call the color 'praying mantis green.'"

"Mary Ruth, I came to say that, by law, I'm everyone's witness. I'll tell what happened with Holcomb, the board, the diversion of money, and the call from D.C. Just tell your lawyers to ask their questions, and I'll answer truthfully," he told her.

His normal radar was muted, or he would have sensed it. She was taping him.

"You're cooperating with them. You're saying bad things about me," Mary Ruth coldly accused, while prodding him to say more. Her eyes were constricted and her mouth twisted into a mask of hate. All hints of innocence were gone. All that remained was a tone he'd heard her use to others but never to him.

"Prove it to me. Prove to me now that you put me above all others!" she demanded.

"What do you mean?" Michael asked.

"I want you to leave Susan now—today," she said without flinching.

And there it was—obvious, hidden in plain sight, but now out where Michael could see what he didn't wish to: the final reduction of the noble crusade, diminished to William Congreve's warning of "Hell hath no fury..."

This—in the middle of a struggle to preserve personal liberty? Madness! he thought. *I thought I was exempt. I don't exist for her. All who enter her life are mere props on her stage, mirrors to reflect an essence of reality that was lost to bad choices or a dance with darkness. Cross her and you're done. I've seen that look in her eyes and on her face. But where? Ah, yes...The snarling, growling dogs at Bull James's house.*

"What?" Michael said. "No, I won't! Are you crazy?! I'm your only friend, Mary Ruth."

With a frozen scowl that made him recoil, she said, "All right. You've made your choice. And don't even think about writing a book! This is my story to tell. I have my legacy to consider."

He stared at her in the golden hues of moonlight and the den's small lamp. Somewhere a cricket chirped, "*treep, treep, treep.*" All that had eclipsed his mind and heart cleared, and he saw clearly what he should have seen before—the emotional vampire Dr. Hartin warned him to flee.

As he turned to leave, he looked back for the last time at the woman he had believed in, silhouetted by her night lamp, hands on her hips. As an afterthought, he noted that her choice of outfit was appropriate, given the propensity of the female praying mantis to devour the male after she'd used him.

He heard the sound of a distant bell and knew it was tolling for him.

* * *

The night before the final briefing for Mary Ruth's trial, Michael couldn't sleep. He rose early and showered for the trip to Atlanta. As he stared up through the bathroom skylight, he could see the slant of an early citrus glow, but all the ambient colors and sounds were muted in his fading world.

Susan was quiet and let him have his distance, but she came to him as he was leaving and said, "You'll be strong and do well, for that's the kind of man you are—the best man I've ever known." She gave him a note with the image of a lone wolf howling in the night, railing against the world.

The commute down Interstate 20 was the longest drive of his life. When he slipped into Atlanta, the city had not yet roared to life. He was soon seated in a small office in the Russell Federal Building, where he was left waiting for a very long time. He took a Xanax—and then another—to calm his nerves. Finally he was called to another room filled with agents—all the agents who had visited his house on the night of his reckoning, plus one young agent he didn't recognize…but no prosecutors.

"What's up?" Michael asked the men with the brooding expressions.

"Nothing much," Agent Booker said, staring at a pile of papers.

With the driest tone Michael had ever heard, Agent Barrows asked, "Any contact?"

Michael didn't know what he meant and asked, "What?"

"Any contact? Knowing how the prosecutor feels about it?" Barrows asked.

"No, I don't know what you mean," Michael answered.

At that moment, Alex Martin burst into the room, crimson-faced, eyes bulging, and screaming at Michael at the top of his lungs. The agents drew back from the erratic, wild flailing of his hands as he yowled, "Liar, you liar…lies, lies, and more and more lies! You do this to me?! To me?! Lock him up!"

The agents moved in to restrain and cuff a stunned Michael. He asked them, "Arrest me? For what? Where're your warrants? Where's due process?"

"Due process?" Agent Booker scoffed. "I tried to tell you, Parker. Things have changed. We have the power to arrest anyone we believe has lied to us, no warrants needed. Just our judgment if we think you've lied to us. They gave us this power to get terrorists off the street while we build our cases." They seized Michael and shoved him against the wall. His pockets were emptied and his hands wrenched behind his back. Heavy chains were draped over his shoulders, around his waist, and between his ankles.

"Today," Booker laughed, "you're a terrorist. Everyone's a terrorist after 9-11!"

Michael's friends had tried to find him, tried to warn him that Mary Ruth had gone in before he got there that morning intending to cut a deal with the prosecutors—a deal that was actually no deal at all. She had waited too long to sign a plea agreement. She got no time off for cooperation and no reward for her last act, a parting gift as she walked from the room.

"Your friend Mary Ruth, the one you seem so protective of?" Agent Barrows smirked. "Let me tell you what she thinks of you. When she was leaving this morning, she turned and said, 'Oh, here, you might find this interesting.' She tossed us the tapes she'd made of your contact with her and your vow to tell the truth in court, even if her lawyers asked you questions that didn't serve our story line. Those were her tapes, not ours. We knew nothing about your attempt to help her until she gave you up. That bought *her* nothing, but she bought a whole *boatload* of misery for you."

Barrows laughed, "What was it you said? 'Tell the truth, the whole truth, and not some lie written in Atlanta or Washington?'"

Agent Booker chimed in, "That wasn't all. She gave us this look of mocking concern and said, 'Oh, and you'd better put him in isolation and watch him closely. He won't be able to take this. He'll try to kill himself—suicidal, very suicidal.'

"You know how she bites down on her lower lip and smiles that little satisfied smile of hers?" he asked mockingly. "She did that this morning and said, 'We may not go to heaven together, but we'll go to prison together.'"

"For someone who's seen all you've seen in your life, you're the most naïve person I've ever known. You have a big blind spot for broken birds with sob stories," Barrows added.

Michael was stunned, but he knew he had no right to be. He now understood what Captain Mark Stuckey had experienced in Jackson—the pop of the gun and the sudden, burning pain, as he fell at the hands of the abused woman he was trying to help.

He was cuffed, chained, and swept away so he couldn't testify and complicate the vendor's trial. The shackling reduced his gait to that of a shuffling old man who took tiny, waddling, penguin steps. He teetered and almost fell, but each time he was righted by the agents with sudden jerks of the chains that ran under and around his crotch, sending searing pain through his genitals.

"You had a sweet deal, Michael, and you threw it away. You should've played ball with us," Booker scoffed.

Michael didn't answer as they dragged him to the elevator and the waiting U.S. Marshals. They locked him in a holding cell until he could be transported to the Atlanta Correctional Detention Center, which contracted to temporarily house prisoners bound for the Federal Bureau of Prisons.

The agent's last words would not let him go—"You should've played ball." It was the echoed translation of Mary Ruth's warning— "You've made your choice."

The manual for would-be heroes lists many roads it claims will lead to truth and justice, but not all paths actually go there. Some don't pass Go. Some go directly to jail, and the Monopoly meters command the travelers, "Don't collect $100, don't take a ride on the Reading, and turn in all of your houses, hotels, and real estate."

Michael had never known such helplessness and fear. He was in uncharted territory. All the things that could never happen, the things that were impossible and unthinkable—they had come to pass in this nightmare that wouldn't end.

He teetered at the edge of madness as his mind tried to initiate a shutdown, to run the survival-mode program which would save and preserve his sanity, which seemed suddenly so tenuous.

Then it hit him. With his considerable assistance, Mary Ruth had done what Fredrick had been unable to do that night in Tupelo. She had killed him.

Back in the room full of agents, they shook their heads.

"Well, he deserved it," Agent Booker said dryly.

"Don't say that," said the young agent fresh out of Quantico Academy.

"What? You have sympathy for him? What he's done is unforgivable," Booker said.

"He may deserve it, but we all 'deserve' it," the new agent said as he pulled out the chain from around his neck and held the cross before them.

You could've heard a pin drop.

CHAPTER THIRTY-EIGHT

*"Cold, cold water surrounds me now and all I've
got is your hand... Lord, can you hear me now? Or
am I lost...I can't let go of your hand."*
—Damien Rice, *"Cold Water"*

*"God comes padding after me like a Hound of
Heaven..."*—Malcolm Muggeridge

The pearly white cotton balls over Atlanta seemed to have been cut and pasted into a windless, opaque sky that was lifeless and in a state of mourning.

The white government van was outfitted with rear cages fit for wild animals and driven by solemn men with angry countenances. It bounced and screeched to a halt in the rear alley of the ACDC, the Atlanta Correctional Detention Center.

Scraps of paper blew here and there amidst the inner-city neglect and decay, and a foul wind rolled and clinked empty wine bottles. A skinny cat slept on top of a garbage pile, and an ancient black woman, wearing an ill-fitting mail-order wig, loitered in the doorway of a building across the street, pooching her lips in kissy gestures at passers-by.

Electric guitars from clubs in downtown dives made twanging licks that drifted by promising respite, hinting of a place where troubled souls could drown their sorrows. An old lady, as white as lard, jogged by in blue spandex tights and high-top jogging shoes in this land of the surreal.

Doors opened and slammed shut again as two barrel-chested U.S. Marshals barked, "This is it. Get up!" With their military brush cuts and muscles that had muscles, they jerked and pulled Michael this way and that. He stumbled and almost fell from the weight and restrictions of the heavy chains that bound him from his ankles to his hands and waist. It took all his effort to keep from falling. The men of indifference spoke in bursts of "Go here, do this, no talking."

The marshals dumped him on the doorsteps of the ACDC. The grizzled officer on duty opened the doors to an atmosphere of stale air and inhabitants with features that were pallid from too little sunlight. It reeked of a slow death and an end-of-the-road destination for inmates and officers alike.

The keepers of the "castle" began to process Michael like thousands before him, some lost and forgotten in the system—Americans mixed with Cubans, Nigerians, Mexicans, and many other nationalities housed in the giant complex, along with the creatures of the street—the crackheads, prostitutes, gender benders, and garden-variety winos.

As they shuffled Michael along each corridor, the smell grew stronger—blood, urine, vomit, and bodily fluids. Altogether it was a toxic stew that disinfectants could never erase. Worst of all was the trifecta of fear, helplessness, and hopelessness, a paralyzing mix that destroyed any remnant of innocence hard-wired into man at birth. Michael thought some of it was familiar—an orphaned remnant of the smell that lingered in his car in Tylertown after the shooting.

"So," said the heavyset, bleached-blonde female officer who was processing him, "it says here you're suicidal."

"What?! No, absolutely not!" Michael answered numbly.

The officer with the bad case of the frizzies answered, "Well, that's what the Fed boys have got down here—to watch you, isolate you, give you no bread knives to cut your meat, not even any plastic forks—like you're going to get any meat here!" That brought uproarious laughter from her partner, the entry officer who looked like Jack Nicholson.

"Jack" stared at Michael, his latest opportunity for torment. "Man, you sure must have made them mad. What'd you do to the prosecutor—steal his Phi Beta Kappa key or something?"

"Something like that," Michael said. He felt sick and wanted to throw up.

"Hey, you're not going to puke, are you?" Frizzie asked.

"Just hang on," she said. "It'll get better. I know it's a bit overwhelming now, but don't be scared. Yeah, there are people here who would shake you down, kill you maybe if they had the chance, but you're so hot, so high profile…you're going straight to isolation. That's here on the jacket—isolation, no human contact."

They suited him in orange, three sizes too big, then photographed and fingerprinted him. After they strip-searched him for the third time and demanded that he assume the most degrading positions for body cavity inspection, they led him down another maze of hallways.

Officers shouted, "This way! … Stand here! … Stand up straight! … What's the matter with you? Are you deaf?" Humanity had gone away, and Michael felt he was inside the belly of the beast, captured within the lightlessness of a netherworld that obscured all gentleness.

They led him through corridor after corridor, and the deeper they penetrated the labyrinths of the huge facility, the worse the smells became. "You got a bed, John?" the escorts called to their fellow managers on each floor.

"No, can't house him here. He's political—too hot for us to handle. They'd kill him on this floor," one faceless voice shouted back from the gloom.

"Let us have the pretty boy," a tormentor called out from the recesses of the cages.

Finally they came to level six. Michael was inspected once more and given a rolled piece of bedding that smelled a hundred years old and contained stains that Michael feared to question. The floor manager walked him to his cell amidst catcalls, whistles, and abusive words in many languages; some Michael recognized and some he didn't, but no translation was necessary.

Calls from the lower and upper levels of the unit rang out.

"Hello, sweetie! Need a friend?" called one disembodied voice that drifted from somewhere in the gloom of the second-story cage.

"Be down to visit later, Pops!" another promised.

"Man, that dude is an old hombre! What'd you do, old man? Assault the President's daughters?" offered a voice with a thick Spanish accent, which was rewarded by uproarious laughter.

They ordered him to step into his cell, and the loneliest sound that Michael ever heard followed—the boom and clang as the huge metal door slammed shut, locking behind him. Michael, who was claustrophobic, was left within a space the size of his bathroom at home. The walls seemed to move, to close in and crush the life from him. He wished to be transported to another time and place before all this began—before Georgia, before Bell and Mary Ruth, before politics, before he forgot who he was. As he drifted into an exhausted sleep to relieve senses that could no longer bear reality, he longed for second chances and for the warmth of Susan's arms.

* * *

A lemon sun, the very point between orange and green, illuminated his cell the next morning. He startled awake to a heart-pounding disbelief that he was still here in what his mind had pretended was a nightmare. He staggered to a tiny window where he could stand on his tiptoes and see the last early blinking and crackling of the pink and blue neon sign advertising cheap and reliable bail bond services.

Silver sheets of rain of Biblical proportions pelted Atlanta during Michael's first night as a prisoner, but no rain could wash away the gagging smell of broken hearts. His nightmares were still fresh, coughed up like furballs from yesterday. Some were islands of escape, images of better days in Parker Grove when Pearl told him stories of when she was a girl.

Her papa, home from his Civil War imprisonment in Ft. Delaware, found two young crows that had fallen out of their nest. He brought them home to Pearl. They became her pets and hopped along beside her to snatch food from her plate and to steal her powder puff.

"One day," she told Michael, "a flock of wild crows flew over, just cawing and cawing. Papa had forgotten to clip the wings of our crows, and they looked at those wild cousins and then back at me for what seemed a long goodbye. They lifted up and up to join those wild ones winging their way toward heaven."

She paused and said, "That's all that most of us really want, Michael, to one day—fly away." Here where Pearl could never imagine him to be, he finally understood what she meant.

The screams of the tormented echoed in the ACDC. The morning banter from the inmates outside his cell swept away those good memories and isolated him from the refuges where his subconscious wanted to go to hide from horror, a place where order and good still reigned.

Michael was in isolation from Susan, the inmates, and the world so he couldn't testify and spoil the prosecutor's new script. He wasn't allowed to tell her what had happened, and he imagined she was frantic. The food served was stale bread, thin, hard slices of green baloney, and small cups of warm Kool-Aid. Weight began to fall off of him. His hygiene faltered as he was denied the mandated twice-daily, fifteen-minute breaks allotted to shower and move around.

"They'll kill you in here, man," the morning shift officer told him. "We got to keep you segregated for your own good. We're going to let you out for a phone call and shower tomorrow."

Michael placed his first call to Susan as a hundred faces watched him from their cells.

They both tried to hold back the floodgates, but eventually the tears came as the enormity of it washed over them, and they were unable to see or touch each other.

"How're you doing?" Michael asked, worried for the woman he loved, who was now without her caregiver. He was acutely aware that his mistakes had left both of them vulnerable and exposed.

"I'm fine, but I'm so frightened for you," Susan answered with a quiet strength.

"I'm okay," he said. "Actually it's kinda like a resort here." They both laughed weakly.

"I'm sorry, honey, so sorry," he said, choking back tears as the lump of grief balled up in his guts and all the way up into his throat.

"Stop, Michael," she said. "I told you once after we watched *Love Story*—love means never having to say you're sorry. Each time you apologize, you're wasting the time we have left."

But there was nothing either of them could say to say to change it all. In the end, they merely employed their usual parting exchange.

"Well, see you later, alligator," he said.

"After while, crocodile," she answered. Then came the long hesitation and the deafening click of goodbye.

* * *

Tyrone "Corleone" Jones, the baritone-voiced, tall, black man in the next cell, began to talk to him through the slots in their doors. He provided the human interaction that some seemed so determined to eliminate.

"I read all about you," Tyrone said. "It sounds a bit too convenient for that woman who testified about you. We can spot liars on the street a block away. Of course, I could be wrong, and you could be the pistol she claims." He laughed with abandon.

"That's me, but maybe not a pistol anymore, just a son of a gun," Michael said in an attempt at forced humor. "Why are you here, if you don't mind me asking?"

Tyrone got real quiet for a moment and said, "Something went wrong and someone died. So someone had to pay, and they picked me." That's all he'd ever say about it, but the two unlikely neighbors talked for hours at a time through the slots in their doors. The conversations ran late one night, and a young, new guard came by while they were still talking. He tried to slam the slot shut on Corleone's arm, but the prisoner grabbed his wrist instead and tried to wrench him through the opening. The guard was screaming. It was quite a scene. The veteran officers laughed, but a shakedown followed to show solidarity.

One thing Tyrone noticed about Michael was that the nurse brought him pills each night, so he asked about them. Michael told him that they were just giving him his usual doses of prescription meds, which had been the practice from the beginning of his incarceration. However, those were abruptly stopped, and he was notified that there would be no more per jail policy.

Michael asked the nurse, "You're going to make me go cold turkey from Xanax? Do you know that Xanax withdrawal can be worse than heroin?" But the nurse was only the messenger and had no reply.

Within forty-eight hours, Michael was living in a different world. He was hallucinating wildly, unaware of where he was, helpless, covered in vomit, and soiling himself. His breathing was shallow, and the sphincter muscles had given way to unbearable stress.

In his dream world, he was standing at a MARTA station in Atlanta. The fog was thick and swirling. An enigmatic figure was standing on the platform with his back to Michael. Tapping him on the shoulder, Michael asked, "Sir, can you tell me where this train goes?"

The man turned. It was the grim-faced border agent from his earlier dreams—the ones when he first came to Georgia. Off in the distance, the hissing and bleating whistle of an approaching engine grew louder. The agent said, "This is the last stop before eternity. Have you found something to believe in amidst this pain, Michael Parker? Are you ready to pick up your cross and serve?"

Michael was in and out of his dream and unable to answer officers who came by his cell. They came not to help, but to curse him for faking and demand that he get up and clean himself. Michael was too far gone to answer them. He was living in a world his drug-starved brain had created, a place to survive until the storm passed—or a place to die.

Tyrone got word out to Susan through trustees he was paying. He told her that he feared they were going to kill Michael, who could no longer answer him. Susan began to call and stir up so much dust that the medical team came to Michael's door, only because they feared his notoriety and the public relations fallout if he died on their watch. Stunned at his condition, Dr. Julius Greene, chief of staff, ordered immediate transport to Grady Hospital.

Even through the haze and stupor of the pervasive twilight he sleepwalked in, Michael insisted on bathing before they left. As he stumbled to the shower, the residents of the ACDC rained comments regarding his nakedness, but he was beyond knowing or caring about their threats or mocking. Two officers, who looked very angry, came and shackled him when he returned from the shower. Michael thought they looked like a dangerous mutation of Mutt and Jeff. They transported him through backstreets that were little more than catacombs.

"I know this boy's faking," Mutt said as the truck bounced along the potholed streets.

"Yeah, thinks he's better than the rest of the inmates—even better than us," Jeff answered.

Mutt laughed, "Yeah, we could take this street here down to the river and drop him in, say that he escaped, and just drown the little rat. We could save the city some money. All the papers are saying that he's involved with that Robinson tramp, and she testified that he made her do it all. We could dispense some vigilante justice."

"Yeah, what you say, Parker? You ready to go swimming?" Jeff asked.

Michael knew—or hoped at least—that this was purely sadism and not an actual plan to kill him. But in his state of mind, he was terrified nonetheless…locked away at the mercy of uniformed thugs who weren't exactly the essence of charity, traveling the back roads of a pitch-black and unforgiving city.

He spent twelve hours at Grady waiting to see a doctor, as inmates were given the lowest priority. They were considered a nuisance by the resident physicians, who appeared improbable candidates for employment at any credible hospital.

When he was returned to the ACDC, he was almost relieved that he was in the confines of the jail, considering his other option was the murky depths of the Chattahoochee River. He saw an officer who had shown him kindness and called out, "They threatened to kill me!" She turned away, and they dragged him down the tunnel to the floor housing the medical unit. He was jeered and mocked, called names that would make even a veteran cop wince. It was a total absence of humanity. It was—hell.

He wasn't isolated in the medical unit, and the three weeks there passed quickly. He had two visitors—the number two prosecutor and an FBI agent. They wanted him to sign papers that were beyond his comprehension at the time—papers that the jail staff could have executed. The two men just wanted to see him, to rub his face in it one last time. Michael decided he preferred the company of inmates.

Dr. Greene came to see him after the Feds left. "How're you today?" the doctor asked during a check-up.

"The shakes are better, and the hallucinations aren't as bad, but the floor still rushes up to meet me when I walk quickly. When we're led to the basketball court, I can't even catch the balls inmates throw at me. They seem to come like missiles. Objects jump around like they're under wild strobe lights. The movement is shocking…frightening! I wouldn't recommend this form of detox to my worst enemy, but I am living proof that cold-turkey Xanax withdrawal can be endured," he said.

Dr. Greene replied, "Well, you have survived it, so I must send you back to isolation on your old floor."

"Already?! Do you think I could be given a bit longer to recover?" Michael asked. His pulse rate began to pound away at the door of a panic attack.

The doctor looked at the floor and said quietly, "No. Someone in the prosecutor's office has complained that you're being pampered."

So Michael returned to the greetings from his fellow residents, who had only seen him briefly—on entry, leaving for the hospital and phone calls. One voice missing was Corleone, who had contacted Susan. He had been transferred to another institution.

The smell from the holding cells just down from him was unbearable—worse than before, if that were possible. He had only been back a few days when he looked through the slot in his door to see four officers. Each one had an arm and a leg of a well-known crack addict who cycled in and out of the jail. He been known to spit on officers and inmates.

They took the man to the far back unit, away from the main body, and began to beat him. The thuds, whacks, and screams from the beating echoed across the floor and were nauseating and overwhelming. Michael began to scream at the top of his lungs, "Stop! Stop! Someone please stop them!" Finally Michael covered his ears to mute the man's wailing and sobbing.

When the sounds of the assault finally ceased, the officers walked out. Two had blood spatters on their teal jail shirts, and one was pulling off leather gloves. He looked at Michael's cell as he passed and said, "You want some of what we gave him? If not, you better keep your mouth shut."

Michael recovered a scrap of paper and a pencil that a trustee had given him. Although it was intended for writing to Susan, he instead penned a letter to the warden, which the trustee smuggled to the mailbox. Michael hoped his carefully crafted letter and his notoriety might move the powers-that-be into action.

The response was almost immediate. The next day, the floor was flooded with brass—four sergeants, two lieutenants, a major, the deputy warden, the psychologist, the chaplain, and more. An officer walked by and said, "See what you caused." The cells were cleaned, and new regulations were established regarding the treatment of prisoners—even those who spit on you.

Michael jolted from a nap the next morning to see a face peering at him through the peephole. "Hello," the man said. "I have something for you, something from those who appreciate what you did. A friend will bring you some food later to sustain you."

Michael rose from his cot and walked to the door. The man said he was a volunteer pastor. He reached through the hole and clutched Michael's hand. He began to pray for Michael and held his hand tightly but gently.

"Father, come to Michael with the good infection. Show him Your coherence, the cohesiveness of the ages. Show him, Father, that the time of last hymns, last prayers, and last chances are near. Show him, Lord, that even now, Gabriel is raising his horn. Even now, You are stepping through the clouds to wash away all tears. Amen."

He ended the prayer for Michael and handed him a Bible. "I hope you find solace here, Michael Parker. You might begin with the passages I've highlighted for you."

As the man rose to leave, Michael said, "Wait! What's your name?"

"Chances," the man with the azure eyes said softly, "because we serve a God of second chances, Michael."

Michael took the Bible and sat on the floor looking at the gift, feeling the weight of the book that beckoned him home. The pastor said, "Before I leave, I have something for you to use as your bookmark, to remind you that Someone has paid your debts—in full."

Michael took the bookmark and on the back side, Michael's name had been inscribed, and underneath it…the image of the Cross. He pitched forward and buried his wet face in the precious Words of Life. When he looked back up, there was no sign of the man, and guards claimed there was no preacher named "Chances" on their security roster. Michael never saw him again.

Michael waited, and the provisions came as promised. The trustee who brought the extra food also smuggled him a dog-eared copy of a novel, *Odd Thomas* by Dean Koontz. Michael identified with the title character, who also encountered the forces of evil. He found himself repeating one of Odd's lines over and over: "Life has meaning…when my last sun has set and my last moon has risen, when the dawn comes that marks the moment when I am born with the dead, there shall be mercy."

Michael also began to pray as Odd did, "Spare me that I may serve."

Not only did Michael pore over the novel, but he began to read the Bible as never before. He labored in the fields of Job and the Psalms—the books for troubled souls. He read and reread them, copied bits and pieces here and there, and soon began to fashion his own prayers.

One day while Michael was studying, he was stunned to see inmates begin lining up at the door, even though few had ever seen him in this asylum of lost and forgotten souls. They sat on their haunches to stare at Michael through the tiny slot in the massive door. The Cubans came. The Nigerians came. The Mexicans came. The crackheads and transvestites came. All the invisible people—those who were rarely acknowledged in a rented world—they came to Michael's door.

They didn't come to gawk or talk. They came to confess hushed recitals of evil deeds they'd committed—murder, assaults, all manner of perversion and man's inhumanity to man. They came to unburden themselves, to seek some sort of absolution—and forgiveness.

Michael didn't understand. He didn't feel worthy. He didn't know what to say to them except for kind words and soft utterances of, "I know, I know. I'm sorry."

Michael prayed, "I don't understand, Lord. Why is this happening?"

Then, the first glimpse of what he thought unknowable swept over him, the first down-payment of many to come. It was an understanding that this was just the beginning of how it would be now with God.

"Michael, Michael. Don't you know Me?" Michael saw the tornado turn in Parker Grove, the discus begin to rise in Tupelo, the miracle in Tylertown. He heard again the voice in his car commanding him to go back and get the bulletproof vests. Playing in his heart was the melody that had soothed and healed him in the hospital, and the softness of the strong hand that held his in the ICU now grasped him again.

"Come out, Michael. Come out to life. I have rescued you from the world that took all you valued. Now nothing remains but your love for Me. You shall be My burning bush to shine brightly for others. In your own version of life, you have pulled people *up* to help them. Here you will know Christ by coming *down* to these lost and forgotten travelers. This is the dialectic of love. There is no path to Me that bypasses your neighbors."

He had spent years of seeking some elusive simplicity, even as he constructed his own complex and artificial existence—one that revolved around Michael Parker. But here, in this womb of brokenness, the Light invaded the dungeon of his ego and called him out of himself. Divine love washed over Michael's world, and he understood for the first time that something more was at stake than his own life and liberty—something tumultuous, essential, and eternal.

He removed his government slippers and fell to his knees. This was a house of horrors and deprivation, but he knew he was now on—holy ground. The Hound of Heaven had not given up on him.

Michael looked out the tiny window in his cell and saw the blinking, white cross above the inner city mission in the distance. Underneath it in red were the words "Jesus saves."

CHAPTER THIRTY-NINE

"There's a man goin' round takin' names. An' he decides
who to free and who to blame. Everybody won't be treated
all the same...When the man comes around."
—Johnny Cash, "When the Man Comes Around"

"The goat...shall be...used for making atonement
by sending it into the wilderness as the
scapegoat."—Leviticus 16:10

"Man, you are famous—or infamous!" said Jason, an excited trustee, as he handed Michael a smuggled copy of the front page of the *Atlanta Journal-Constitution*.

The headlines and excerpts quoted all the players in the trial underway, including Mary Ruth Robinson, the chief witness for prosecutor Alex Martin.

"I didn't know what he was doing. He kept me out of the loop," the former superintendent said.

"Where is this Michael Parker who can shed light on the facts of this case? Why is the government keeping him locked away? What are they afraid of?" Josiah Bates, lawyer for the vendor, asked.

"He's irrelevant to the vendor trial. Parker will go to prison, and Superintendent Robinson will go to prison. *This* is the trial for Russian Action Communications, Incorporated," Assistant U.S. Attorney Alex Martin stated.

"My client is a victim of this Michael Parker. She trusted the wrong man," claimed Elbert Johnston, attorney for Mary Ruth Robinson.

John Mendez, Michael's lawyer, was also quoted. "This is classic. Whoever's not here in the courtroom must be the mastermind, the Big Kahuna who led Robinson astray. She assumed by default what was to be Michael's role as government witness in the RAC trial. When my client made some poor decisions, the superintendent betrayed him. She is telling her lies and playing victim with all the conviction of a seasoned actress.

She's the classic 'woman scorned.' The government conducted numerous interviews with my client, collecting the facts about what really happened in this whole ordeal. In the end, they used none of it. They say *now* that the information wasn't true, but they were prepared to build their entire case around it—until they abruptly changed game plans."

After the trial, Mary Ruth was told that Michael had almost died inside. A friend sent word to him that she was inconsolable and had asked if she could write him in the ACDC.

"Mail call, Michael," Jason said. "It looks like the wicked witch has sent you a letter."

Dearest Michael, the note began. *I'm sorry. I know nothing I say can make it better, but I wanted you to know I did what I had to do. They were threatening my family for putting their names on vendor donations. I'm obviously sorry for any harm that I caused.*

"Okay, c'mon and tell me. What'd she say?" the trustee asked.

"It wasn't what she *said* so much as what she omitted. She failed to explain how anything she mentioned was connected to the tape she voluntarily supplied to the government or why she went out of her way to tell them to lock me up in solitary," Michael answered through the slot in his door.

He paused. "But then, that's classic. Nothing's ever her fault. In all of her 'woe is me' stories, it was her father's fault, her husband's fault, the Democrats, the Republicans, the teachers, and so on. Personal responsibility never visited her door. She was always Flip Wilson as Geraldine—The devil made her do it."

Michael paused again, remembering the story of her night in the woods and the day of the exorcism. He said, "Those six words may be the truest ever uttered to describe Mary Ruth."

* * *

John Mendez came to visit Michael. "We can try for a second bail if you want, Michael, but it will be tough."

"I know. That's what the jailhouse sages here tell me every day," Michael said.

The ACDC housed many repeat offenders, including one who had also served time up in New York. He had even shared a cell with a member of Donnie Brasco's former gang. Overhearing Michael's conversation with his attorney, this inmate yelled out, "You got no chance of winning a second bail—no chance at all, Michael. That prosecutor hates your guts, and you becoming a Jesus freak ain't gonna save you neither!"

"Yeah, I hear him," Mendez said, "but this hearing isn't about guilt or innocence. It's about whether you can go home to Susan, who's so terribly sick. It's about getting your affairs in order."

"Let's go for it, then," Michael said.

* * *

The courtroom was formal, sterile, and impersonal—a place where lives were changed forever, for better or worse. The stale breeze smelled of recycled air that barely registered in any visible sense. The tables for both prosecution and defense were of the same shiny, oak veneer. Behind them, the spectator benches were uniform, almost like church pews, but absent warmth and divine Presence.

An emaciated Michael was unshackled and led into the room by the U.S. Marshal assigned to the court. He only had the t-shirt and jeans he was wearing when he was arrested. The faces of the character witnesses registered shock at his appearance, but that was quickly followed by kind smiles from these friends and acquaintances who had come to testify on his behalf.

Alex Martin's face, however, was contorted into a barely controlled scowl. His eyes seethed with an unbridled loathing of the one-time star witness for the prosecution.

"All rise! The Honorable Federal District Judge Harrison Stockman now presiding," the bailiff said.

"Gentlemen, we have a hearing before us today for bail consideration for Mr. Michael Parker," Judge Stockman said.

"Mr. U.S. Attorney, do you object to the granting of bail?" the judge asked.

"The government of the United States *does* object, Your Honor. Mr. Parker was already out on one bail. He violated his agreement with the government and was arrested for contact with a defendant he was to testify against. He is also, we believe, a danger to the safety of that witness, who testified for the government and now fears the defendant. By her testimony, he is also a danger to himself if released," Martin said, telegraphing his intent to bury Michael.

"Mr. Mendez, how do you respond?" the judge inquired.

"Your Honor, my client has been a good citizen all of his life. He made a mistake, but he is no threat to anyone. Also, his wife is critically ill. He would just like to be with her to make arrangements for her care and to get his affairs in order before he leaves for prison. We have witnesses who will support our contention," Mendez said.

"Very well, please call your first witness," the judge ordered.

Michael's neighbor, Juanita Brody, came and testified about his care for Susan, his qualities as a neighbor, and his character.

"Isn't it accurate to say that you barely know Michael Parker? How then, could you know his mind? You hardly see him, isn't that true?" Martin asked her.

Brody looked at the prosecutor without blinking. "Oh, I do see him when he walks each night. He stops to pray with us and our children."

She reached into her purse and produced a small rock she extended to the prosecutor. "If you are without sin, Mr. Martin, why don't you cast the first stone here today?" Martin was stunned, taken aback at her audacity, and his placid façade began to crack.

Michael's physician, Dr. Todd Hartin, was called to the stand and questioned by Mendez. Then Martin strode to the witness chair, intending to set things straight this time. "Dr. Hartin, isn't it true that your diagnosis for Mr. Parker is faulty? This so-called 'obsessive-compulsive disorder' which you say compels him to set right what he sees as wrong—isn't it true that it's not consistent with the American Psychiatric Association standards that I hold in my hand?"

"Those standards are out of date. My diagnosis is consistent with *current* guidelines," the doctor answered. He went on to cite chapter and verse, and Martin's confidence began to wilt.

It was dealt a further blow when Judge Stockman said, "I have a question for Dr. Hartin. Is Mr. Parker a danger to himself or to anyone else, in your opinion?"

"No, sir. It's not in him to do harm to anyone, including himself," Hartin answered.

Martin was furious and tried to punish the doctor, much as he had Michael after the ill-fated visit to Mary Ruth. "Isn't it true that this isn't your medical opinion—just an attempt to help a friend?" he spat in a sudden tantrum.

The unflappable physician looked at the prosecutor and said, "Well, I do admire Mr. Parker, because I saw him go out of his way time and again to help Bell employees who needed counseling. He went far and above what I'd ever seen anyone in his position do. He has cared for his wife through thick and thin, seeking the best medical advice from around the country to try to save her when it seemed hopeless. But do we see each other outside the office? No. If I saw him in the grocery, I would speak to him, I suppose," the doctor said, as the slightest smile of mocking satisfaction appeared on his face. Martin was red-faced and humiliated.

After the questioning had run its course, Judge Stockman said, "I will retire to my chambers to make my decision."

When he left the courtroom, Michael was taken to a holding room, where he fell to his knees and cried out to God in the Puritan prayer he had memorized.

> *Lord, in the daytime stars can be seen from deepest wells, and the deeper the wells the brighter thy stars shine; Let me find thy light in my darkness, thy life in my death, thy joy in my sorrow, thy grace in my sin, thy riches in my poverty, thy glory in my valley. Deliver me Lord, if it be your will. Amen.*

They finally came for Michael, escorting him back to sit next to his lawyer. Then the judge returned.

"After deliberation, I have decided to grant bond and allow Mr. Parker to go home to his wife. He isn't a threat to anyone, despite the government's contentions, and no evidence has been presented to prove that he is. Mr. Mendez, Mr. Parker will surrender any prescriptions he has at home to you, and Dr. Hartin, you'll be the only one to write new ones for him. Unless there are further items, we will be adjourned," Judge Stockman said.

At that moment, a wild man leapt to his feet. The hearing was no longer a matter of justice or even professional pride. It was personal. The hate was visceral, the purest Michael had ever seen. Alex Martin's bugged eyes were frantic as he jumped from his chair, shaking and jabbing the air with his forefinger, aiming it at the judge.

"You can't do this, Your Honor. I demand he be held until sentencing. I don't want him to go home. He betrayed me…uh, the government!" Martin screeched in a raspy voice that got higher by the moment. Spittle from the prosecutor landed on the court reporter's machine.

"Mr. U.S. Attorney, I have ruled. You can sit down," Judge Stockman ordered.

But Martin's rant continued unabated, driven by an uncontrollable rage that burned within. He wouldn't have it. This could not be! There could be no mercy for someone who had dared to defy him, to embarrass him, and to put his career ambitions at risk.

"No, Your Honor! I'll bring more charges against him. Keep him locked in isolation, and I'll go before the magistrate tomorrow to officially charge him with lying to a federal agent."

"No, you won't," Stockman snapped. "I'm the federal judge. You won't make an end-run by going around me to a lower court. I'm the federal judge!" he angrily reiterated as he leaned over his bench, incredulous at what he was hearing.

"Then we'll bring these new charges against him, and you can sign the orders. This man who mocks me—an officer of the court! You can't let him go home," the U.S. Attorney insisted.

The judge was now equally enraged. Shaking his gavel at the prosecutor, he declared, "No, you will not! You knew we were consolidating everything into this hearing. Anything you were going to do should have been done before today. You knew it, but you were arrogant. Now sit down, Mr. U.S. Attorney, or be held in contempt of this court!"

But Martin was out of control. He had passed the point of reason and rose again in his irrational rage. The federal agents at his table looked stunned and pale. Spectators in the courtroom were terrified.

"But, Judge Stockman, you, you just can't…" His voice trailed off in what was now a whine as the judge raised the gavel to twelve o'clock high, preparing to declare the attorney in contempt. The other assistant prosecutor and agents subdued Martin, and he fell back into his chair in disbelief, stunned that a member of the judiciary would challenge his power to act as prosecutor and judge in the modern criminal justice system. He had run into an adjudicator who wouldn't yield what authority he did have.

Michael laid his head on the defense table and spread his arms across it to praise God for deliverance. "Thank you, Lord. Thank you."

People in the courtroom looked at the repulsive and crazed actions of the prosecutor in stark contrast to Michael, who was quietly—even reverently—praising God. A hush fell over the courtroom, and some present said they would never forget what they had seen. It was a moment of revelation for them.

Michael was remanded to the custody of the marshals until paperwork came down. He was given one call before returning to his cell. He called Susan.

"Honey, I'm coming home," he told her.

"Oh, thank God," she said. She began to cry and then called neighbors to arrange a homecoming party.

Mendez rode down on the elevator with the federal agents and the prosecutors. He later told Michael he had never seen such a dejected crowd.

The defense lawyer was also a former prosecutor, but he had been disgusted by the circus that took place in the court. Through a thinly veiled contempt, he told them, "Look, Michael's going to prison, yet you people look like you just lost your last friend. Get over it!"

The usually stoic U.S. Marshal transporting Michael had barely engaged his cuff locks and didn't secure them to the belly chains. On the drive back to the ACDC, the marshal said, "You must hate that no-good…"

"Yeah, maybe once I did, but now I could no more hate him than I could a blind man who stepped on my foot. He doesn't know Who I know," Michael answered, surprising himself.

The marshal looked uncomfortable, but he said, "Well, at least you were bailed out."

Michael replied, "I'd already been ransomed."

* * *

Michael waited two weeks for processing, thanks to the prosecutor's foot-dragging. Shortly, and just before his lawyer came to pick him up, a package came from Mary Ruth. There was no note that could be leaked or used, just a book—the classic novel by George Orwell, *1984*.

As he thumbed through it, a passage had been highlighted in blue.

"I betrayed you," she said baldly.

"I betrayed you," he said.

"Sometimes," she said, "they threaten you with something— something you can't stand up to, can't even think about. And then you say, 'Don't do it to me, do it to somebody else, do it to So-and-so.' And perhaps you might pretend, afterwards, that it was only a trick and that you just said it to make them stop and didn't really mean it. But that isn't true.

"At the time when it happens you do mean it. You think there's no other way of saving yourself, and you're quite ready to save yourself that way. You WANT it to happen to the other person. All you care about is yourself."

"All you care about is yourself," he echoed.

"And after that, you don't feel the same toward the other person any longer."

"No," he said, "you don't feel the same."

And then—perhaps it was not happening, perhaps it was only a memory taking on the semblance of sound—a voice was singing: "Under the spreading chestnut tree, I sold you and you sold me..."

Three hours later when they came to open Michael's door, he walked across the concrete floor of the ACDC for the last time. He was thin as a rake and hollow-eyed, and much of his hair had fallen out from stress, bad food, and rapid weight loss. Nevertheless, the response from some of the inmates cheered him.

Well wishes and a smattering of applause were offered by the men he had prayed with as they confessed their crimes. And somewhere in the recesses of the cell blocks, he heard a mournful solo of Patty Griffin's "Up to the Mountain," a tribute to Martin Luther King, Jr.: "Sometimes I feel like I've never been nothing but tired, and I'll be walking till the day I expire. Sometimes I lay down, no more can I do. But then I go on again, because you ask me to."

That same voice called out to him. It was the regular visitor to the ACDC, back in custody again—the man who had been badly beaten by the guards, causing Michael to write his letter. He yelled to Michael, "Don't come back, Christian! God bless you!"

CHAPTER FORTY

"Steal a little, and they put you in jail;
steal a lot, they make you king."—Bob Dylan

"Maybe you will hear me calling...Won't you come
back soon to the one that will always love you."
—Maura O'Connell, "A Stor Mo Chroi"

One of the first dreams Michael had in his own bed was of a night in 1976 when he and Clay watched while CIA mercenaries loaded a plane with guns bound for the armies of Central America. The pilots returned with their payload—drugs that would subvert the American dream, all the while earning money from their handlers in an attempt to buy that same illusion. At the same time, the MBN was also under siege by Governor Davidson and his own band of mercenaries.

These were moments of disillusionment for the two drug agents. Within his dreamscape, Michael listened again as Clay began to wax philosophical about the pursuit of happiness and those who confuse happiness with pleasure.

"We think *things* equal happiness, Michael—that joy can be compressed into a pill. Here we live in prisons of our own making. You and I combat drugs while our government hires people to fly them in. We ignore the true beauty all around us as we try so hard to be better people, celebrating small triumphs and failures. We ask what life is all about, what it means, but anyone who truly seeks God has found it. He's all around us. We can't be better or happier with the praise of man, nor worse for the world's condemnation. We remain who we are. The world sees the outer man and actions, but God knows our hearts and our motives."

When Michael woke, he couldn't shake the dream. He picked up a copy of *USA Today* which trumpeted the declaration from Washington, "We've saved the Department of Education." The article said that some Republicans would prefer to abolish the department, but that effort had been defeated. In fact, the administration claimed that No Child Left

Behind would actually expand the power of the education department and transform the landscape of public education.

As the White House congratulated themselves, with no mention of the consequences visited upon Georgia, Michael arranged for Susan's care, as his time in the free world was growing short. John Mendez called to tell him that Mary Ruth had been sentenced to ninety-six months—eight years. "What she did to you got her zilch, nada, nothing!" he said.

Michael set about constructing the first outlines of a novel about the Bureau days. The title would be inspired by an old song called "A Whiter Shade of Pale."

Tim Charles, who was Michael's old professor and the second Bureau director, came to support him at sentencing. He had written to the court about Michael's kidnapping in Tylertown; the contract killers at Horn Lake; the ambush by the sniper; his steadfastness while running the internal affairs investigation; and the award from Ole Miss as one of its distinguished alumni.

"This is who Michael is and has always been. It's all right and wrong, no stretch of gray in between. He went too far in this case—much too far—in his crusade to defeat what he viewed as wrong. But the type of action he has been lauded for in the past—well, it is the very same thing for which you want to imprison him now. I just wanted you to know who he was and all he did."

On the day of sentencing, Charles put his arm around Michael's shoulders and looked at him with sad, basset eyes. "Crime pays, Michael. Not this made-up stuff that they're after you for; *your* transgressions provide cover for the real crime … the kind that pays. There's a high cost, a terrible price to misguided heroism. Sometimes love covers, Michael, and sometimes it exposes. There's a reason for all of this, one that you can't see yet…but you will. The sign you saw with Robinson that night, the one that said you were on the highway to hell? Don't believe it for a minute. This is your road to Damascus, and someone's waiting on that road Who'll change everything for you."

The courtroom was abuzz when Michael and Tim arrived. All at the party donned their costumes for the masquerade ball. An observer and freelance writer from Georgia Tech wrote, *The pigeons were dreaming under the eaves, the blindfold on the lady of justice seemed to cover leaking eyes, the statutes were bleeding time away for Michael Parker, and when the clerk announced the case of the United States versus Michael Parker, the words seemed to burn right through him. He seemed to be looking at something high above the judge's bench as if he had retreated to some better place—old memories, first loves, football Saturdays, holding hands, sad movies, and bad jokes. In the poignancy of his ashen pallor, you just knew that he could never be the same person he once was. Everything had changed and he could never ever go back.*

Witnesses testified and asked for leniency, but their tunes were off-key and they were barking up the wrong tree. The judge was impatient. The die was cast in the rigidity of the sentencing guidelines. Michael's haunted look bore testament to the moment.

Alex Martin strode to the front of the court like the Tin Man with no heart. His lips curled into a sneer. "We would like to see him receive a sentence of twelve to fourteen years. Make an example of him, Your Honor. All these people here to testify…they don't know him like I…we do. He deserves the maximum for his disrespect for power…ah, order and justice."

Finally, Judge Stockman spoke. "I am sentencing you to ninety-seven months, Mr. Parker." It was one month more than Mary Ruth. The weight of Stockman's words broke the silence; a court recorder paused, and somewhere behind Michael, someone in the courtroom gasped. The prosecutor smiled, and federal agents at his table quietly congratulated him as he stared at the defense table, willing Michael to look at him.

The judge frowned at the gallery and continued, "That's the lower range under the guidelines. Do you have anything that you wish to say, Mr. Parker?"

Michael thought of those convicted for the Watergate scandal. Bud Krogh had commented, "A six-month sentence is not all that bad." Chuck Colson's one-to-three turned out to be eleven months with parole. But that was 1974. Since then, sentences had tripled and quadrupled, and there was no more parole.

In the whispery, dry voice of a man now facing the finality of his fate, Michael said, "I want to thank you for the time you allowed me with my wife. I'll never forget that kindness."

The judge with the sagging bags under sad eyes said quietly, "It could have been more if I had adhered to the upper levels of the guidelines. I'll allow you to self-surrender in sixty days."

Defense Attorney John Mendez left the Federal Building with a group as a diversion for the media pack outside—as his client went down a side hall. Sam the informant stepped out of the shadows, much as he had that first night in the parking deck, to shake his hand. With tears tracking down his face, he shook Michael's hand and whispered, "It's not right. This isn't right! The boys downtown go free. Robinson betrays her loyal captain, and the choir boy goes to prison. This is like the final act of some Greek tragedy."

He stepped back, wiped his leaking eyes and nose with the back of his hand, and said with a forced smile, "So you wanted to fight the system."

Michael smiled, shook his hand, and said, "I fought the law and the lawless won."

* * *

The new editor for the newspaper, whose candidate Michael defeated in Augusta, mocked the judge, saying that Michael should have been given more time. Unaware of what such a sentence entailed, the same journalist would have been incapable of surviving even a portion of the judgment he dismissed as too lenient. A talk show host, whose wife had chased him from their home after he assaulted her, pounded Michael relentlessly in a newfound morality. Representative Joey Tomlin's friend, an editor for another paper owned by the daily, joined in to relentlessly attack Michael and use him as a not-so-subtle example of the consequences for crossing the clique. But Michael's amends were to be made with God and Susan, not the world. His peace was to be found with them as well.

He returned home to savor what time he had left with Susan. Late one evening, he heard a noise from the bathroom and rushed there to find her on the floor. She was dazed from what he recognized immediately as the stroke doctors had predicted for so long. The look on her face drove a spear through his heart as he strained against unbearable pain.

"It's okay, Susan. It's going to be okay," he said to her as a lone tear trickled down her face.

The red-and-white flashes illuminated their driveway as the ambulance came quickly to rush her to the ER. Doctors rushed about trying to save her as she looked around in confusion and uncertainty. She motioned Michael to come closer as she tried to form words.

"What is it, honey?" he asked.

She pulled his ear to her lips and whispered, "I was back in the tunnel of light again, like that time in ICU. I saw Jesus smile at me tonight, Michael. He said, 'If God be for you, who can be against you?'"

CHAPTER FORTY-ONE

"I said to the man at the gate of the year: 'Give me a light
that I may tread safely into the unknown.' And he replied,
'Go out into the darkness and put your hand into the Hand
of God...' So I went forth, and finding the Hand of
God...He led me towards the hills and the breaking
of day in the lone East."—Louise Haskins

"Death is at your doorstep, and it will steal your
innocence but...not...your substance. You are not
alone in this. As brothers we will stand and we'll
hold your hand."—Mumford and Sons, "Timshel"

There was a gentle drizzle falling outside the two-story brick residence that had been home to Michael and Susan for eighteen years. Michael could hear the steady *splatter-splot* on the window panes and then the *drip*, *drop*, and *roar* of rain in the gutters as the storm increased—common yet endangered sounds that he now cherished more than silver or gold.

The air in the house was salted with sorrowing. The walls of their bedroom seemed to sweat or bleed with an aching of farewell. The nightlight backlit a cross on the dresser and cast a giant shadow on the wall. The streetlamps popped on and off, struggling to illuminate the curtain of night that would too soon yield to the grim reality waiting in the morning ahead.

The nurse was downstairs. Michael lay awake, listening to Susan's labored breathing. He was aware it might be the last time he would hear the irregular rhythms he had listened for in times of trials. It was his last time to be there for her—the last time to feel the warmth of her. She slid her hand over his and clutched it tightly as he fell into a restless and fearful shallow sleep.

He finally rose and went to his study at 1 a.m. He began to gather the books he hoped he would be allowed to take to prison—volumes to become his insulation and refuge in a foreign world.

These books had been given to him by Wayne Thatcher and Lon Burton, old friends who had rallied to Michael's side—the wheat separated from the chaff. They had compiled an eclectic assortment of books: a large study Bible, works by C.S. Lewis, Shakespeare, and Ravi Zacharias, and *Born Again* by Chuck Colson, once known as President Richard Nixon's "dirty tricks man." And lying on his desk was the classic he was in the process of reading.

He picked up *Les Miserables* again and began to pore through the novel he'd read as a student long ago but couldn't fully grasp until now— a story of the tender ground where justice and mercy met, where grace and law clashed.

Reading the novel had reminded him of scenes from the 1998 cinematic release. When he and Susan had seen it at the theater, he had felt a natural affinity for Javert, the officer of the law. Over and over in his mind rolled the images of the single-minded policeman—a man whose existence was consumed by his view of justice, who couldn't believe in redemption and only saw Jean Valjean as a convict.

So sure that he was right in his beliefs about humanity, Javert told Valjean, "Reform is a discredited fantasy. Modern science tells us that people are by nature law-breakers or law-abiders. A wolf can wear sheep's clothing, but he's still a wolf." Javert's god was the law, and his unrelenting devotion to it gave him a feeling of self-righteousness, as well as a certainty of Valjean's guilt and sinfulness.

While Michael had identified with the policeman when he saw the movie, he knew that was no longer the case. Now, after his own journey of redemption, he felt more of a connection to Jean Valjean, for it was the convict who realized the depths of his sin and received God's mercy. Javert couldn't. It was the conflict between law and grace he could never grasp or reconcile. This realization caused Michael to feel his first stirrings of pity for prosecutor Alex Martin, a modern-day Javert.

Something else that Michael couldn't shake was the words of the priest to Valjean—"I have ransomed you from fear and hatred, and now, I give you back to God." It echoed the love and mercy in the voice he heard before the ambush that cold day in Mississippi. It mirrored the grace he had seen in the eyes of his visitor in the ACDC.

He called Lon early that morning. "Lon, I was so good at being 'good' that I didn't know it wasn't enough and never would be. Free will, that freedom to choose between good and evil or sin and righteousness, can be a tricky thing. I can't say that I'm without fear, but I had to learn that I was lost before I could be found."

Michael could almost see Lon smile from beneath his gold-rimmed glasses when he said, "You are in the eye of the world's storm, but the world only seeks vengeance. God desires justice, reconciliation, and mercy. There's not a wasted tear in the valley. Who better than you, Michael, to go and proclaim the forgiveness of the Lord?"

* * *

Friends, neighbors, and healthcare workers milled around the den of the house where Michael and Susan had spent so many happy years. No one seemed to want to make eye contact, and the false cheer was overwhelmed by the smell of sorrow and finality that flavored the gathering of goodbyes.

The time had finally come. The nightmare that wouldn't go away was now the permanent view in the unwelcomed light of day. It suggested two thousand nights away, which he knew Susan could not survive. He leaned down to her chair and kissed her at the soft, wet corners of her eyes.

He choked back a sob and whispered in her ear, "See you later, alligator."

She answered through frightened eyes overcome by a flood of tears, "After while, crocodile."

He slipped her a card and turned to walk away. Susan struggled to raise herself from her wheelchair to see over or around the well-wishers, to catch one last glimpse of Michael as he walked like a condemned man out the front door of their home with Wayne.

Michael looked back and saw love, real and lasting love, in her eyes, the reflection of another love that was undeserved.

As he was lost to her view, Susan was sobbing and desperately ripped open the envelope to reveal his card, which read: *A woman's heart should be so hidden in Christ that a man should have to seek Him first to find her.—Maya Angelou*

In the corner, he'd written, "When I need you, I always know where to find you. I love you, Michael."

There was a rumble of distant thunder as he walked to the car, and he heard someone say that the devil was rolling watermelons.

* * *

Wayne drove to the countryside outside of Edgefield, South Carolina, escorting the sentinel who had abandoned his post on his forced march of surrender. He pulled over in front of the medium-security prison above the camp, trying in vain to clear his throat and to not look at Michael.

"I want you to know that no matter what happens, you have a job when you come home—and you will come home, you hear me? You're a survivor. You'll harness this pain and plow this hard ground with it," Wayne said.

Michael saw the big teardrops in Wayne's eyes. "It'll be okay, Wayne. I'll be in paradise by sundown. I walk by faith now, not by sight," Michael said.

Wayne bear-hugged him in a rib-cracking embrace and then left Michael under the vastness of a cold, gray December sky. Michael was breathing short, halting breaths. The temperature had suddenly dropped, and his breath crystallized as it exited his nose and mouth and seemed to fall frozen to the ground.

The sun was setting over Edgefield Prison Camp—over all that had been his life. Despair was clawing at his insides, yet somewhere to his left, a bluebird perched atop the rolled razor wire that encircled the prison. It was like the one he had seen outside the BellSouth president's window in Atlanta on another dark day. With all its might, it sang a familiar, tender tune of hope, just as its Creator had designed.

Michael took his last breaths as a free man and walked unsteadily into a foreign world just before his first Christmas apart from Susan in thirty-seven years. Thomas Scribner, a gray and grizzled career employee of the Bureau of Prisons, waited for him inside. As the man opened the door, Michael heard a lone radio playing—"Silent night, holy night. All is calm, all is bright."

"Sorry," he said, "but I'm the only one on duty today in receiving—Christmas holidays and all, you know. It may take a moment to process you.

"I'm going to have to strip-search you," he said, and Michael, the loner and private man, stripped his clothes so the man could see that he hadn't hidden any weapons or drugs.

"That's fine," Scribner said, "but what's that around your neck?"

"That's my cross, given to me by my wife," Michael answered with a sudden alarm that it might be taken from him, the last vestige of her.

"I'm not supposed to let you keep it," the guard said. "The rules say you can't bring it in, but I'm going to pretend I didn't see it, okay? You need to know that you must hide it, because even if you buy an approved cross from the government commissary, you won't be allowed to display it. Other faiths can show their symbols inside, but not the cross. That's federal policy."

Michael looked at the floor and whispered, "Something about the cross scares them, I think."

"They have you marked as a special, high-profile political case on your jacket. It's so all will know to go out of their way to deny you common courtesies extended to other inmates. They want to be certain you're not going to threaten the tranquility of the yard. They're assuring the population and outside interests that you're—finished and powerless," he said.

"I understand," Michael said, his tongue as dry as sandpaper. "Thank you for warning me."

The first phase was complete, beginning his transfer from freedom to confinement of thought and movement. They left the processing section for assignment.

Four vultures circled the drab animal farm as they walked up the hill. Guard towers, once used to watch the high-security facility next door, were off to the right. Everything was dull, lifeless, colorless, and barren—

except for the red, white, and blue American flag that rippled in the breeze. The flag seemed lost in this alien universe, there only to remind Michael that the country he loved no longer knew him.

Michael carried his bed roll and a one-inch-thick plastic cushion which would serve as a mattress over the hard steel of his bunk—all that the government had decided was necessary in this life. He walked up the steep hill, which was covered with yellow-brown grass and fraught with deep holes that could turn a man's ankle.

Each step was like a thousand, and 538 men clad in green pants, ancient faded t-shirts, and black military-style boots came out onto the grounds to watch this figure of curiosity. They loitered near the doors and hung on the balconies of the gray concrete buildings.

"Those dorms are filled with large brown recluse spiders that inmates call 'atomic bugs,'" the officer told him. "They are known for their nighttime attacks, which routinely send men to the hospital. Their venom will rot the skin. Avoid them whenever you can."

Mary Ruth had done a serialized interview with a TV station in Augusta, which was local to the prison. Curiosity drove the inmates to come out and see the man the superintendent had used as her whipping boy night after night in the series. She was the helpless *femme fatale* and Michael the evil Svengali who manipulated her. To paraphrase Butterfly McQueen's famous line from *Gone With the Wind*, she knew nothing about birthing no contracts.

"I trusted him with everything," Scarlett breathlessly confided to a reporter, who only days before had been her worst enemy. Like the tape that had derailed his chance to testify for the prosecution and her comment that had landed Michael in solitary, Mary Ruth's words struck one final blow. It wouldn't ease her conditions, but it *would* bring danger and hardship to Michael, just as Dr. Hartin had warned.

Inside what would become his home, Michael's picture hung on the boards. Some of the inmates viewed him as a privileged man who had abused a helpless woman. To many of them, he was also a man who had worked for the government that imprisoned them. They vowed to make his life miserable, to mock him relentlessly every day and show him that he was now like them—nobody.

Some of the staff, whose wives idolized Mary Ruth and believed her story, vowed they would make his trips to the commissary and kitchen as difficult as possible. They determined to render his food portions as lean as possible, although it was already stamped "unfit for human consumption." They promised to make his stay at Edgefield "a living hell."

Michael paused for a moment halfway up the hill, squared his shoulders, and held his head up when he wanted to look down. He began to sing softly and sublimely—"Prone to wander, Lord, I feel it, prone to leave the God I love. Here's my heart, Lord, take and seal it. Seal it for Thy courts above. Bind my wandering heart to thee."

The old guard turned to him and asked, "What's that you said?"

Michael didn't answer. He was watching a small band of smiling Christians walk down the hill like apostles of old, but they were holding Bibles and items from the Samaritan's Purse—gifts for new arrivals. Their hands were already extending in friendship, their lips were forming precious words—"Welcome, brother in Christ."

A zephyr swept across the compound under a chrome sky, and tiny stars began to pepper the fading peach and emerging blue-black of nightfall. The vultures had retired from the hunt, and the vapor lights around the prison began to pop on. Michael thought of Clay's warning, of Pearl and peppermint, and of Susan, who told everyone who would listen, "God will use him in prison in a mighty way."

Michael turned to the officer as normalcy and liberty receded and asked, "Did you ever see the movie *The Natural*?"

"No, I didn't," he answered.

"Iris tells Roy Hobbs, 'We have two lives...the life we learn with and the life we live with after that.' I've been born again, Mr. Scribner. I think I'll go live that second one now," Michael said.

He rubbed the silver cross around his neck, the one that Susan had pressed into his palm as he left her. Then he looked up toward the vault of heaven and whispered, "It is well with my soul."

Not the end, but the beginning.

EPILOGUE

Former Governor Holcomb ran again and lost. The GOP hired Billy Joe. Atlanta was infused with "born again" Republicans. Former Rep. Ricky Garcia went to prison. Rep. Joey Tomlin, who continued to knock down utility poles until it couldn't be covered up, was rewarded with a leadership role for the repeated betrayals of his party. Editor Bill Cook became a lobbyist and campaign adviser.

Michael never again heard from Gayle Powers, the U.S. Assistant Secretary of Education. No Child Left Behind resulted in indictments for cheating, as Michael had predicted. The retired U.S. Ed Secretary was dogged by questions on the "Texas Miracle." Freedom of Information requests revealed no record of who was on the conference call to Michael or that it took place.

"Corleone," who called Susan when Michael was dying, was put in witness protection after he prevented a jail break by a man who killed a state judge. Alex Martin's outbursts were mysteriously deleted from the transcripts of Michael's hearing. Mary Ruth Robinson wrote to say she could barely live with the pain she caused Susan. She served her sentence and remarried.

Lobbyist Jack Abramoff pled guilty to corrupting U.S. House leaders and to a case involving a mob-style execution. He was ordered to pay $21.6 million, sentenced to six years, and was out before Michael. No one was ever prosecuted for the diversion of funds that Gayle Powers asked Michael to prevent. No civil action was filed to recover the millions that were central to the case. Michael was the first to pay $200,000 in restitution of the $600,000 Mary Ruth issued in contracts, though no funds accrued to him.

Susan Parker died after Michael left for prison. Joey Tomlin's media allies used her obituary to attack Michael again. Judge Stockman ordered the Bureau of Prisons (BOP) to escort Michael to her funeral. They refused and appealed to run out the clock until the funeral had passed. Susan's last words to Michael were—"Be good until we meet again."

Michael began a Christian movie ministry. During his 2,000 days of confinement, it would become the most successful inmate-conducted ministry in the history of the BOP. The Cougar Club's Carmen Rodriguez attended regularly and worked in Atlanta's soup kitchens after his release.

> *"To forgive is to set a prisoner free and*
> *to discover the prisoner was you."—Corrie ten Boom*

Coming next, the third in the trilogy—***The Redeemed***